TEXAS HILL COUNTRY

A SCENIC JOURNEY

ERIC W. POHL

Schiffer Publishing Ltd
4880 Lower Valley Road • Atglen, PA 19310

Library of Congress Control Number: 2017935085

Designed by Justin Watkinson
Type set in Gotham/Minion Pro

ISBN: 978-0-7643-5392-5
Printed in China
8 7 6 5

FSC
www.fsc.org
MIX
Paper | Supporting responsible forestry
FSC® C104723

Published by Schiffer Publishing, Ltd.
4880 Lower Valley Road
Atglen, PA 19310
Phone: (610) 593-1777; Fax: (610) 593-2002
E-mail: Info@schifferbooks.com
Web: www.schifferbooks.com

For our complete selection of finebooksonthisandrelatedsubjects,pleasevisit our website at www.schifferbooks.com. You may also write for a free catalog.

Schiffer Publishing's titles are available at special discounts for bulk purchases for sales promotions or premiums. Special editions, including personalized covers, corporate imprints, and excerpts, can be created in large quantities for special needs. For more information, contact the publisher.

We are always looking for people to write books on new and related subjects. If you have an idea for a book, please contact us at proposals@schifferbooks.com.

FRONT COVER: The afternoon sun highlights sloping canyon walls rising above the cool, clear waters of the Colorado River as it winds through Colorado Bend State

This book is dedicated to my loving and supportive wife, Beth.

ACKNOWLEDGMENTS

Thank you to my loving parents, Ben and Paula Pohl, for always supporting my photographic and artistic endeavors throughout the years!

Thank you to all the Texans who contributed their time, effort, knowledge, or support to this effort.

INTRODUCTION

The Texas Hill Country—the soul of the Lone Star State. This unique region of central Texas is known for its rugged natural beauty, charming historic towns, and distinct cultural heritage. It is here, deep in the heart of Texas, where the flat Gulf Coastal plains and south Texas brush country collide with the Edwards Plateau, forming an undulating landscape that inspired the region's name.

EVERY ROUTE IS THE SCENIC ROUTE

An excursion along the byways of the Texas Hill Country reveals an awe-inspiring land brimming with scenic wonders that are perhaps unexpected, yet quintessentially Texas.

Blissful spring-fed streams and crystal-clear rivers crisscross the region, snaking their way through verdant valleys and past craggy limestone bluffs. Spectacular displays of bluebonnets, Indian paintbrush, and other wildflowers blanket rolling meadows in the spring. In the fall bald cypress trees paint the river banks in a spectacle of rust-colored foliage.

Infinite hilltop vantage points, rising over 2,500 feet, offer sweeping panoramas of this stair-stepped landscape, often stretching as far as the eye can see. Waves of juniper-covered slopes rise and fall into the distant haze by day and silhouette against spectacular sunsets in the evening. Beneath these towering sentinels feathery oceans of yellow Indian grass ripple in the wind.

CULTURAL CROSSROADS

Punctuating the landscape, winding rural roads fan out across the region dotted with sprawling Texas ranches, award-winning wineries, and historic dance halls amid charming hamlets—each seasoned with their own blend of cultural influences and distinct flavor.

Lining picturesque main streets and town squares, nineteenth century boutique storefronts and quaint knick knack shops mingle alongside opulent Victorian courthouses and nationally recognized barbecue joints. Weekenders and friendly locals congregate at the bustling mom-and-pop café by day and scoot their boots at the local dance hall by night.

Amid these towns, elements of the architecture, cuisine, music, and other nuances nod to a variety of ancestral influences, including Polish, Czech, French, British, Spanish, Mexican, and Anglo-American. Despite this medley of influences, it was the Germans who truly left a lasting cultural mark on the Texas Hill Country.

In 1831, Johann Friedrich Ernst brought his family to Coahuila y Tejas, a province in the northern part of Mexico—becoming the first Germans to settle in what would later become Texas. Ernst secured a homestead, and as part of his land grant was required to colonize his territory. Ernst wrote letters to friends in Germany painting a picture of paradise and encouraging others to emigrate. His glowing letters were widely circulated and at least one was subsequently published in a German newspaper.

Soon after groups of German emigrants were making the long voyage to the Texas frontier for the promise of free or inexpensive land with fertile ground. Families from the same German village and cultural traditions would make the trip and settle together, forming pocket ethnic communities across south central Texas.

Although largely from agricultural backgrounds, German immigrants in Texas were socially and culturally diverse, including among their ranks artisans, tradesmen, academics, and intellectuals. These immigrants were also religiously distinct, including enclaves of Protestants, Jews, Catholics, and even atheists, known as the "free thinkers."

For many Germans, Texas seemed the promised land—a place of bountiful open space, religious freedom, and personal liberty. At a glance it was a place to start fresh, where prosperity was not a question, it was practically guaranteed.

However, life on the Texas frontier was less than perfect. Increased suppression of religious freedom and personal liberties by the new centralist Mexican government were sowing the seeds of the Texas Revolution. In 1836, Texas fought and won its independence from Mexico and German immigration continued in the newly formed Republic of Texas.

In 1842, a group of German nobles formed a society called the Adelsverein, with philanthropic and commercial goals of promoting large-scale emigration and establishment of German settlements in Texas. Though the group was ultimately a financial disaster, it successfully settled more than 7,000 Germans in Texas by 1853, and founded the Hill Country towns of New Braunfels and Fredericksburg.

In 1844, Henri Castro emigrated from France and founded Castroville, just west of San Antonio. Castro recruited and helped bring over 2000 German speaking settlers from the Alsatian region of France to Medina County.

In 1845, Texas was annexed by the United States. German immigration remained strong throughout the remainder of the nineteenth century, peaking in the 1890s—making Germans one of the largest ethnic groups in Texas. The surge of Germans in the 1800s would help set the stage for farming and ranching traditions and impart cultural elements that remain part of the fabric of Texas.

Today, tens of thousands of annual visitors to the Hill Country enjoy the patchwork of towns that proudly flaunt their "willkommen" signs, German schnitzel and wurst, and celebrations like Oktoberfest in Fredericksburg and New Braunfels' Wurstfest—an annual ten-day festival saluting German-Texan culture with sausage, music, and craft beers.

Other celebrations of spirit reign in the Hill Country, as there is a festival for just about anything you can think of: from a variety of music festivals like blues and jazz, to lavender and chocolate festivals, dozens of art and antique shows, quilt exhibits, chili cook-offs, and that is just the tip of the iceberg.

Outdoor recreation is also a quintessential part of the culture in the Texas Hill Country. One of the area's biggest seasonal draws is "floating" or "tubing"—short for inner-tubing. On any given summer day, in certain areas flotillas of fun-loving folks can be seen floating shady scenic rivers like the Comal, with its aquamarine waters, or the cypress-lined Guadalupe—also known for its world class fly fishing.

Wild adventures abound amid a myriad of wilderness parks like the steep rocky canyons and autumn color of Lost Maples State Natural Area to the half-mile long stair-stepped cascades of Pedernales Falls State Park. From underwater cave diving, bouldering, and whitewater rafting to birding and star gazing, the Hill Country is undoubtedly an outdoor lover's paradise.

AN UNDEFINABLE REGION, DEFINED

Although the Hill Country's exact boundary lines will vary depending on who you talk to, it is generally outlined by the pronounced topography of the eastern part of the Edwards Plateau—a contiguous geological uplift in central Texas.

Distinguishing the eastern and southern boundary is the Balcones Escarpment—an abrupt change in elevation and topography that rises from the Coastal Plains, nearly bisecting the middle of Texas. This conspicuous uplift—the result of ancient faulting activity—begins north of Waco and follows Interstate 35, skirting the west side of Austin, San Marcos, and New Braunfels. To the south it grazes the outer suburbs of northern San Antonio and roughly trails above US 90, going west before dissipating near Del Rio.

The northern and western boundaries of the Hill Country are not as easily definable; the topography gradually becomes less pronounced and melts away into more arid desert plateaus of West Texas, near the Pecos River valley.

GEOLOGICAL AND SUBTERRANEAN WONDERS

The Hill Country's alluring canyons, spring-fed rivers, and caves are all the result of natural forces over time. The stage was set during the cretaceous period, about sixty-five to 145 million years ago, when central Texas, as well as much of the state, was covered by a warm shallow ocean. During that time marine organisms such as coral, clams, and oysters died and their remains settled on the bottom of the ocean. Over time their shells and bones were broken up into sediment and compacted over millions of years, forming limestone.

Eons later, geologic instability along the Balcones fault created an uplift known as the Edwards Plateau. Over time the softer deposits on the eastern edge of the plateau were eroded by the elements, exposing the harder Lower Cretaceous limestone and leaving the chalky cliffs, valleys, and outcroppings that we see today in the Hill Country.

Amid the geologic wonders of the region lies a billion-year-old pink granite monolith known as Enchanted Rock. The massive dome protrudes from the surrounding countryside just north of Fredericksburg in a geological zone called the Llano Uplift. The uplift forms an island where the exposed rocks are millions of years older than the surrounding countryside. Many gems and minerals occur in this region, such as iron ore, copper, silver, and gold, and it is the only place you can find blue topaz—the state gemstone of Texas.

Below ground, tectonic movement and the dissolution of softer sediment subsequently birthed subterranean honeycombs of tunnels, fissures, sink holes, and caverns such as Longhorn Cavern State Park, in Burnet County, and Cave Without a Name near Boerne.

As it rains, surface water permeates this underground world via fractured limestone, sink holes, or other porous layers. Known as karst topography, these geological characteristics are prevalent throughout the region, essentially converting Texas Hill Country into an enormous cistern. Amid this karst landscape, aquifers like the Edwards and Trinity supply water to a large swath of Central Texas. Under pressure, this water bubbles to the surface, creating artesian springs and feeding creeks, rivers, and lakes across the region.

DEEP IN THE HEART OF NATURE

Tucked away in tranquil canyons, the descending chirp of the canyon wren mingles with the sounds of trickling spring water echoing off lush fern and lichen-covered limestone walls. In these protected environments small stands of big-tooth maples and witch hazel thrive—relics of an ice age when Texas was much cooler and wetter.

Amid the subterranean world of the Hill Country, the abundance of caves, grottoes, and sink holes is home to multiple millions of Mexican free-tailed bats which live in central Texas during the warmer months, creating one of the largest maternity roosts of bats in the world. Other cave creatures like the rare Texas blind salamander also thrive in these dark cavernous environments.

Towering old-growth bald cypress, pecans, sycamores, and hackberry trees flourish amid the sprawling riparian corridors of larger rivers like the Colorado, Guadalupe, and Frio. Endemic Hill Country species like the Cagle's map turtle and Guadalupe bass make their home in these areas.

In the uplands, sheltering forests of ash juniper and live oak supply essential cover for the endangered golden-cheeked warbler and black-capped vireo, as well as other creatures like gray foxes, coyotes, javelinas, and porcupines.

The diversity of this ecological crossroads and location along the North American migratory central flyway makes it a perfect stopover for throngs of monarch butterflies and migratory birds on their way to winter in Mexico and south Texas.

▶ Each spring visitors flock to Central Texas to marvel at the famous displays of bluebonnets, like these near Marble Falls. From March through April, the official state flower dots landscapes across the Hill Country.

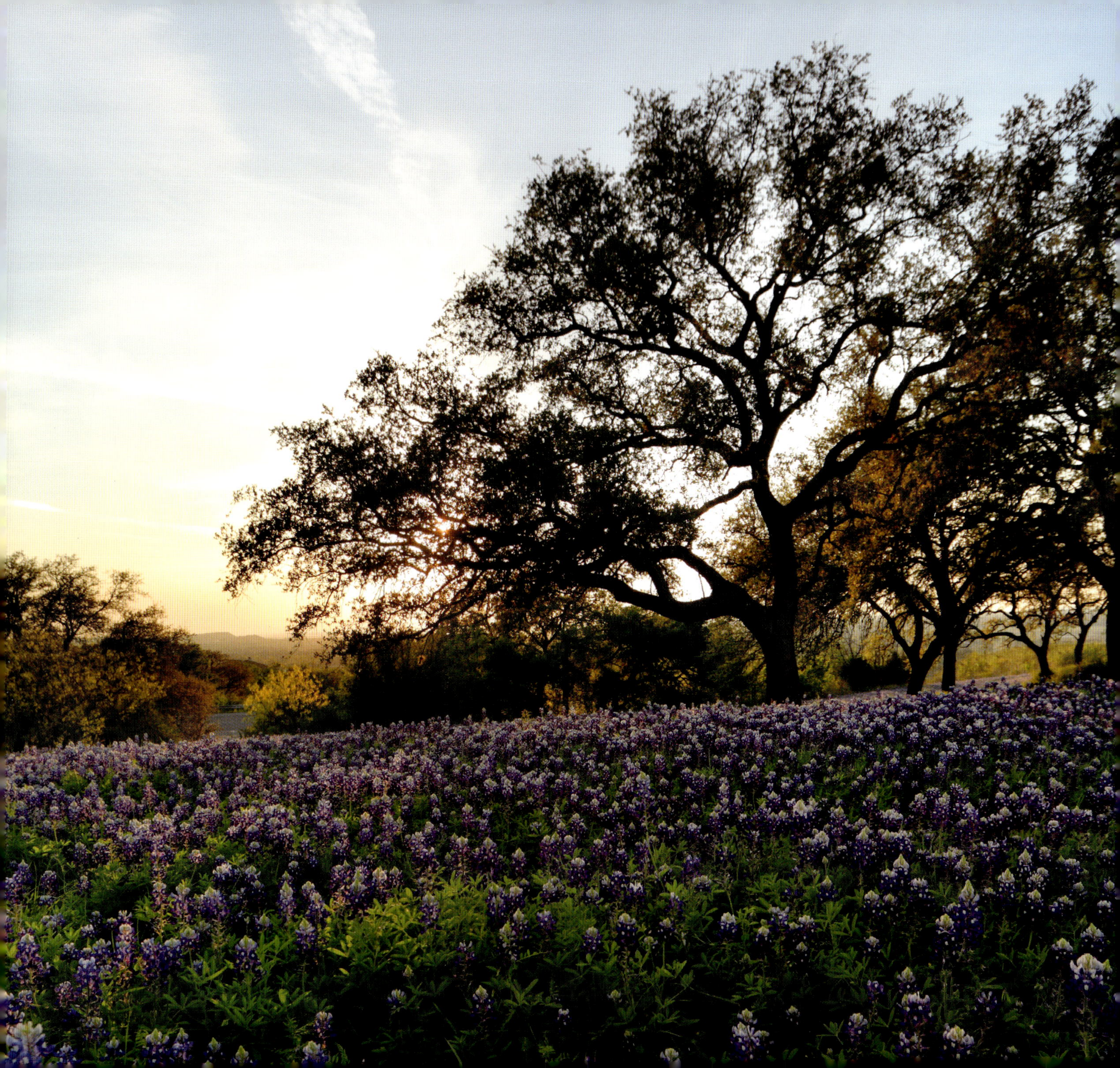

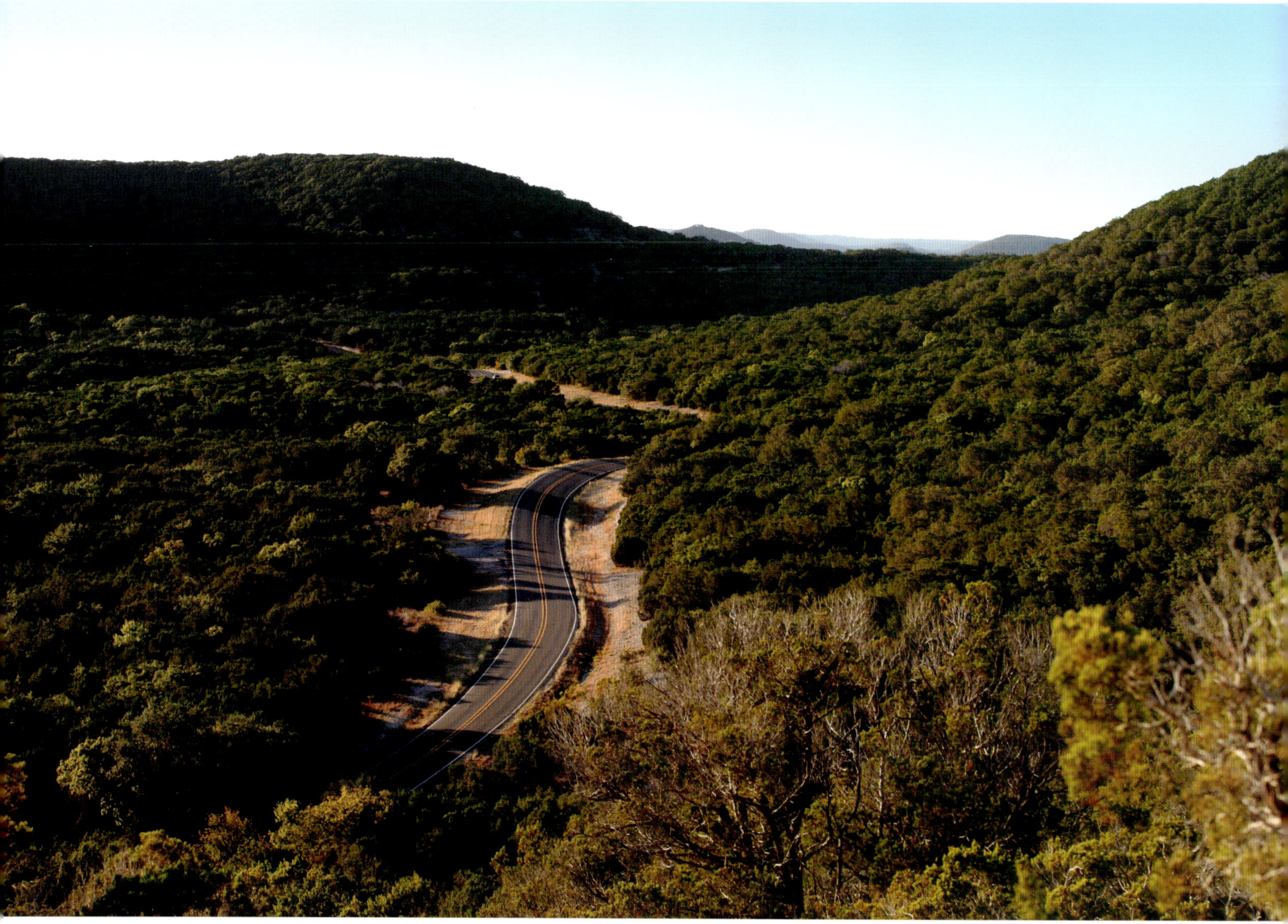

▲ Scenic Farm-to-Market Road 1431 traces the edge of the Balcones Canyonlands National Wildlife Refuge. The refuge, which covers 19,000 acres northwest of Austin, is a haven and nesting site for protected species like the golden-cheeked warbler and black-capped vireo.

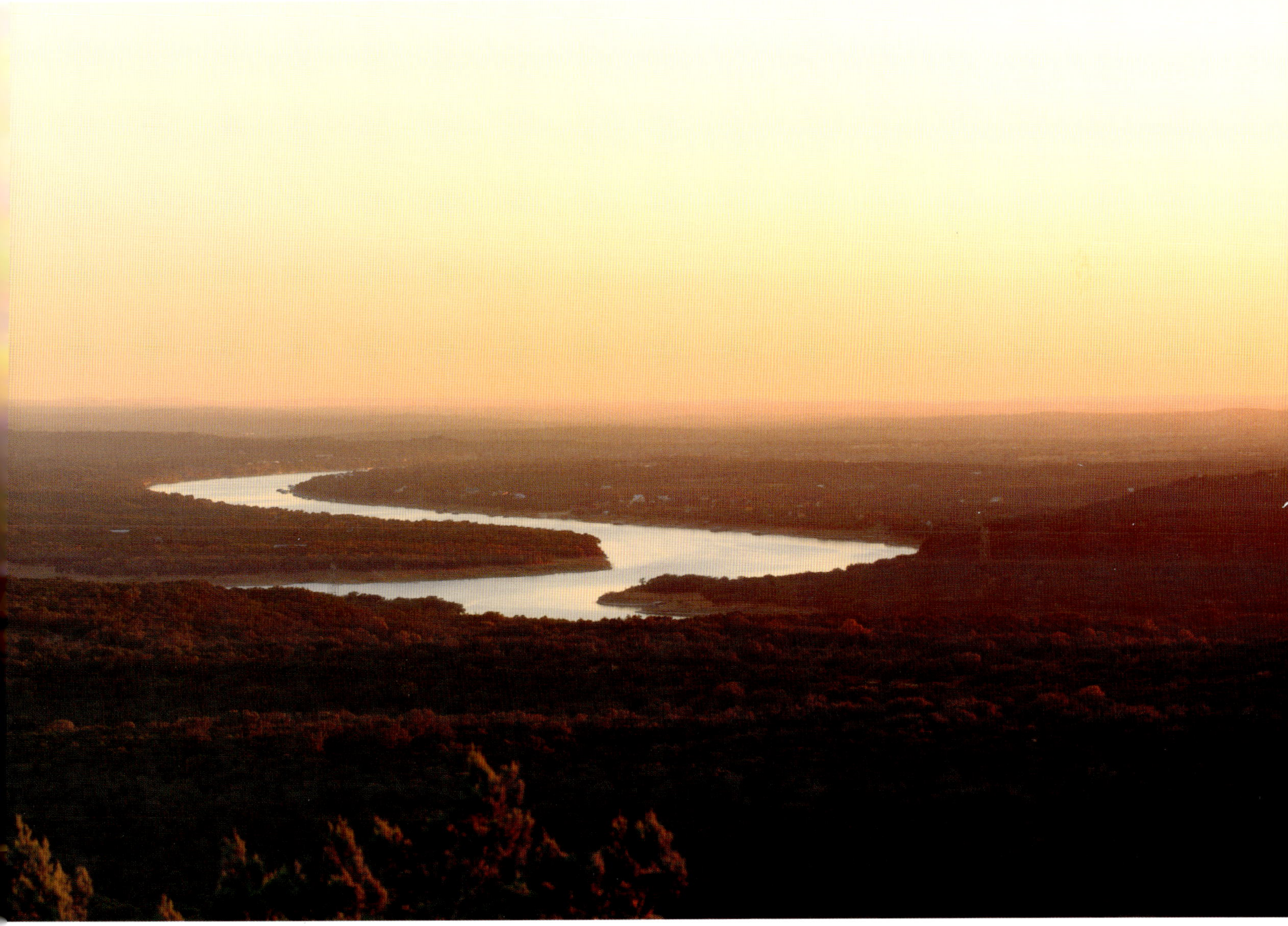

▲ Lake Travis, the largest of the Texas Highland Lakes on the Colorado River, winds its way for sixty-five miles through the rugged slopes of the Hill Country. This view is from the Sunset Deck at the Warbler Vista Unit of the Balcones Canyonlands National Wildlife Refuge.

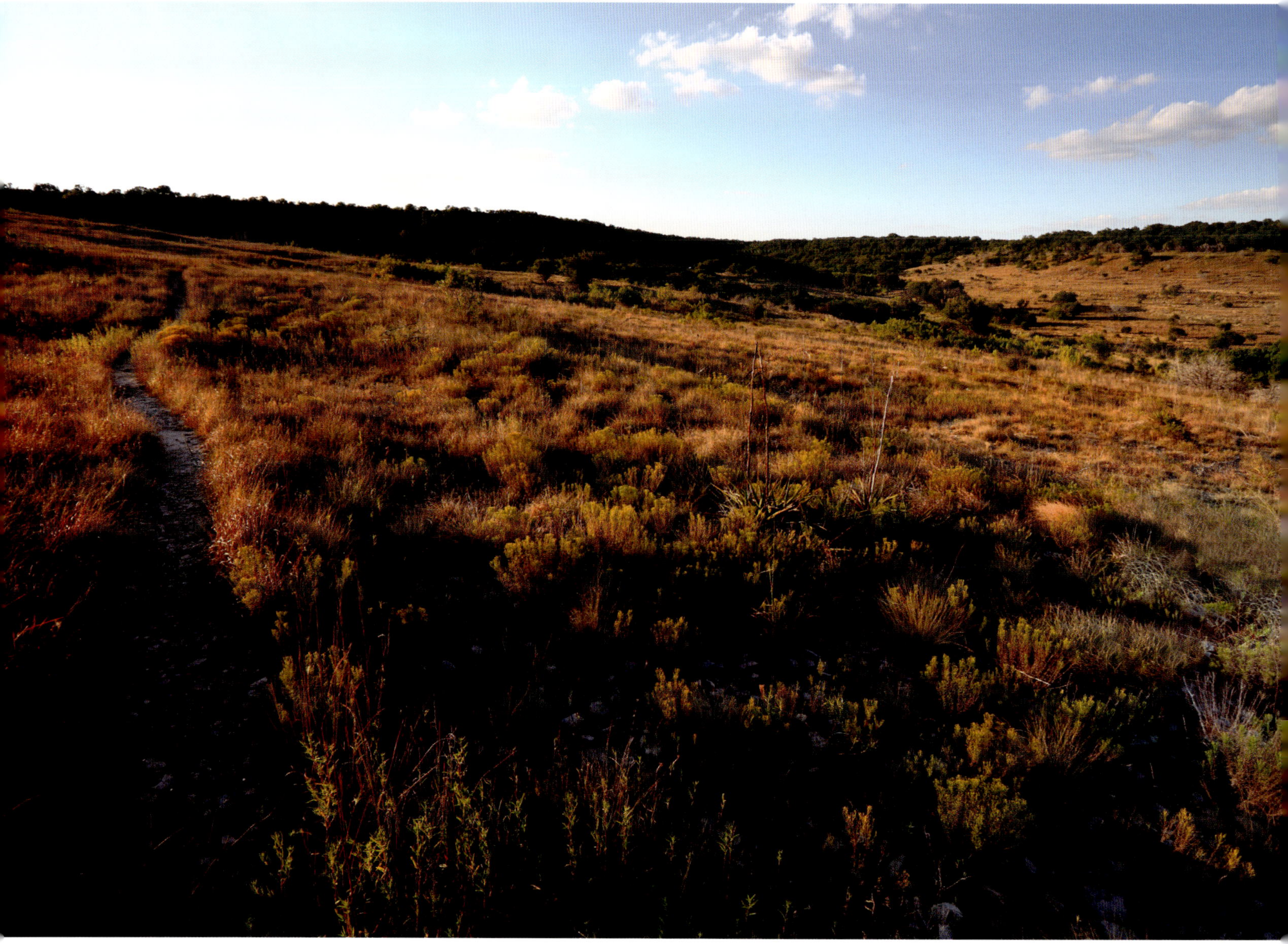

▲ The Doeskin Ranch Unit of the Balcones Canyonlands National Wildlife Refuge offers miles of trails traversing terraced grassland prairies, creeks, and juniper woodlands while offering panoramic Hill Country views.

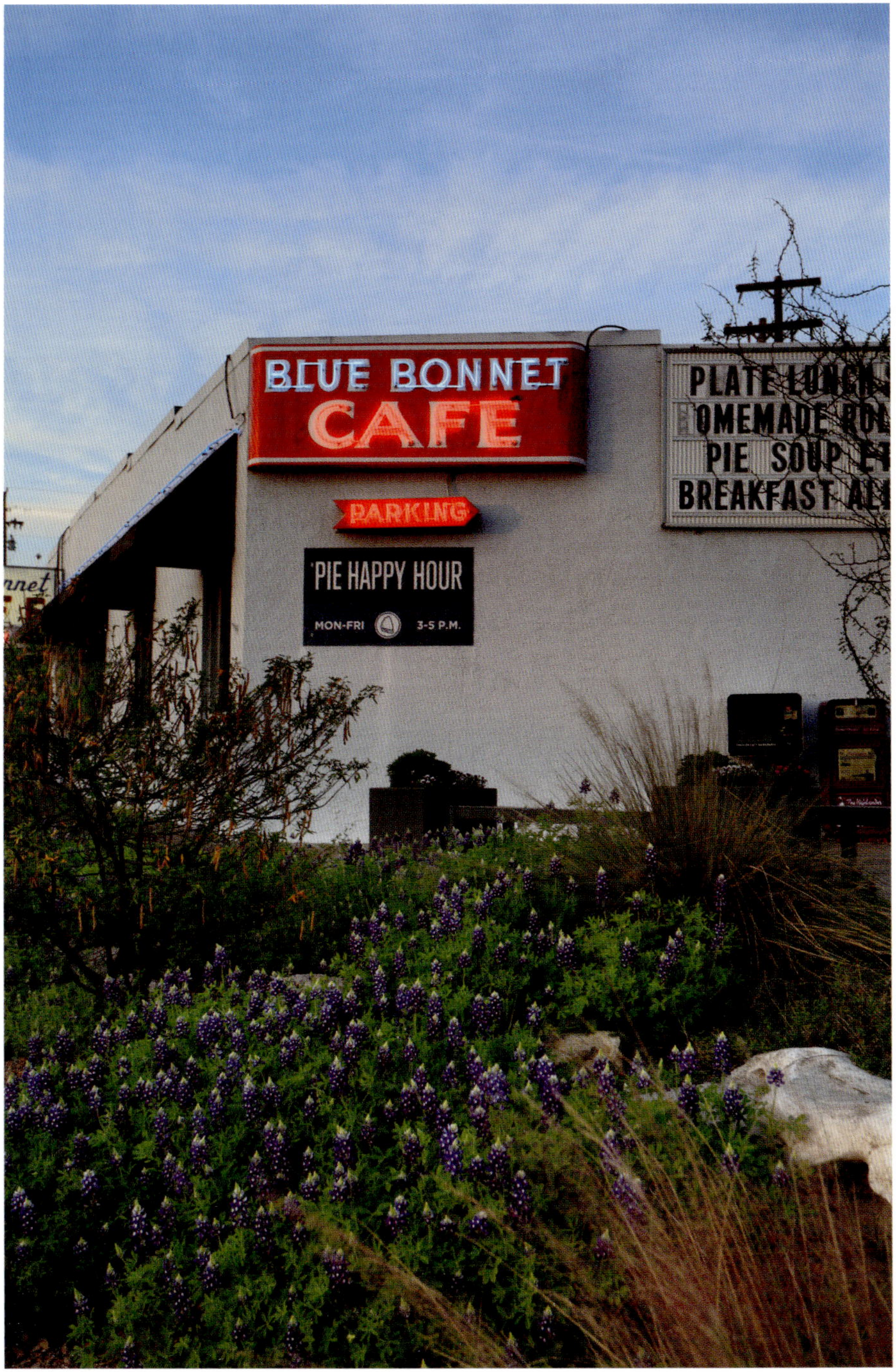

◀ The Blue Bonnet Café, famous for its classic diner fare and fresh-made pies, opened in 1929, in downtown Marble Falls. The café moved to its current location in 1946, and its iconic neon signs have been a beacon to hungry travelers on Highway 281 ever since.

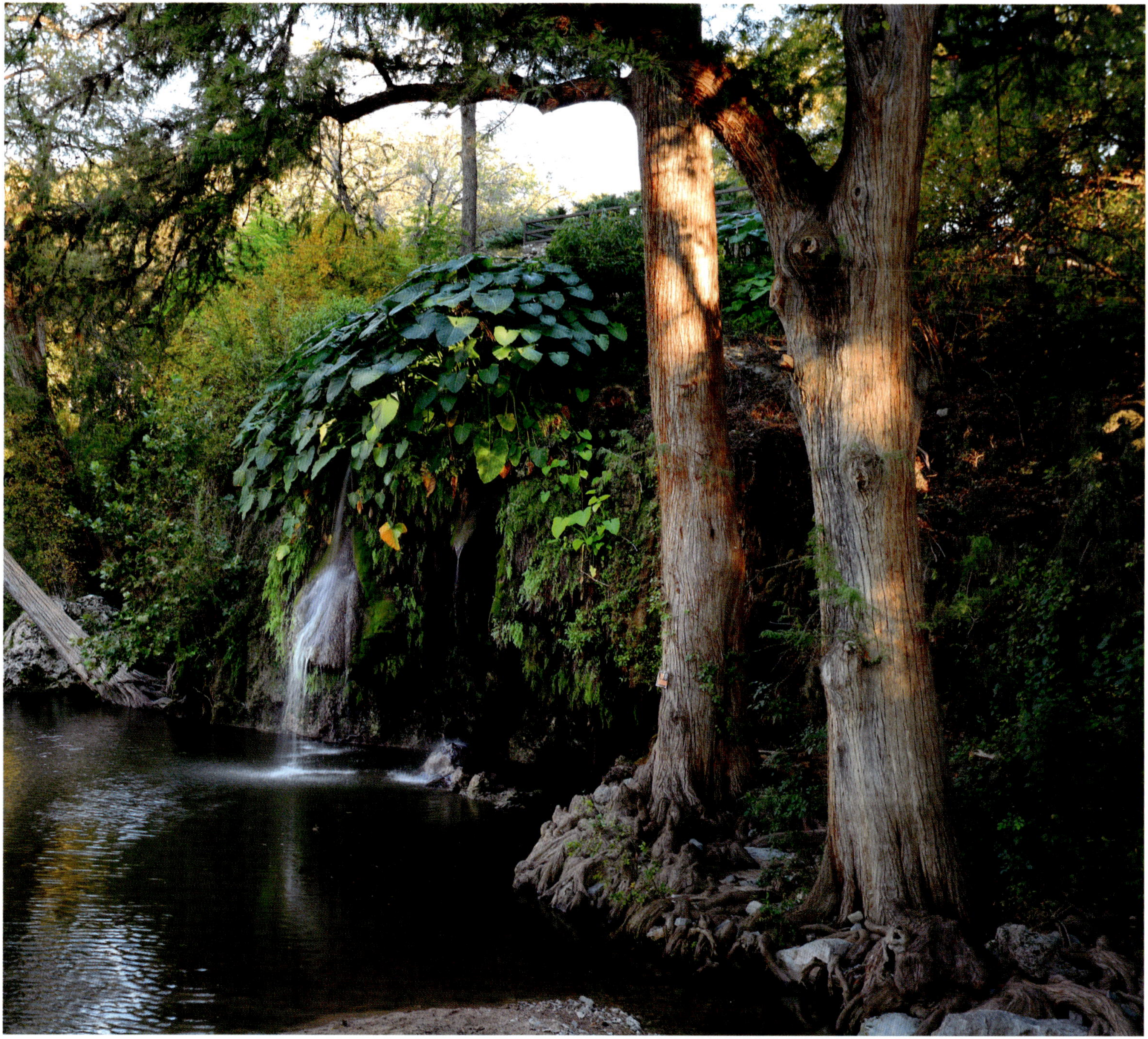

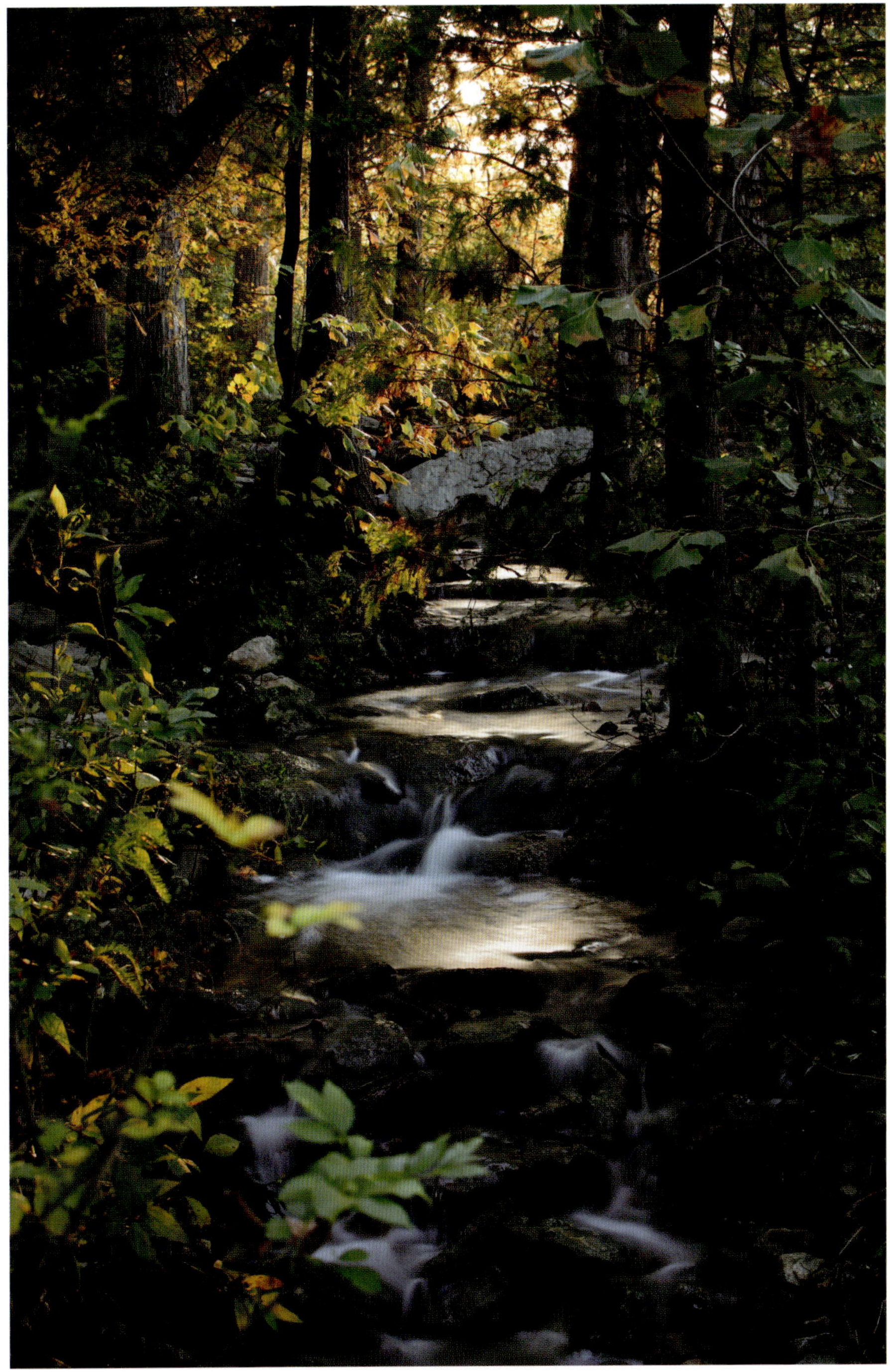

◀ Fern-draped waterfalls, spring-fed streams, and a famous swimming hole make the 115-acre Krause Springs a popular camping and swimming destination near Spicewood.

▶ Dozens of bubbling springs feed Little Cypress Creek as it cascades over stair-stepped limestone and meanders through Krause Springs before flowing into Lake Travis.

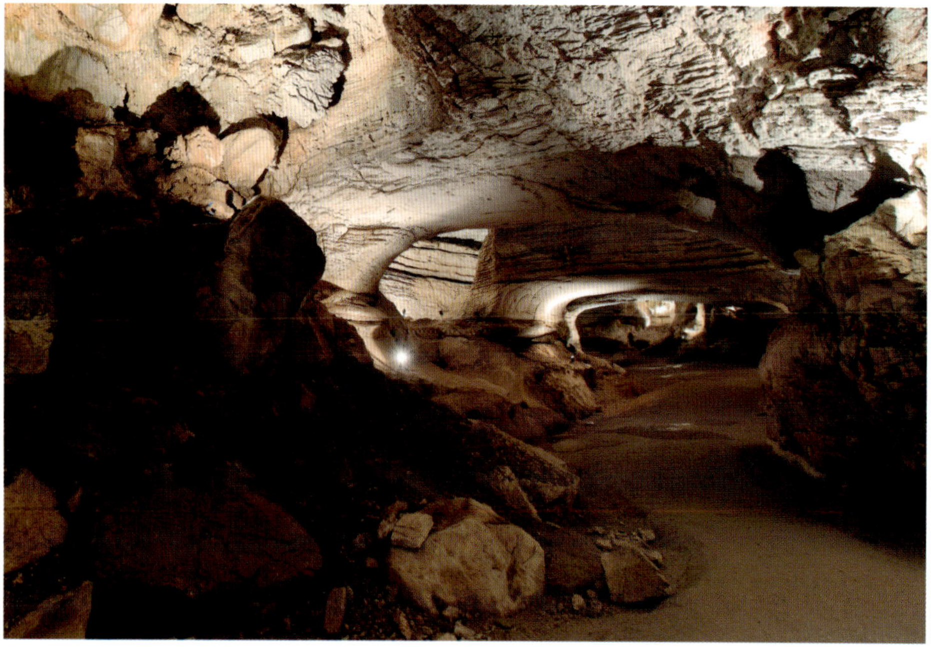

◀ The smooth undulating walls and expansive chambers of Longhorn Caverns were formed millennia ago by a subterranean river. Historically, the cave was used for secret activity, such as a confederate gun powder safe house during the Civil War to a speak-easy and dance hall during prohibition.

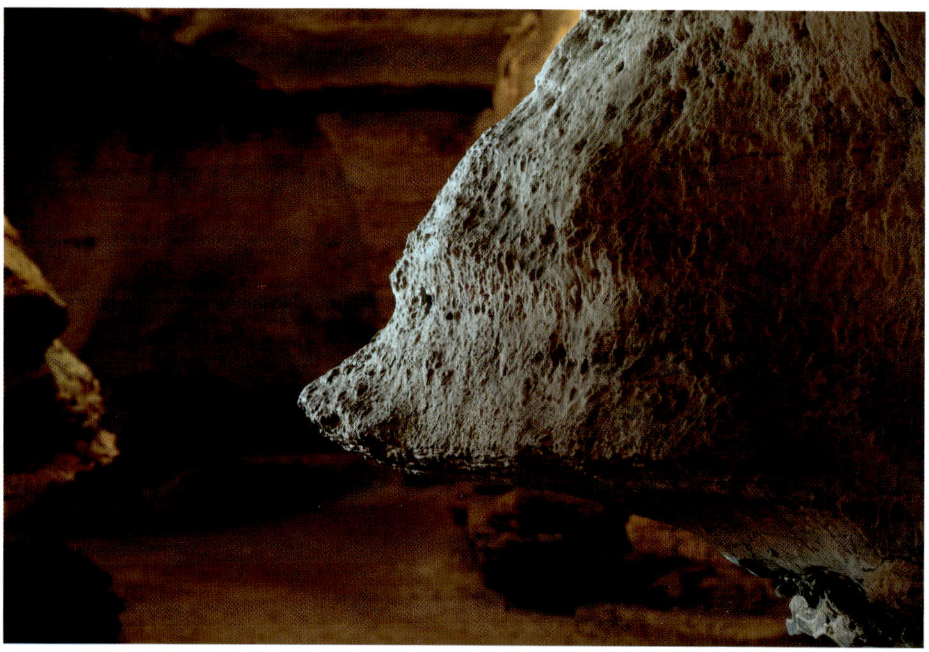

◀ A natural rock formation inside the depths of Longhorn Caverns jumps off the walls in the shape of a large bear head.

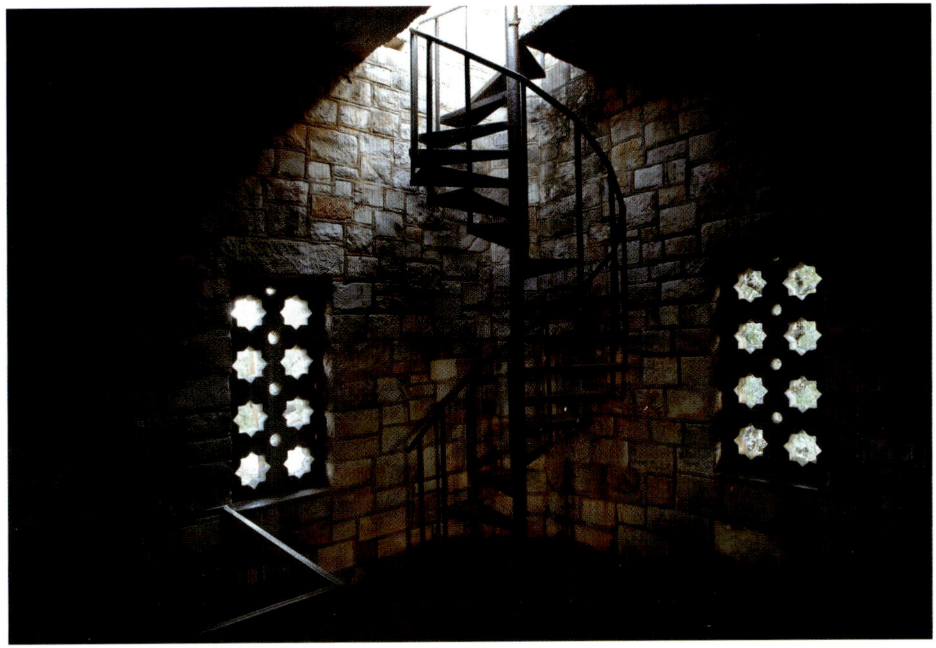

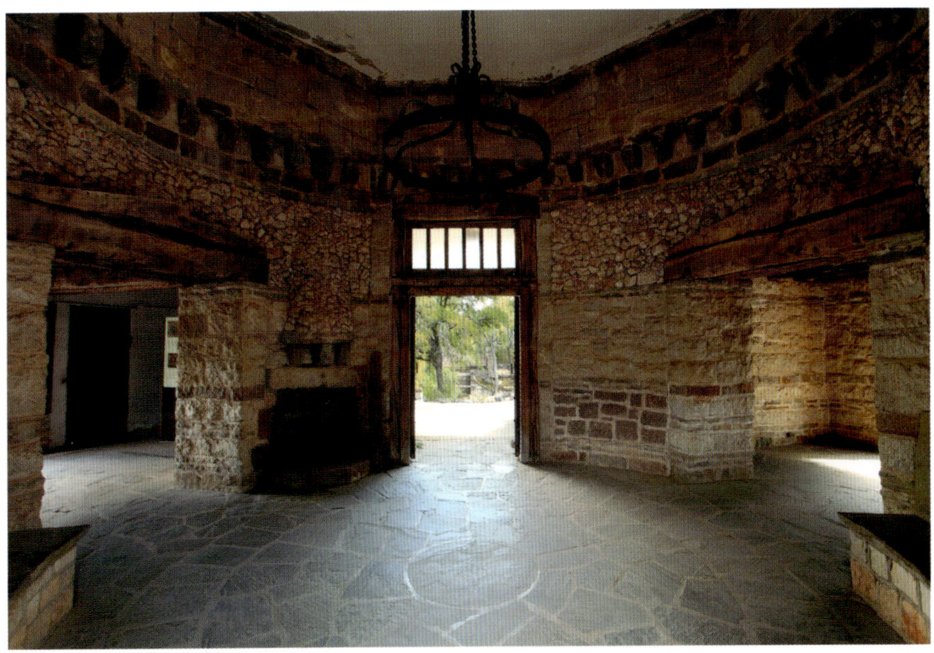

◥▶ Texas parks are peppered with historic stone structures hand-laid by the Civilian Conservation Corps in the 1930s and 1940s. Two wonderful examples are the observation tower (above) and administration building (below) at Longhorn Cavern, constructed using stone quarried on site and rubble removed from the cave.

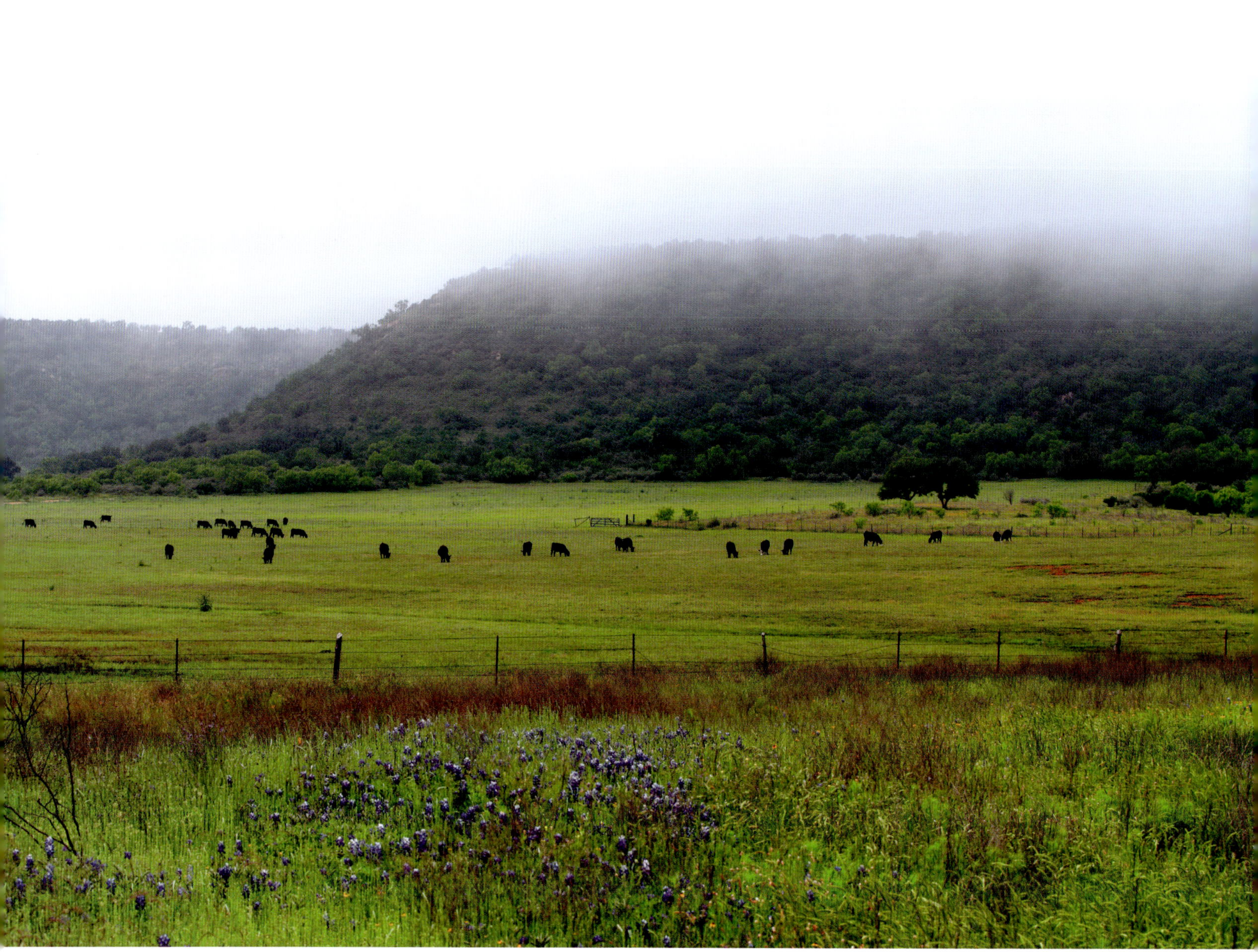

▲ A small patch of bluebonnets in eastern Llano County overlooks a sprawling verdant pasture beneath towering hills partially shrouded in fog.

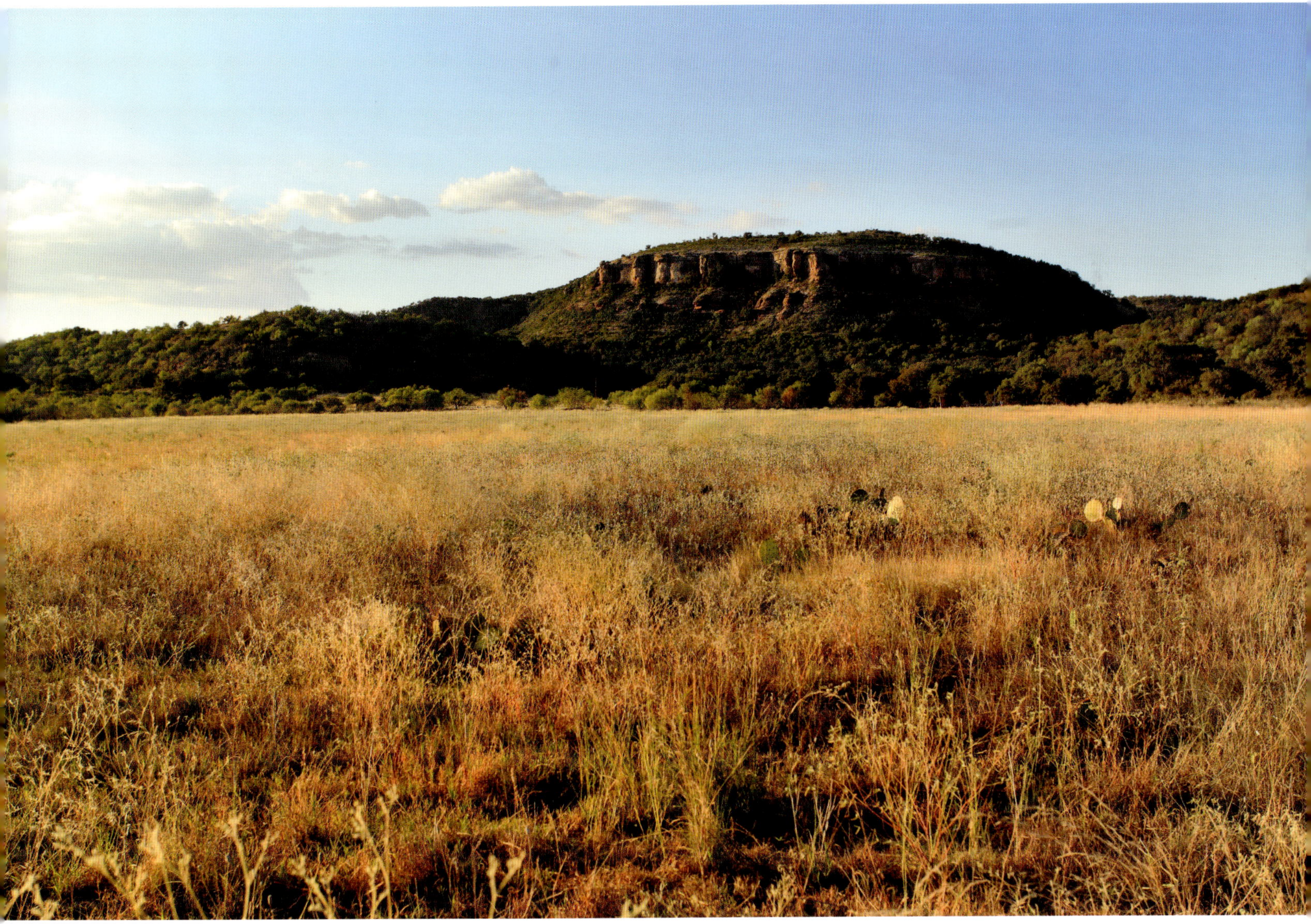

▲ Rising above the rolling plains southwest of Kingsland, the striking layered sandstone and limestone face of Packsaddle Mountain stands as a prominent Hill Country landmark. The mountain endures as a testament to Texas history—from old legends of Spanish gold and silver mining and an Indian battle in 1873 to modern ranching heritage.

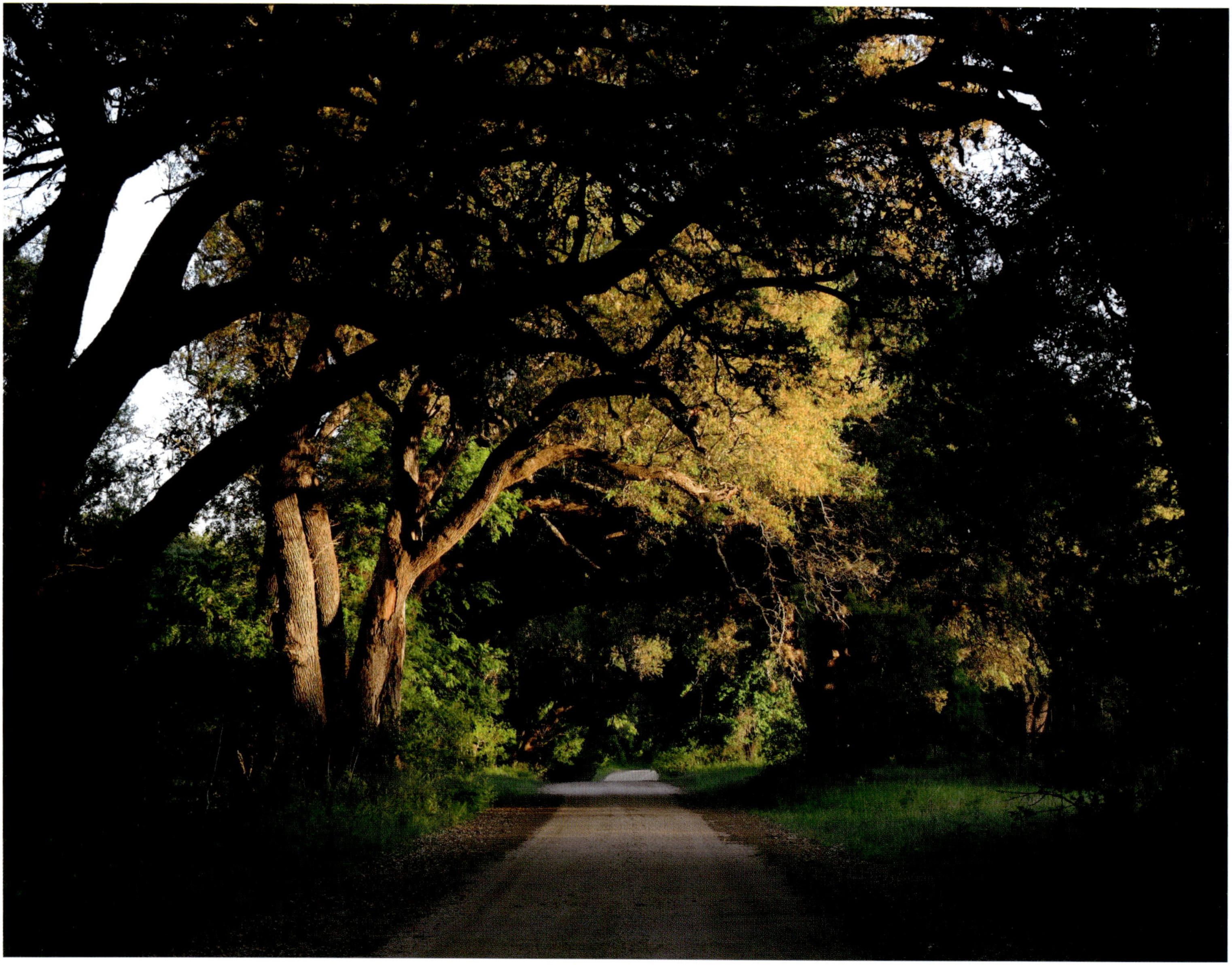

▲ Live oak trees flank a stretch of country road in Llano County as their meandering branches twist and arc across the road, forming a tunnel-like appearance.

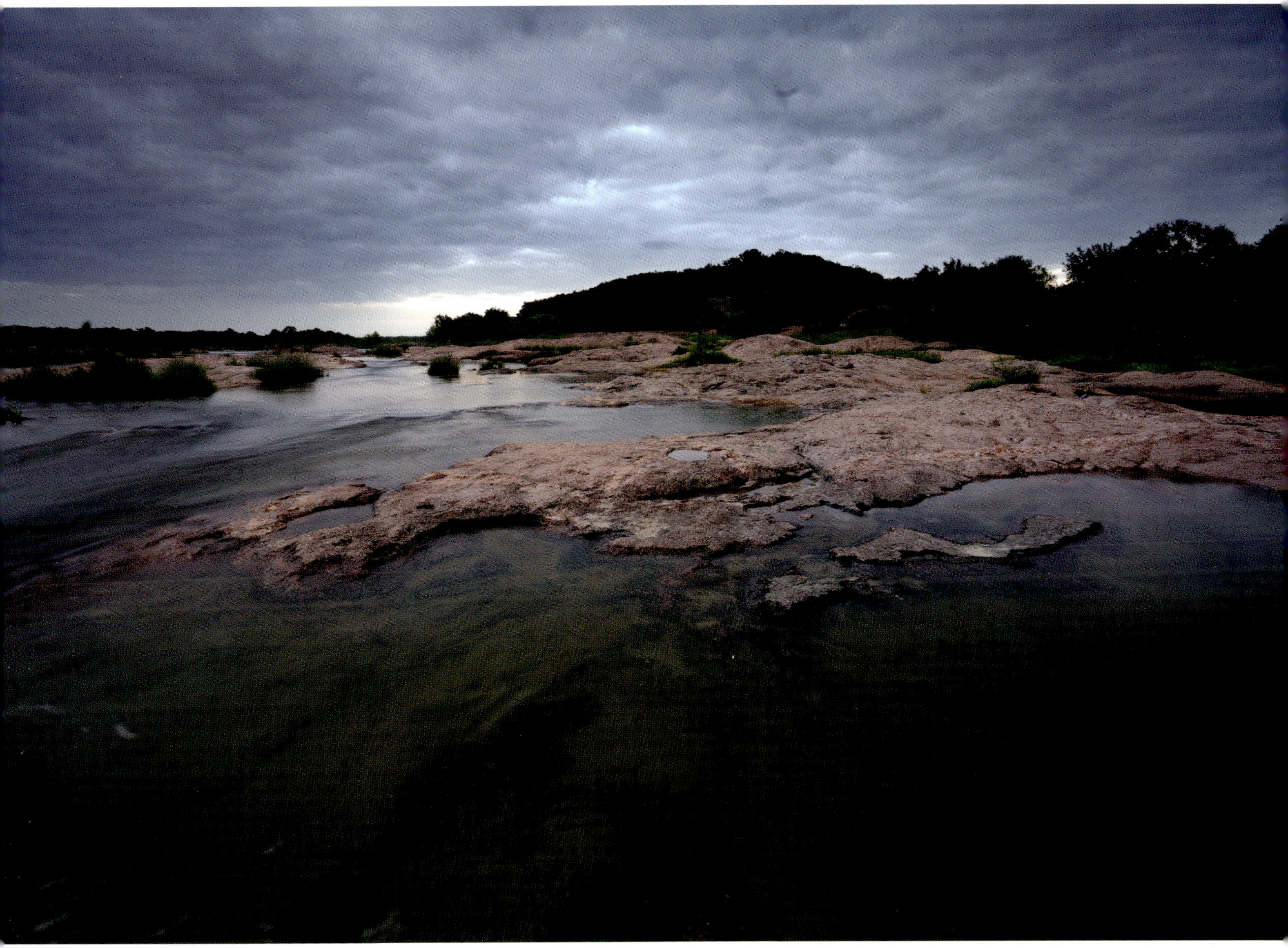

▲ The clear waters of the Llano River flow over a wide bed of pink granite outcroppings, forming channels, pools, and rock islands. This two-mile stretch of river known locally as "The Slab" has become a popular summer swimming hole near Kingsland.

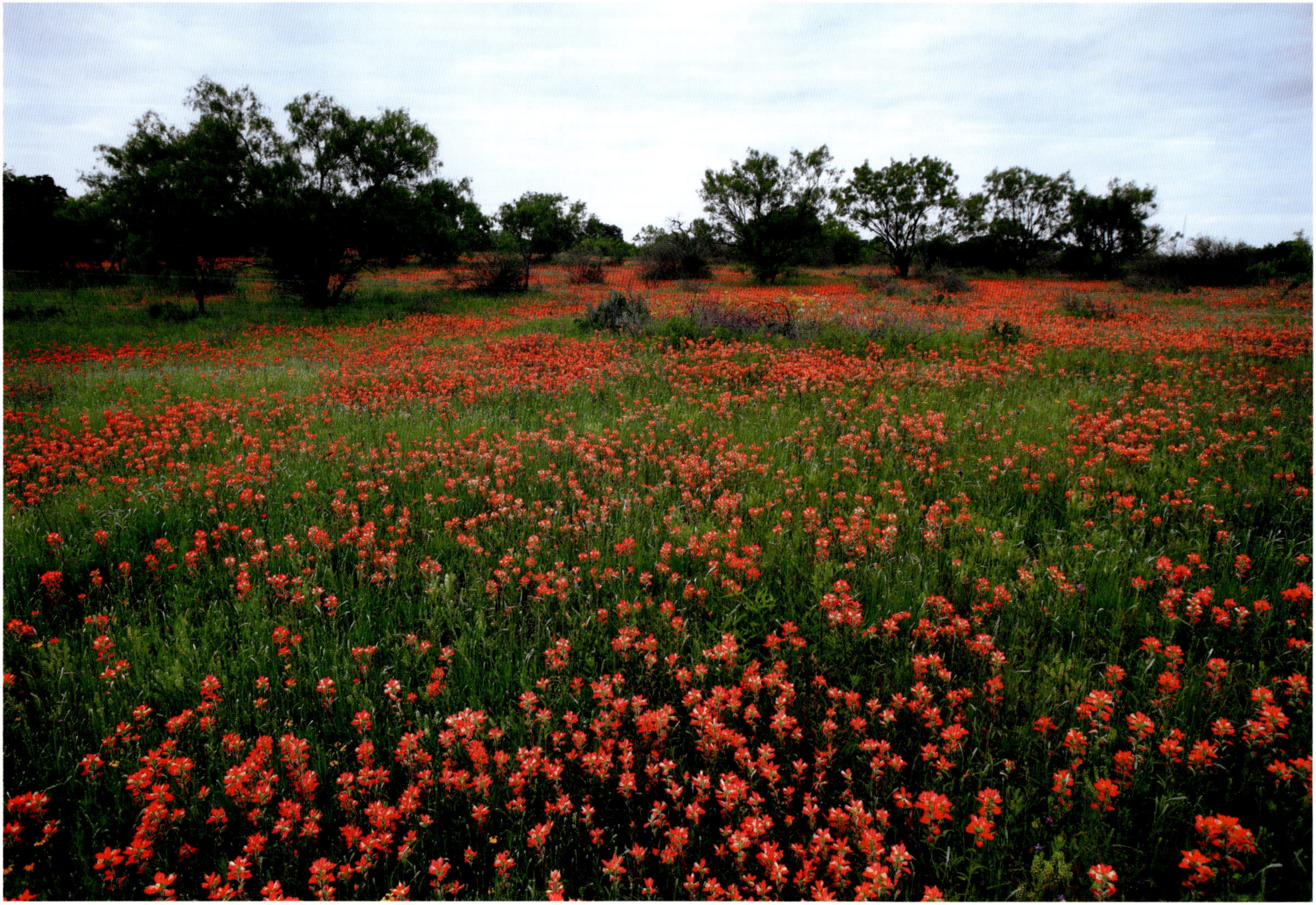

▲ Named for the tufts of brightly colored red bracts that cluster around the top of the plant, Indian paintbrush can be seen blooming in the spring throughout Central Texas and beyond, like this scene in eastern Llano County.

▶ Carpets of vivid yellow basin sneezeweed with splashes of red firewheels cover a meadow near Kingsland.

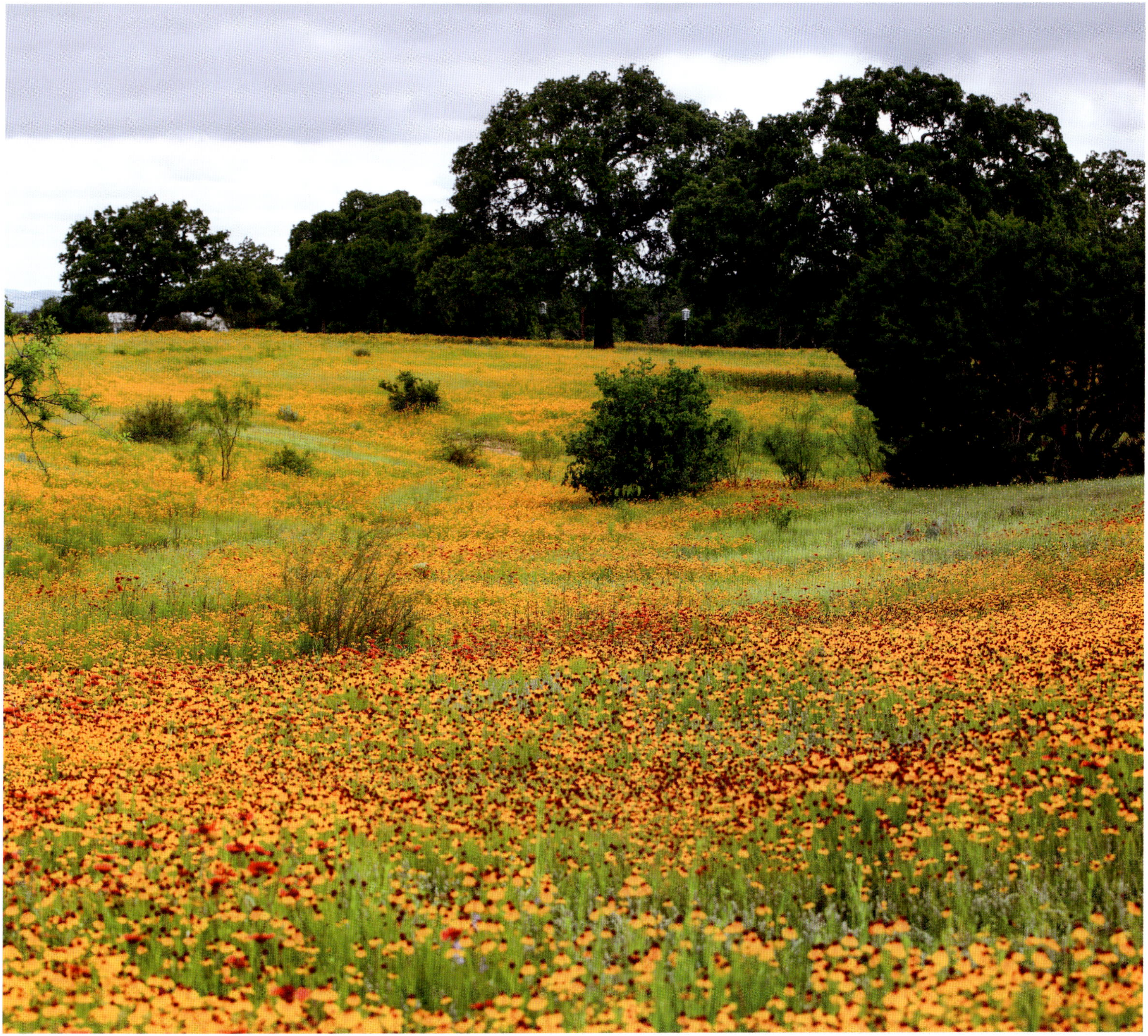

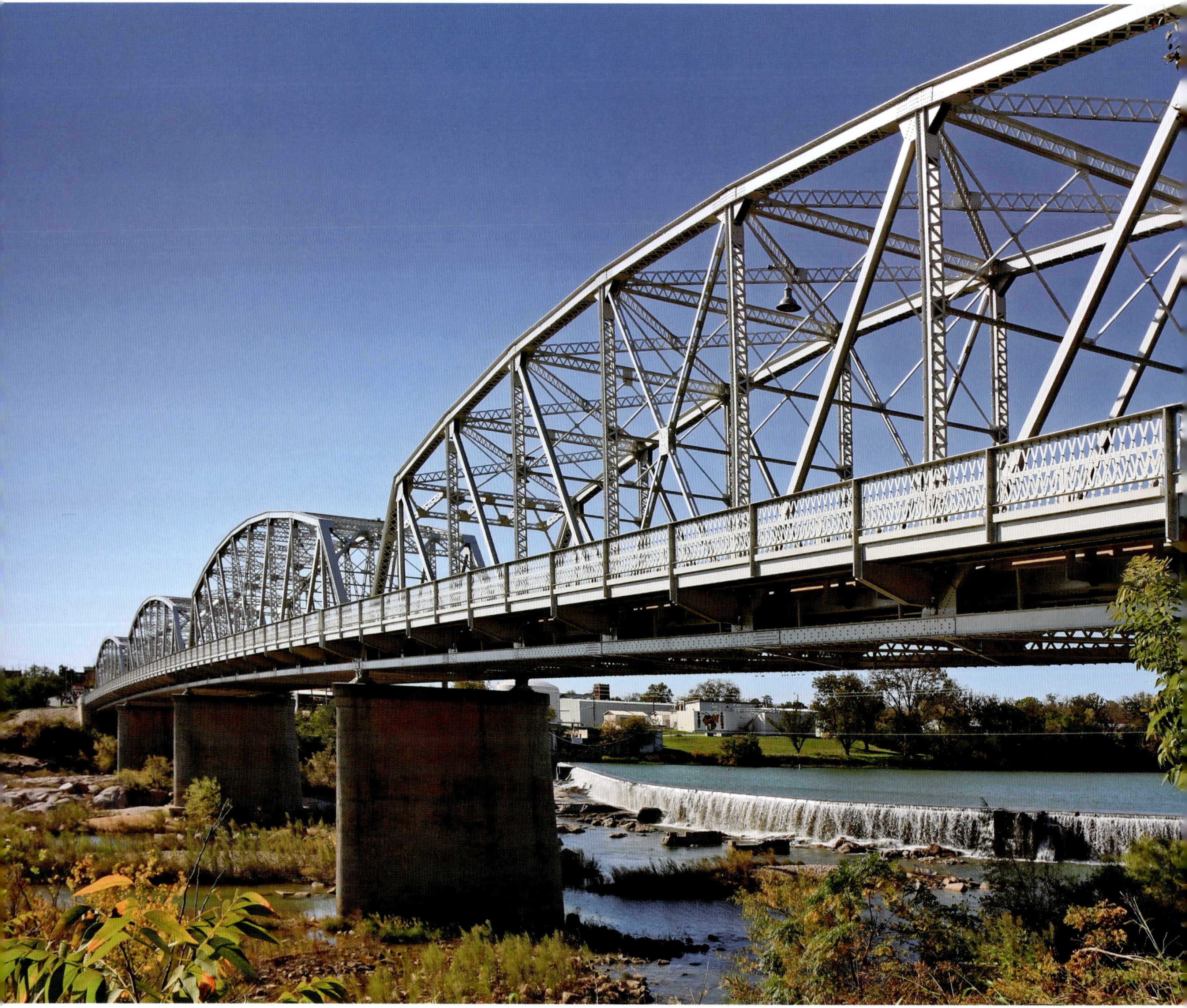

◀ Named for a former mayor of Llano, the 1936 Roy B. Inks Bridge is an impressive four-span steel truss structure spanning nearly 200 feet across the Llano River. It was constructed after a devastating flood washed the previous bridge away in 1935.

▶ Located on the central square in downtown Llano, the 1892 Llano County Courthouse features ornate exterior detail in sandstone, marble, and granite. The square surrounding the courthouse is known for its variety of shopping boutiques.

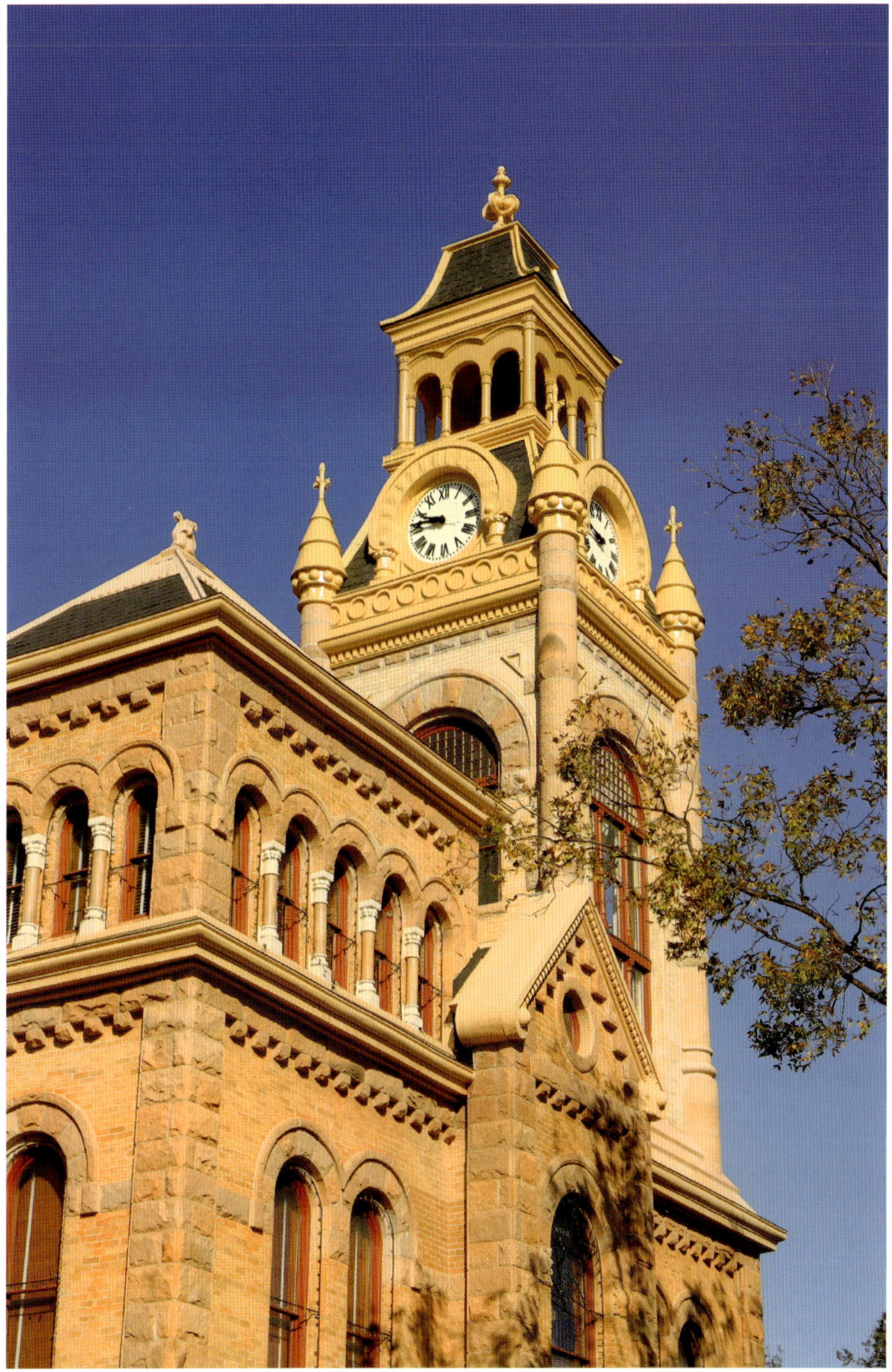

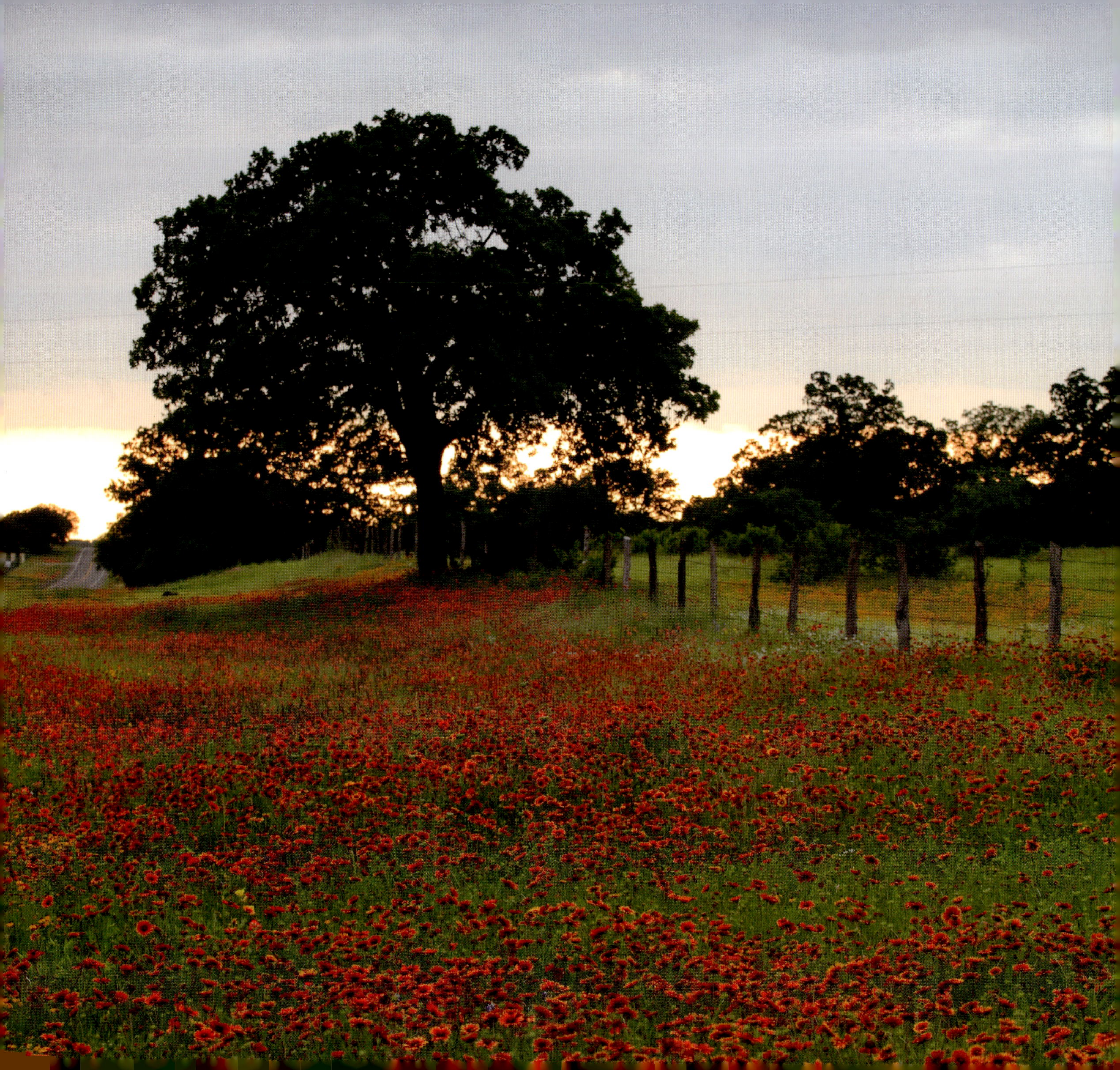

◀ Firewheels, also known as Indian blankets, enliven a highway roadside with fiery red-orange blooms as the sun sets between Llano and Mason.

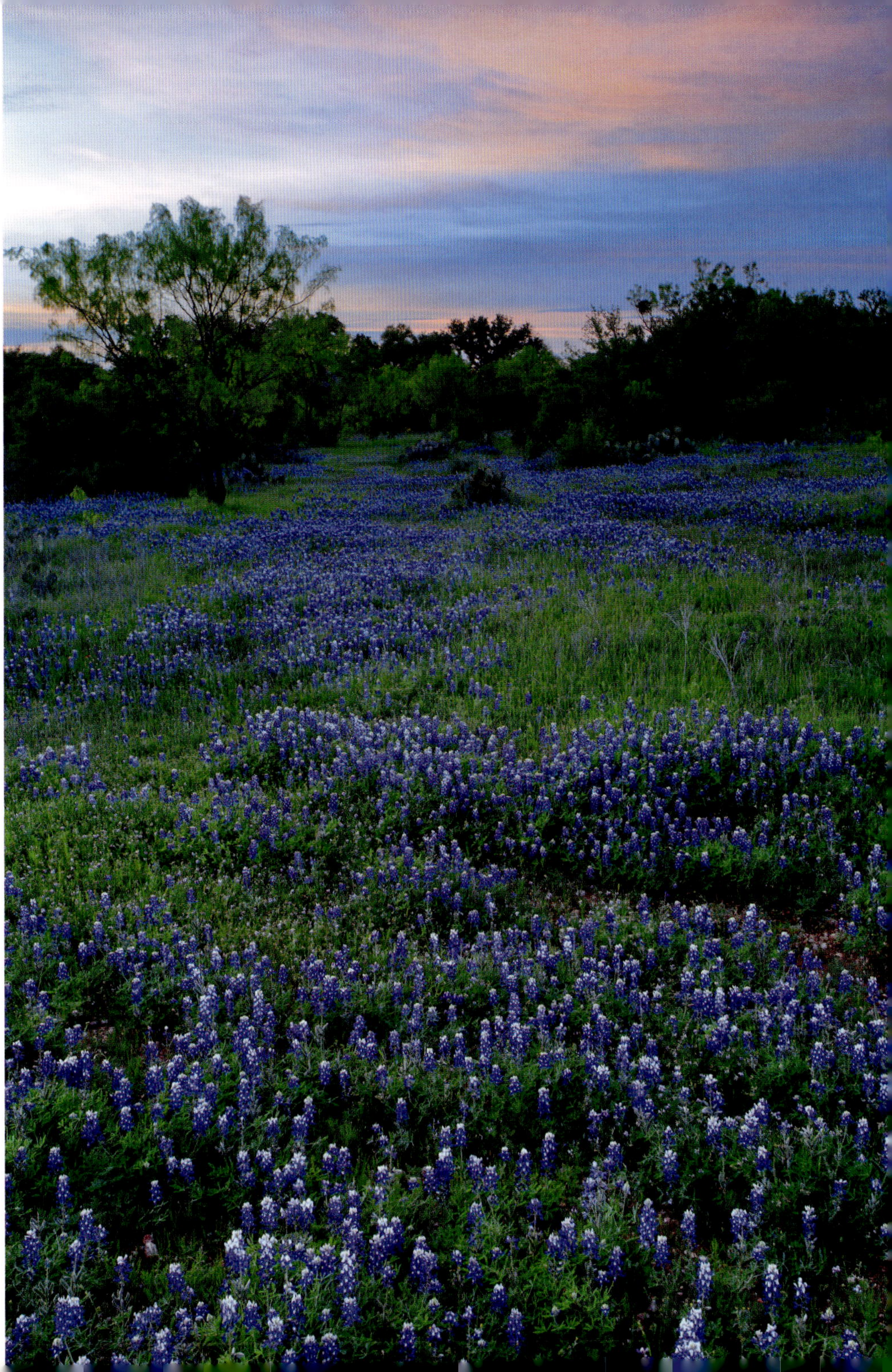

▶ Dense clusters of bluebonnets give the impression of meandering streams of water flowing across a meadow south of Llano.

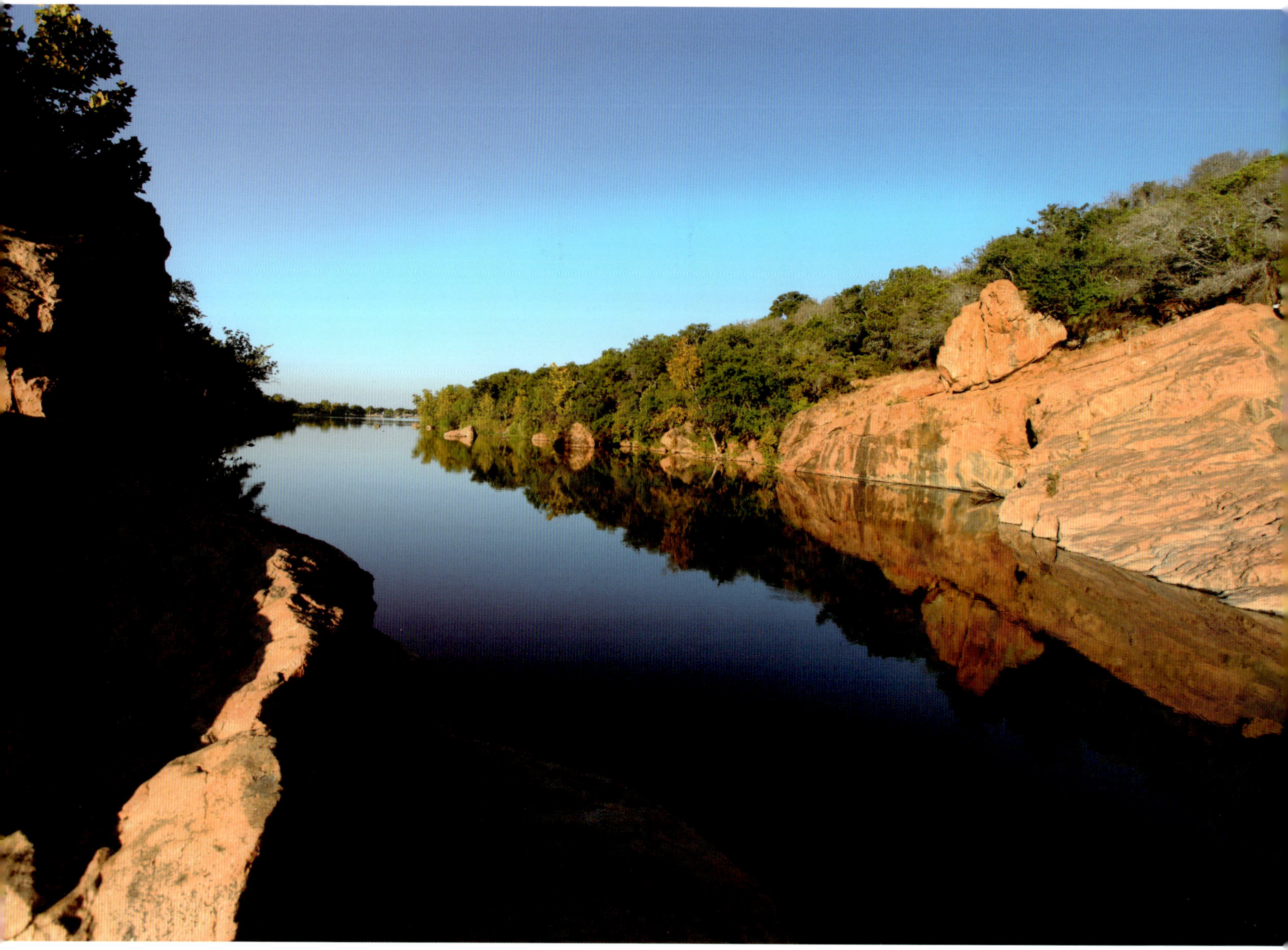

▲ Islands of pink granite-like rock called gneiss jut up to form rocky outcroppings, hillocks, and boulders at Devil's Waterhole in Inks Lake State Park. The rocky shoreline and deep clear water make the inlet a popular summer swimming hole.

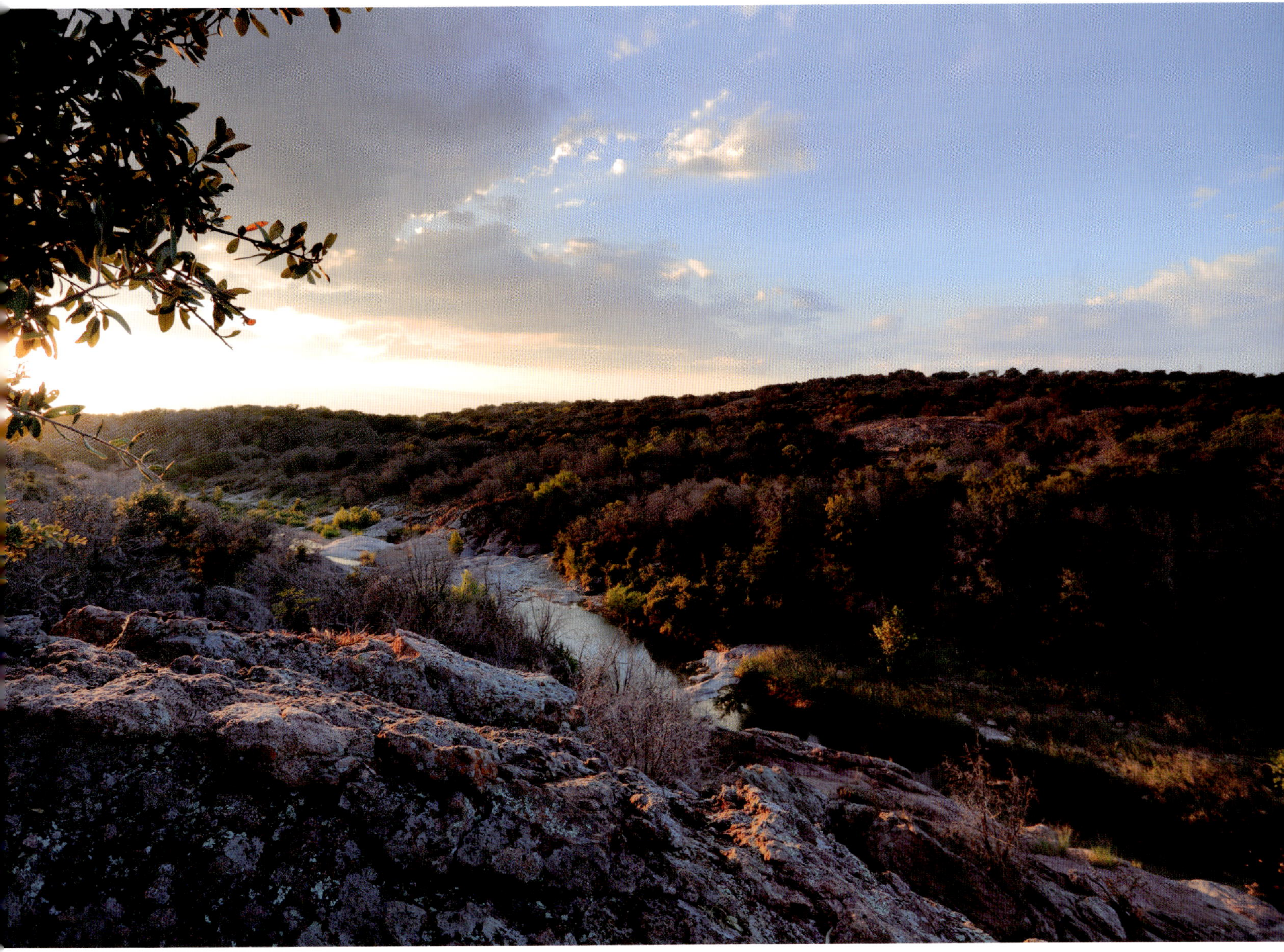

▲ The setting sun illuminates gneiss rock outcroppings and rolling terrain in a valley carved by Spring Creek, one of several streams that feed Inks Lake.

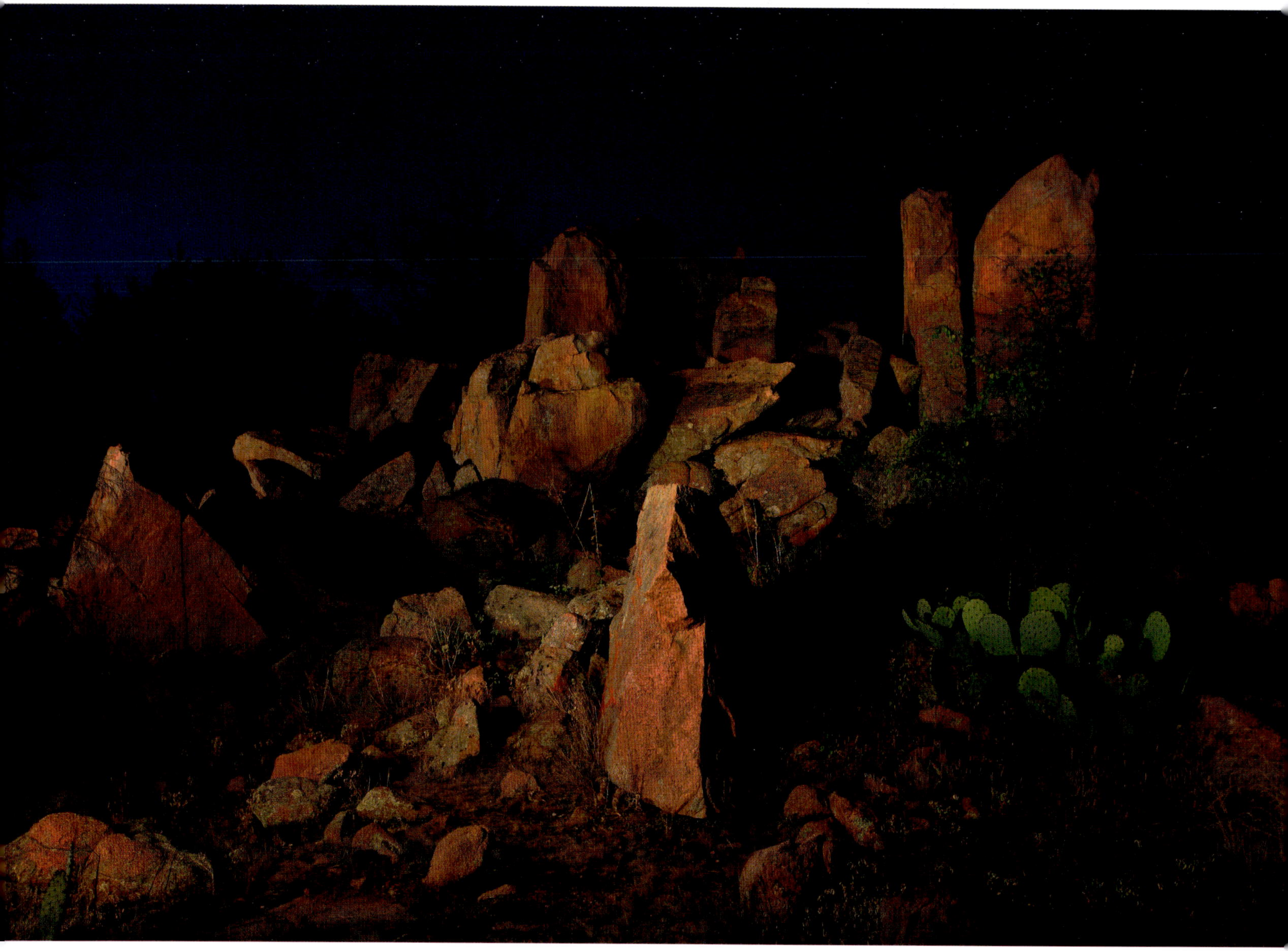

▲▶ Crumbling stacks of boulders punctuate the landscape at Inks Lake State Park. The ancient 600-million-year-old exposed rock often has a carpet of colorful lichens and moss which slowly break down the rock over time.

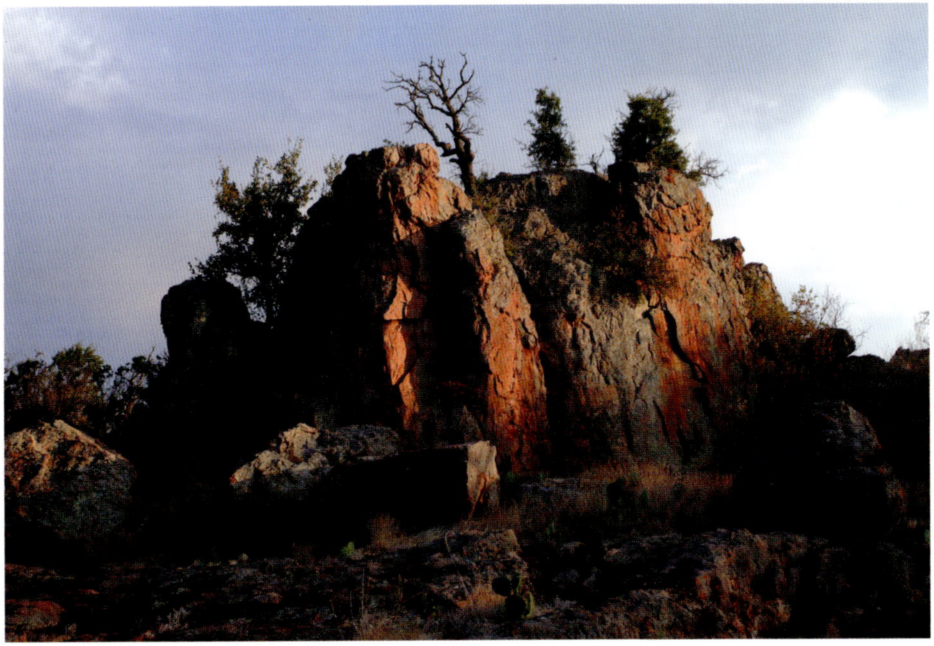

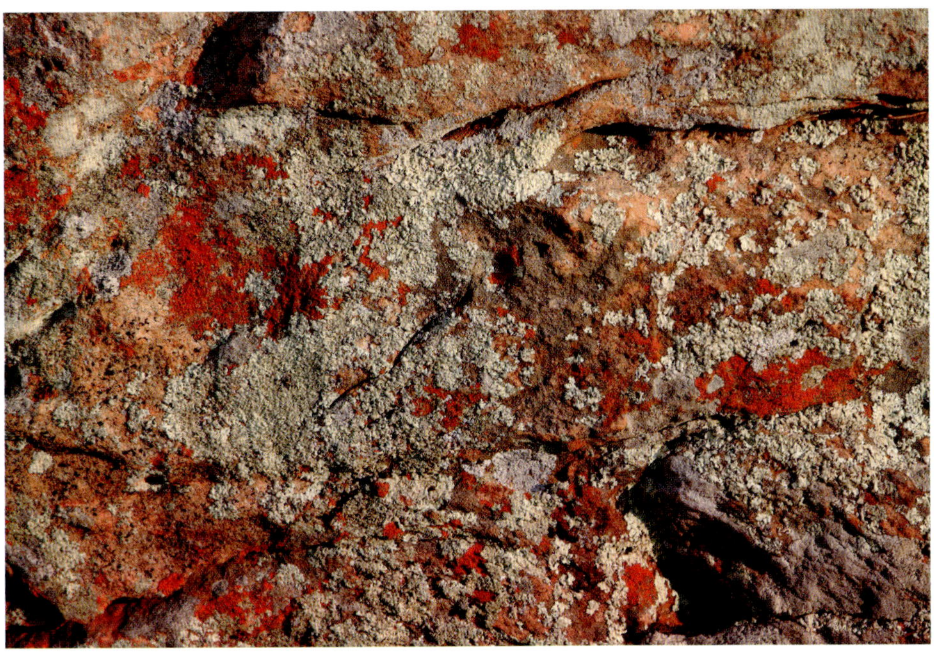

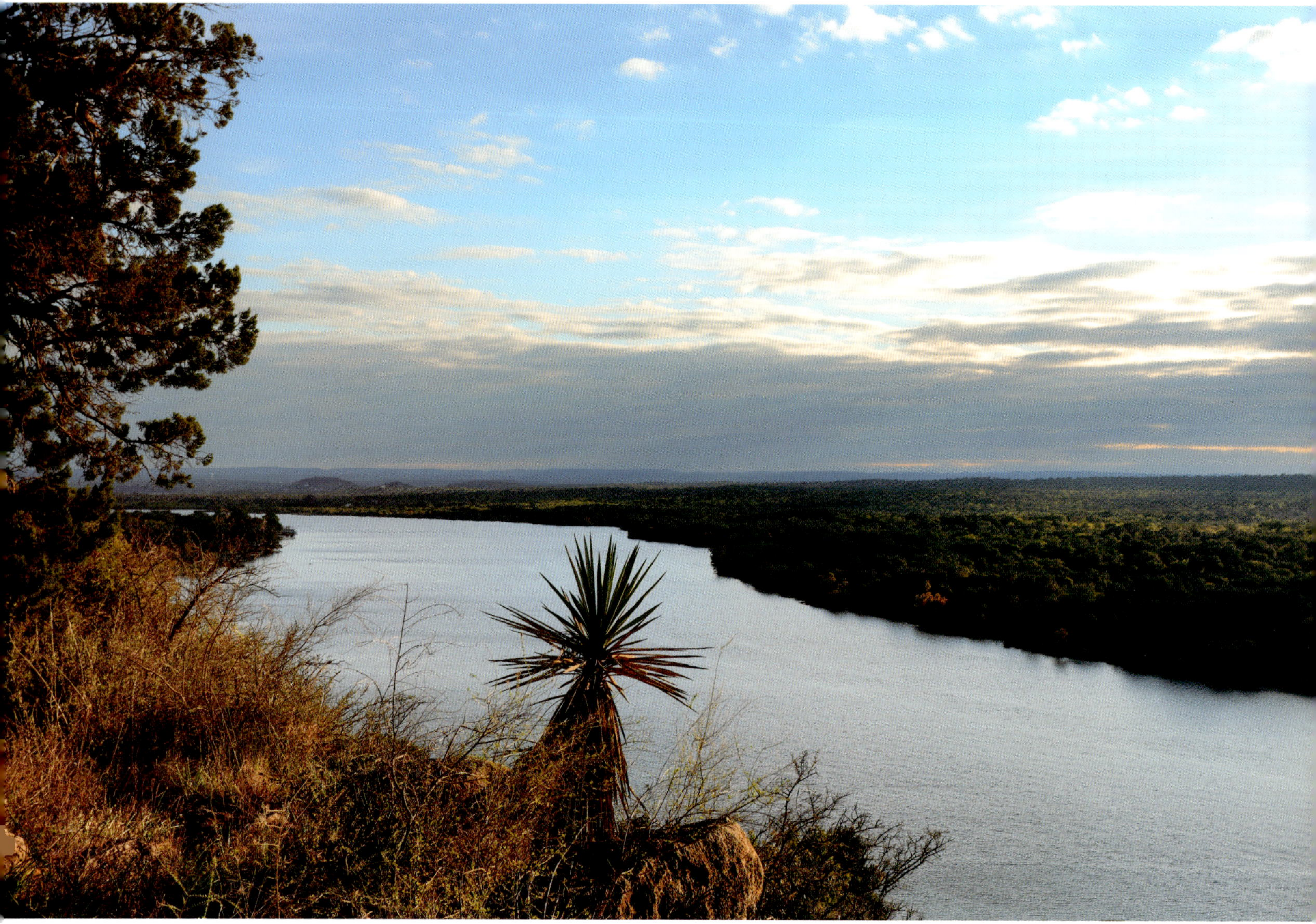

▲ As the Colorado River winds its way through the Texas Hill Country, reservoirs like Lake Lyndon B. Johnson provide flood control and hydroelectric power throughout the region. Known as the Highland Lakes, the chain of six Colorado River reservoirs also includes Lake Buchanan, Inks Lake, Lake Marble Falls, Lake Travis, and Lake Austin.

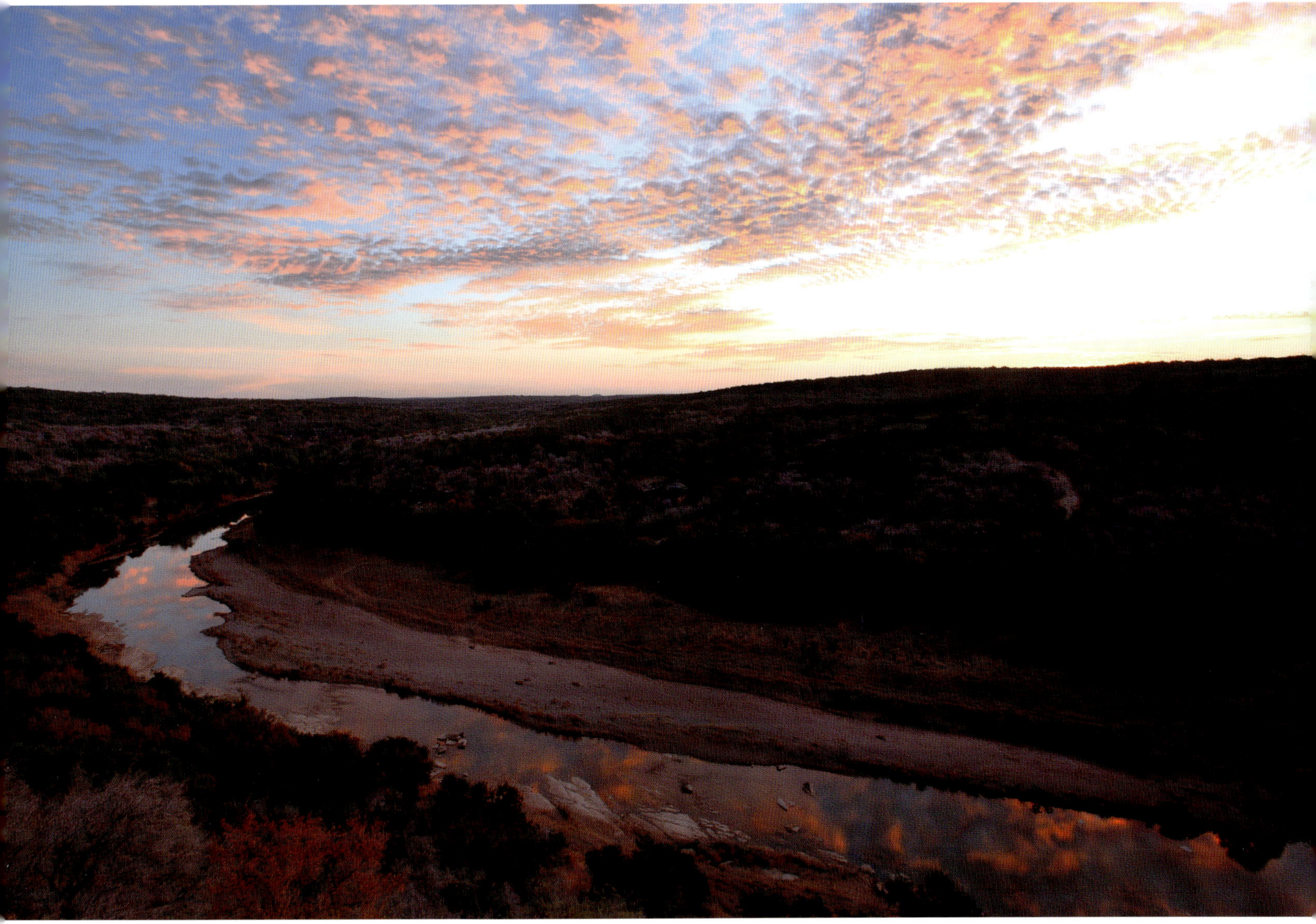

▲ Dramatic cliffs, deep canyons, cool cascading spring-fed creeks, and a slow-moving, shallow stretch of the Colorado River characterize Colorado Bend State Park—a 5,328-acre preserve west of Lampasas.

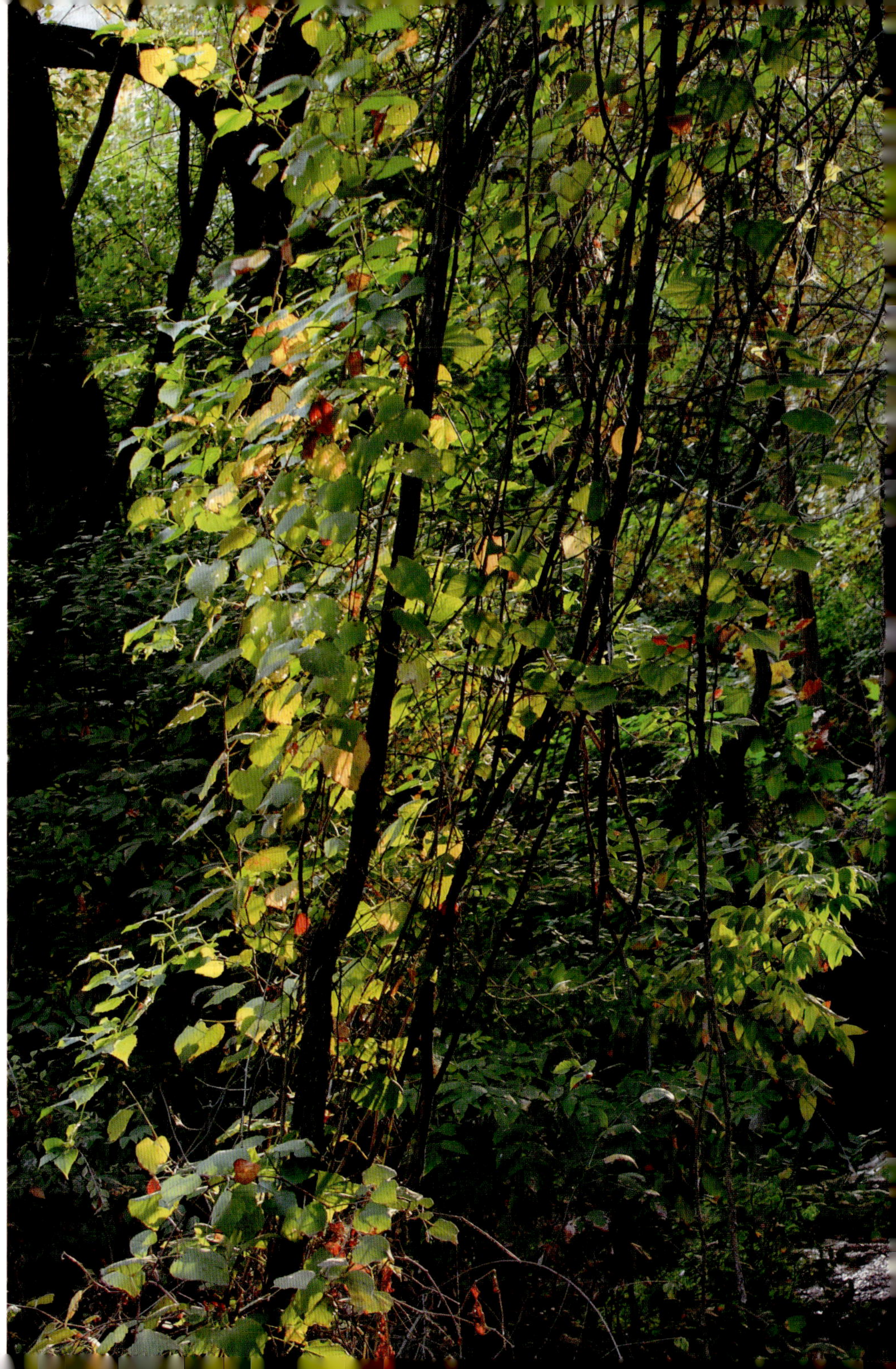

▶ The morning sun highlights lush maidenhair fern, moss-covered travertine formations, and swirling mists at the base of Gorman Falls—a terraced, seventy-foot waterfall and the jewel of Colorado Bend State Park.

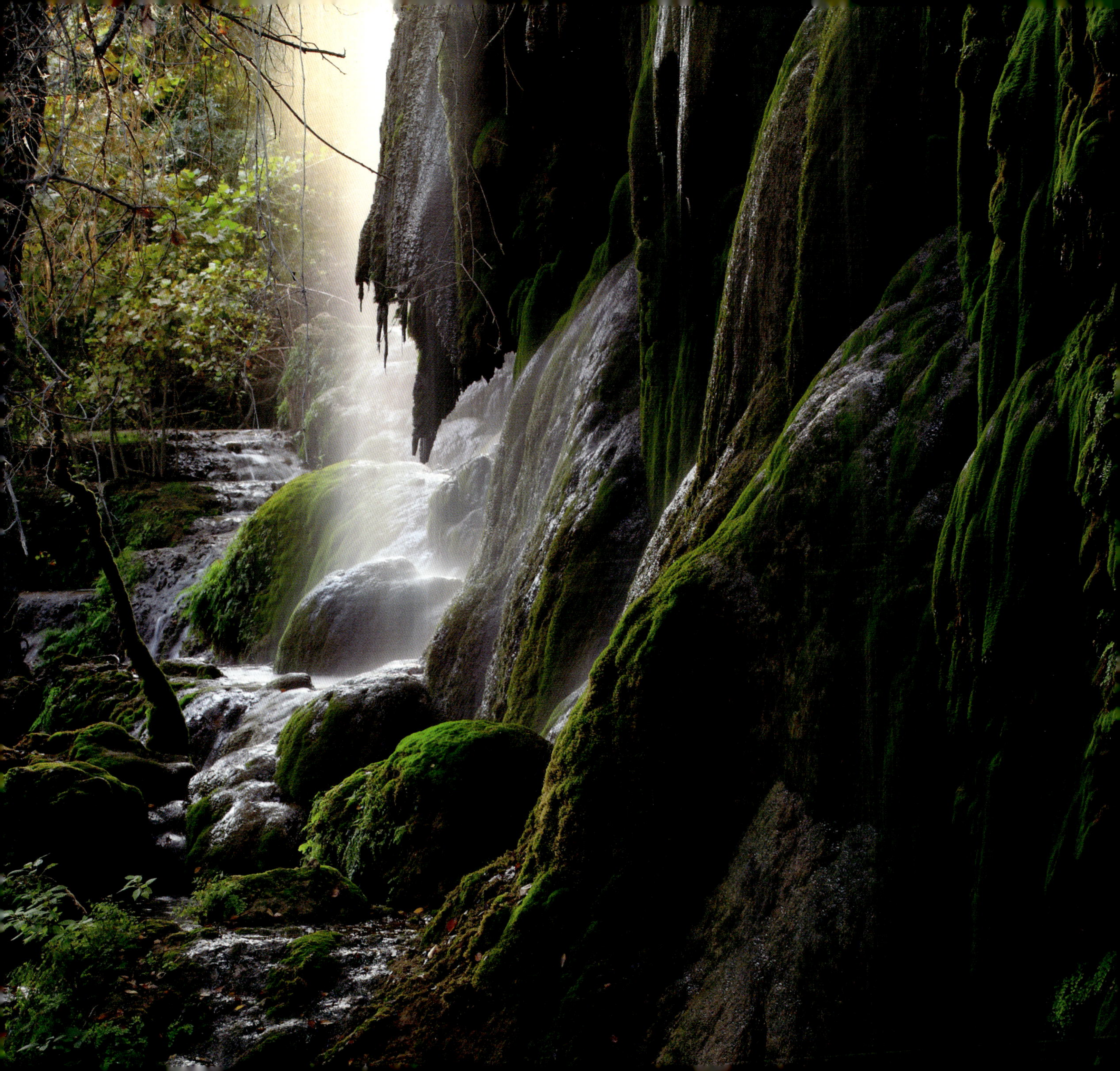

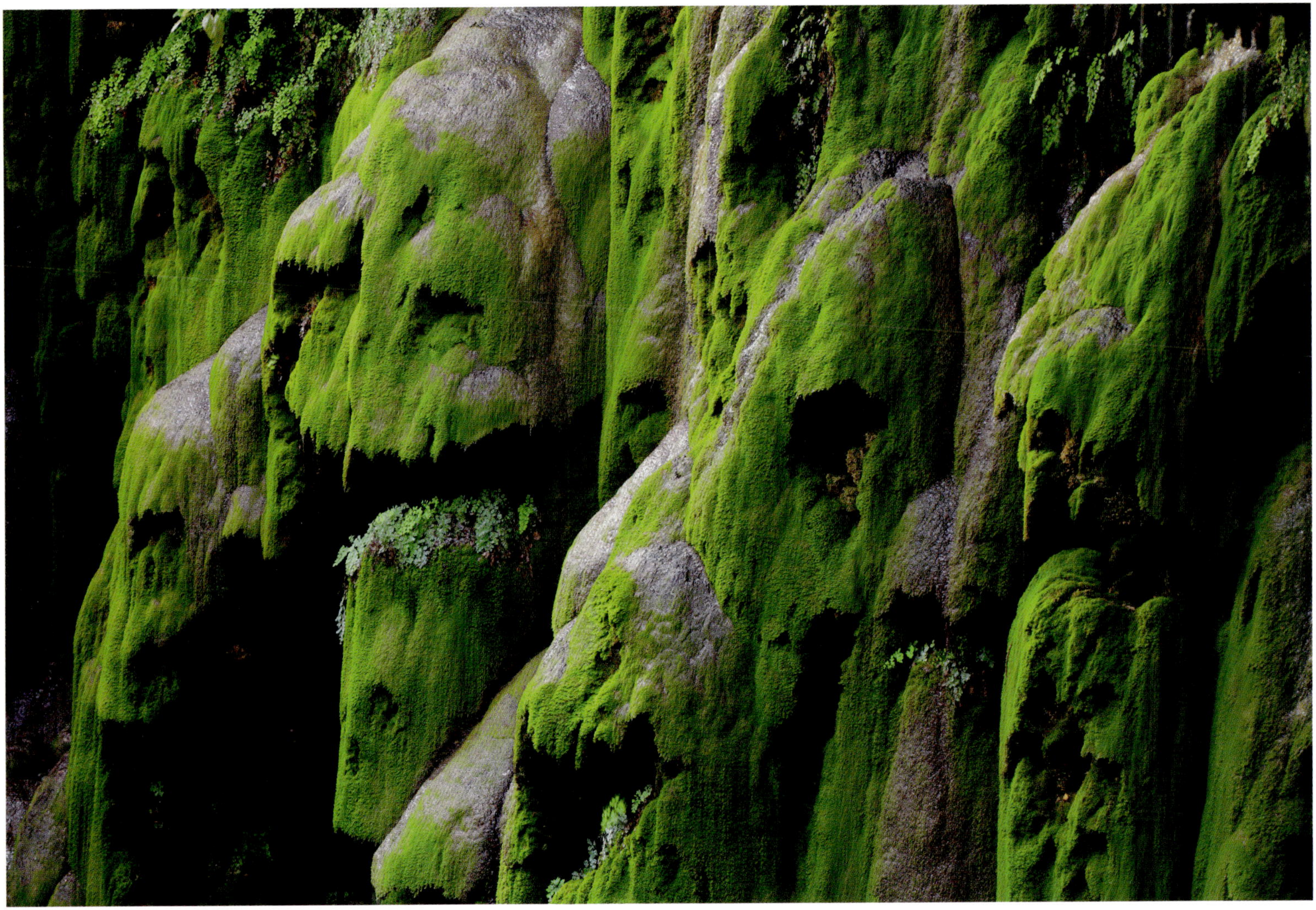

▲ As mineral-rich water cascades down the face of Gorman Falls it deposits layers of calcium, forming travertine formations seen here covered in a carpet of moss.

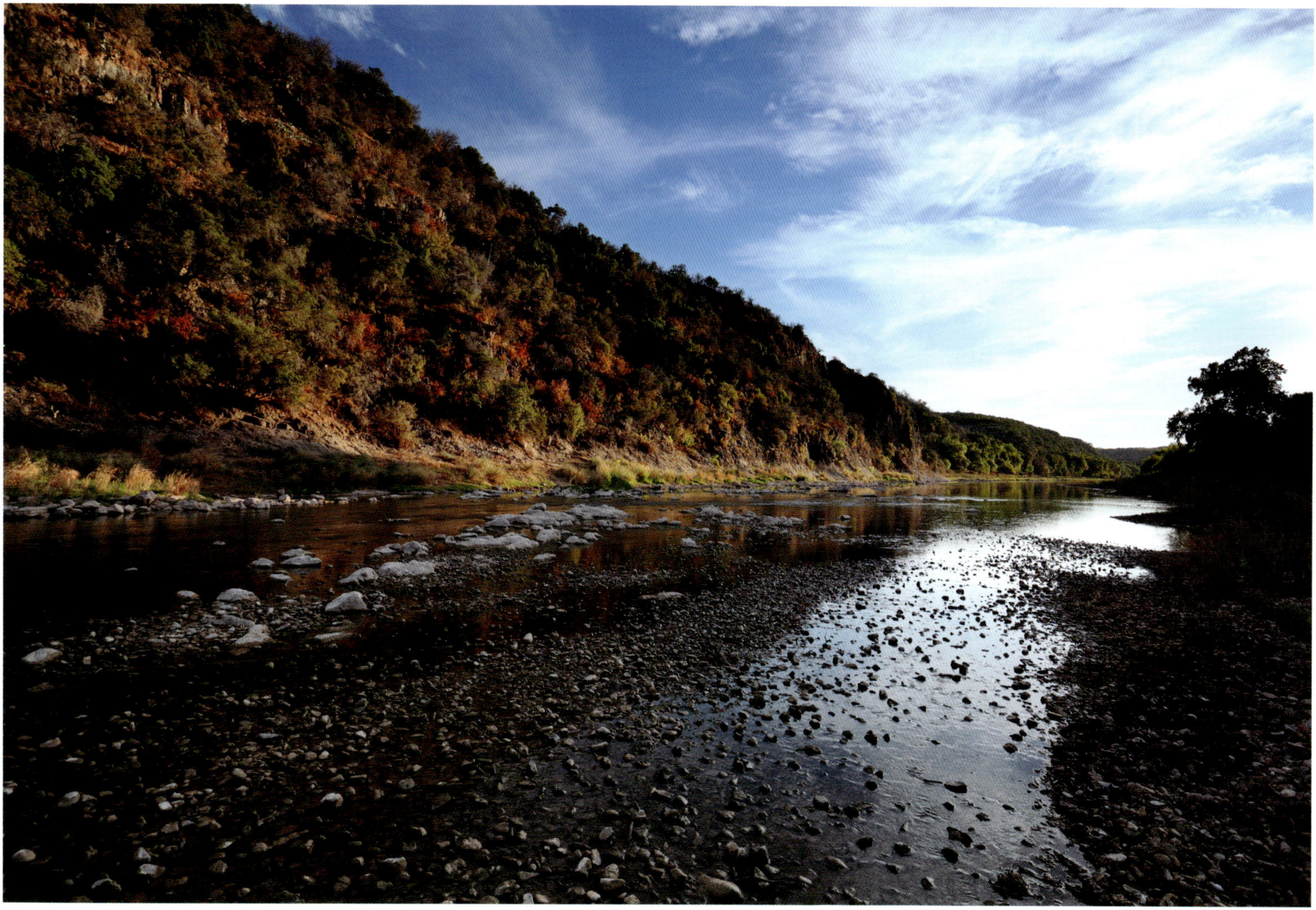

▲ In Colorado Bend State Park autumn hues pepper the limestone cliffs in early fall above the Colorado River.

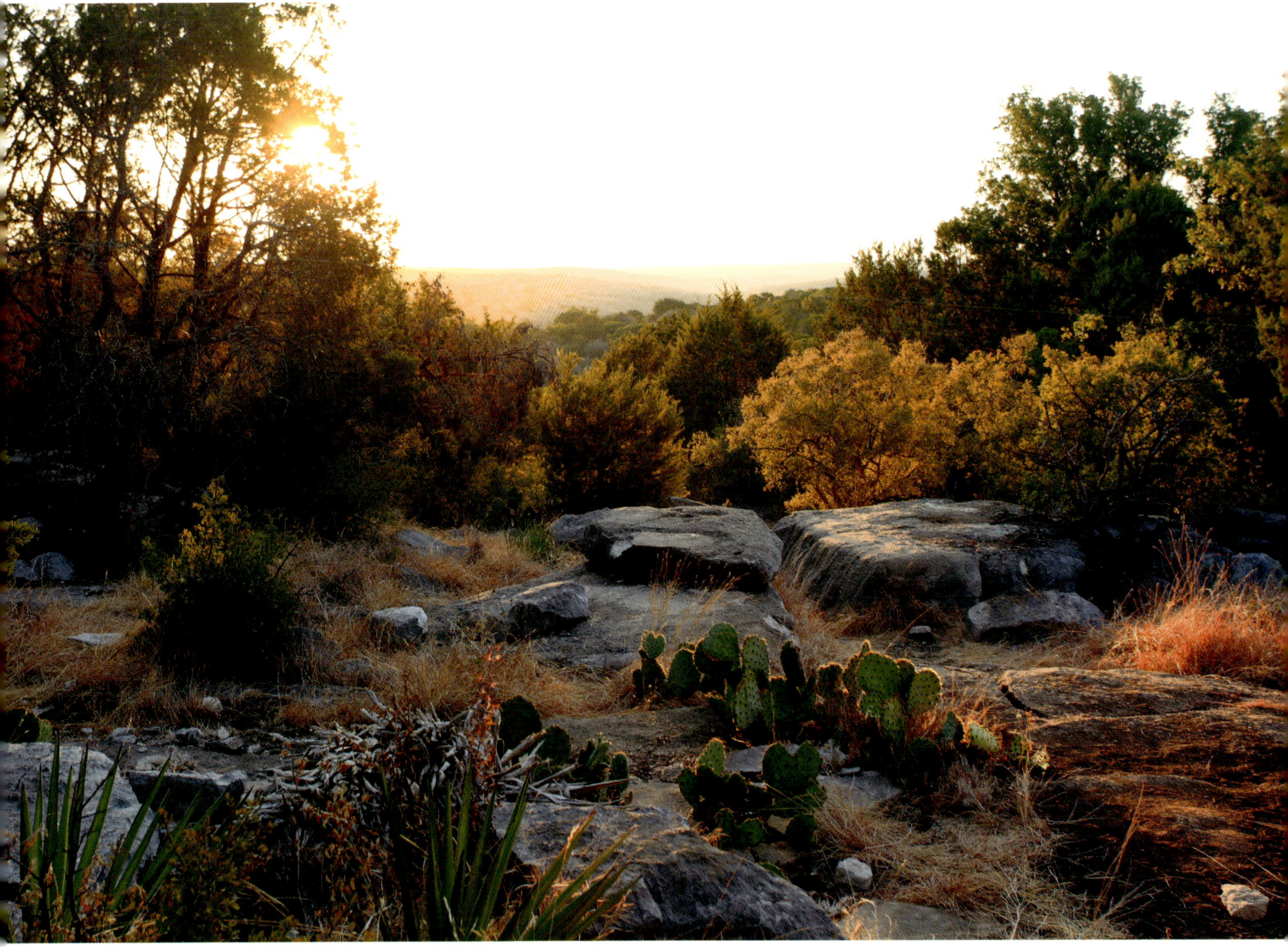

▲▶ Sunlight filters through the hardwood and live oak trees, highlighting prickly pear cactus and native Hill Country grasses like sideoats grama and little bluestem.

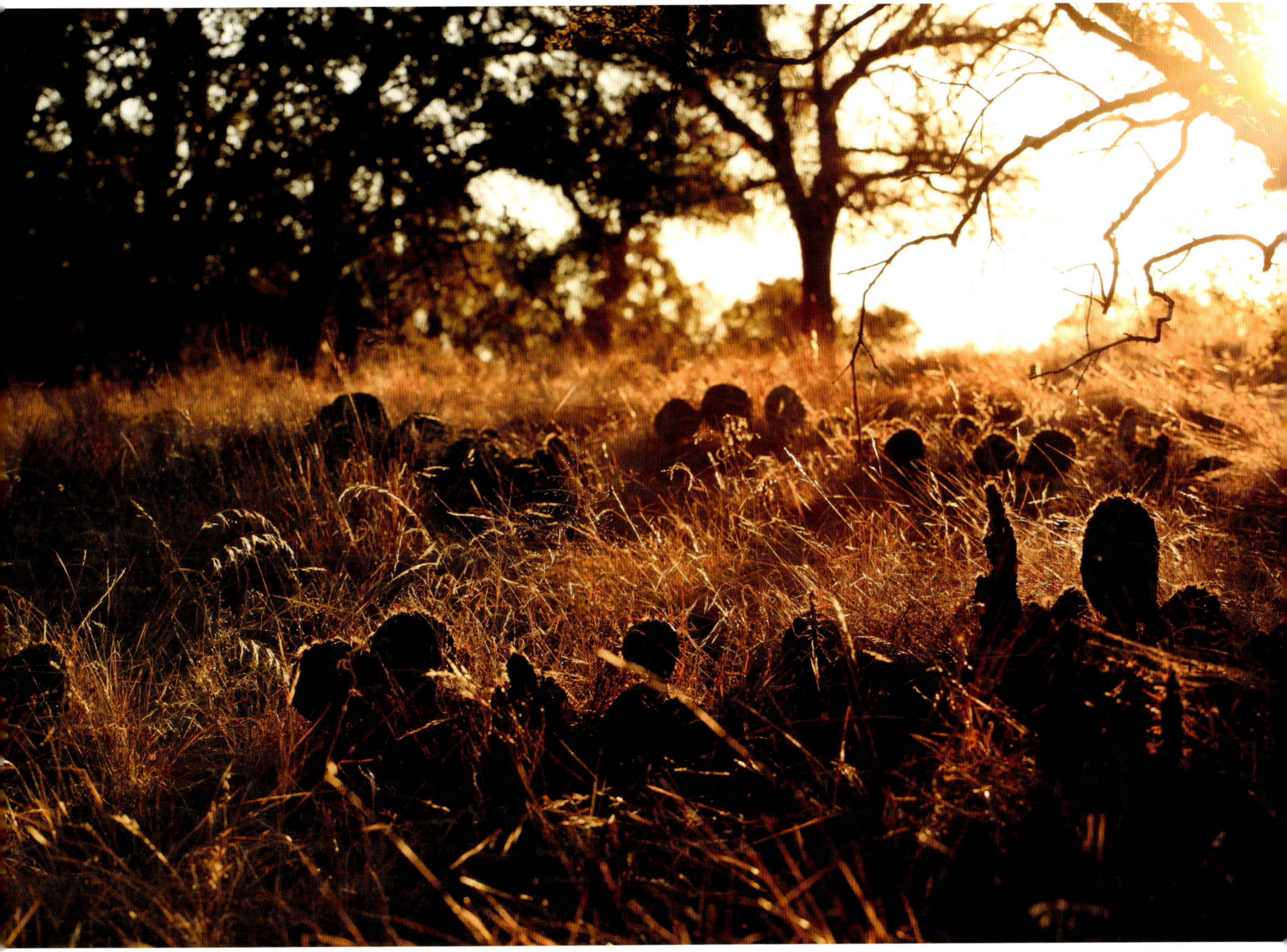

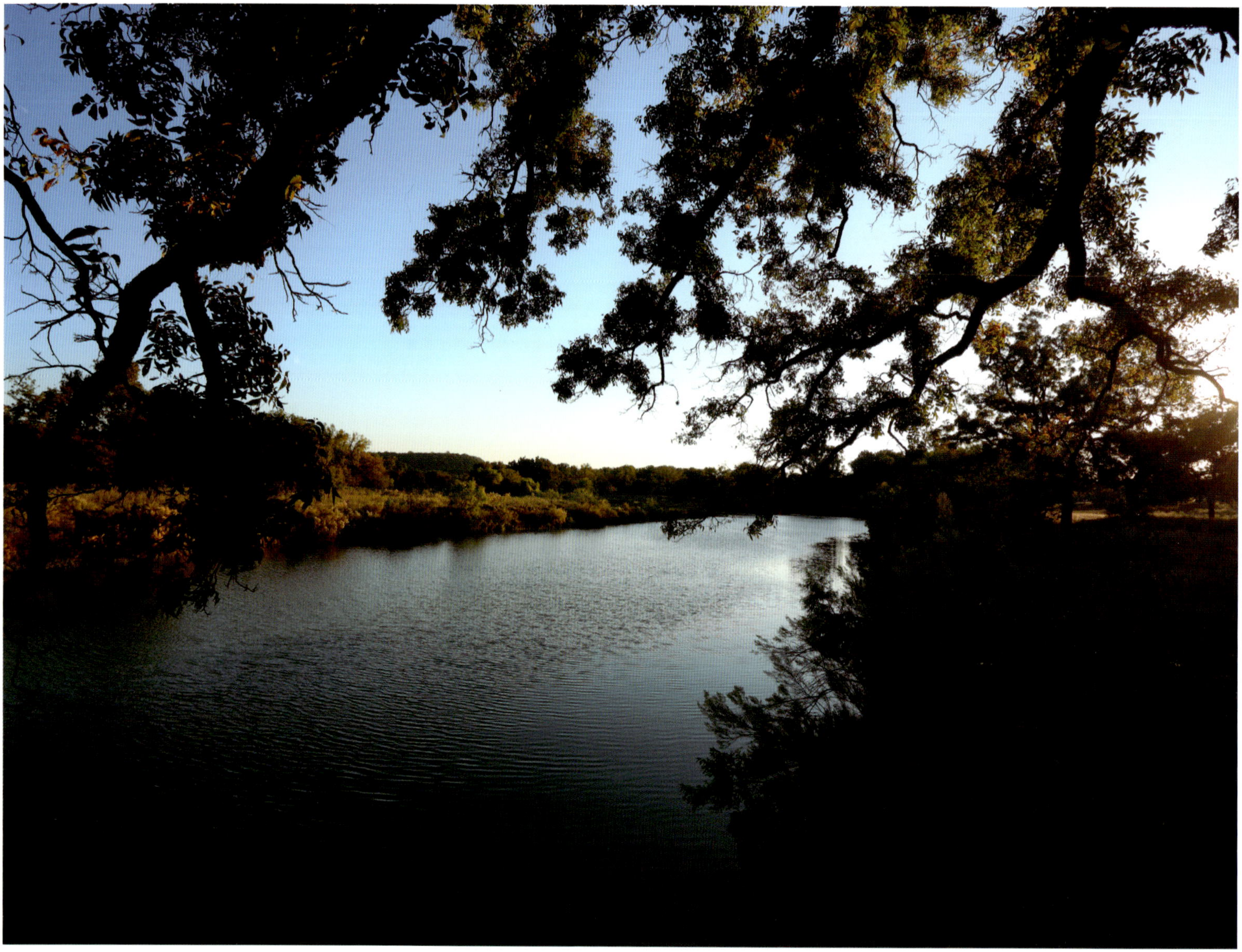

▲▶ South of Junction, 507-acre South Llano River State Park contains heavily wooded pecan bottomland along two miles of the South Llano River. The park provides important habitat for a population of Rio Grande turkeys that roost in the bottomland during the fall and winter months.

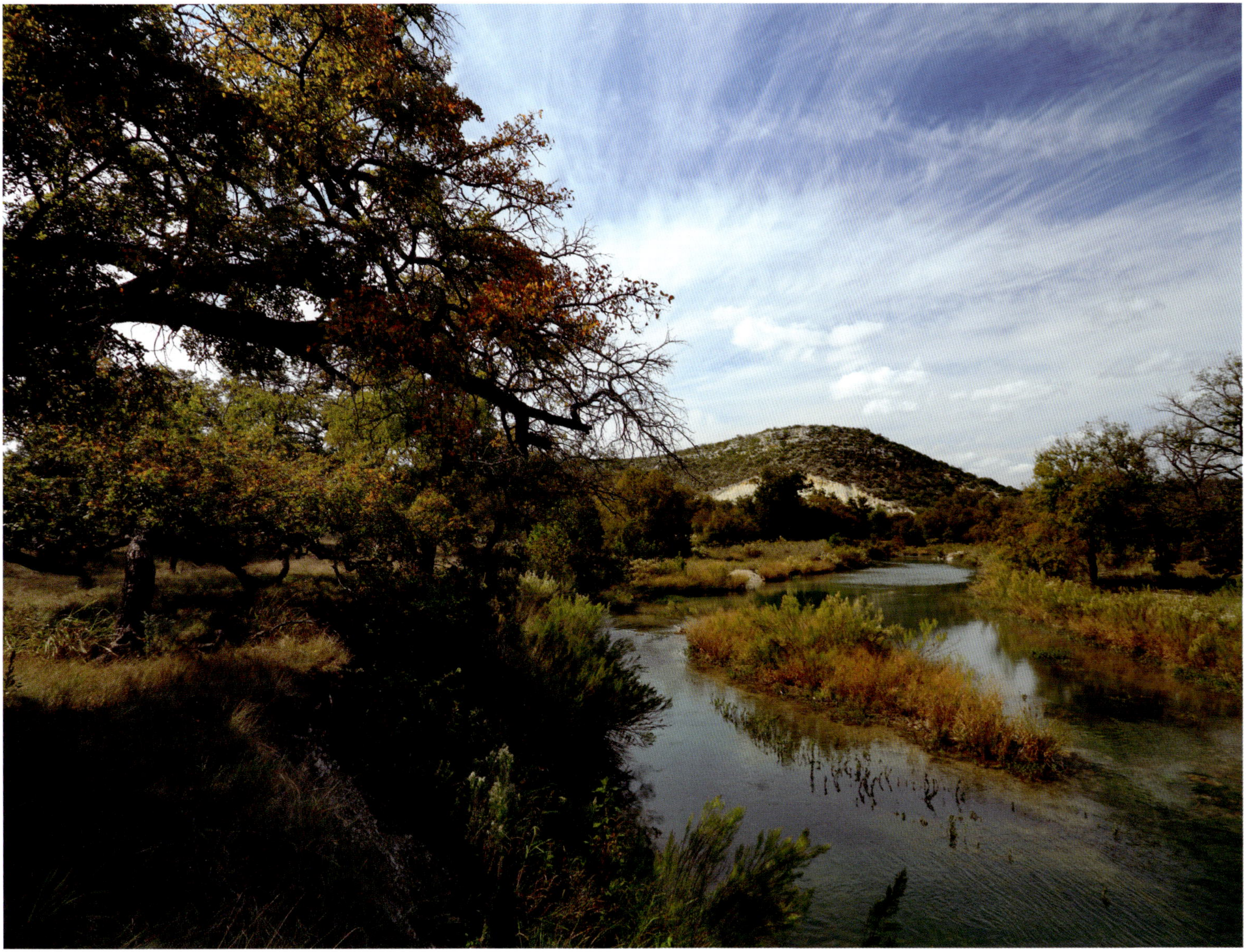

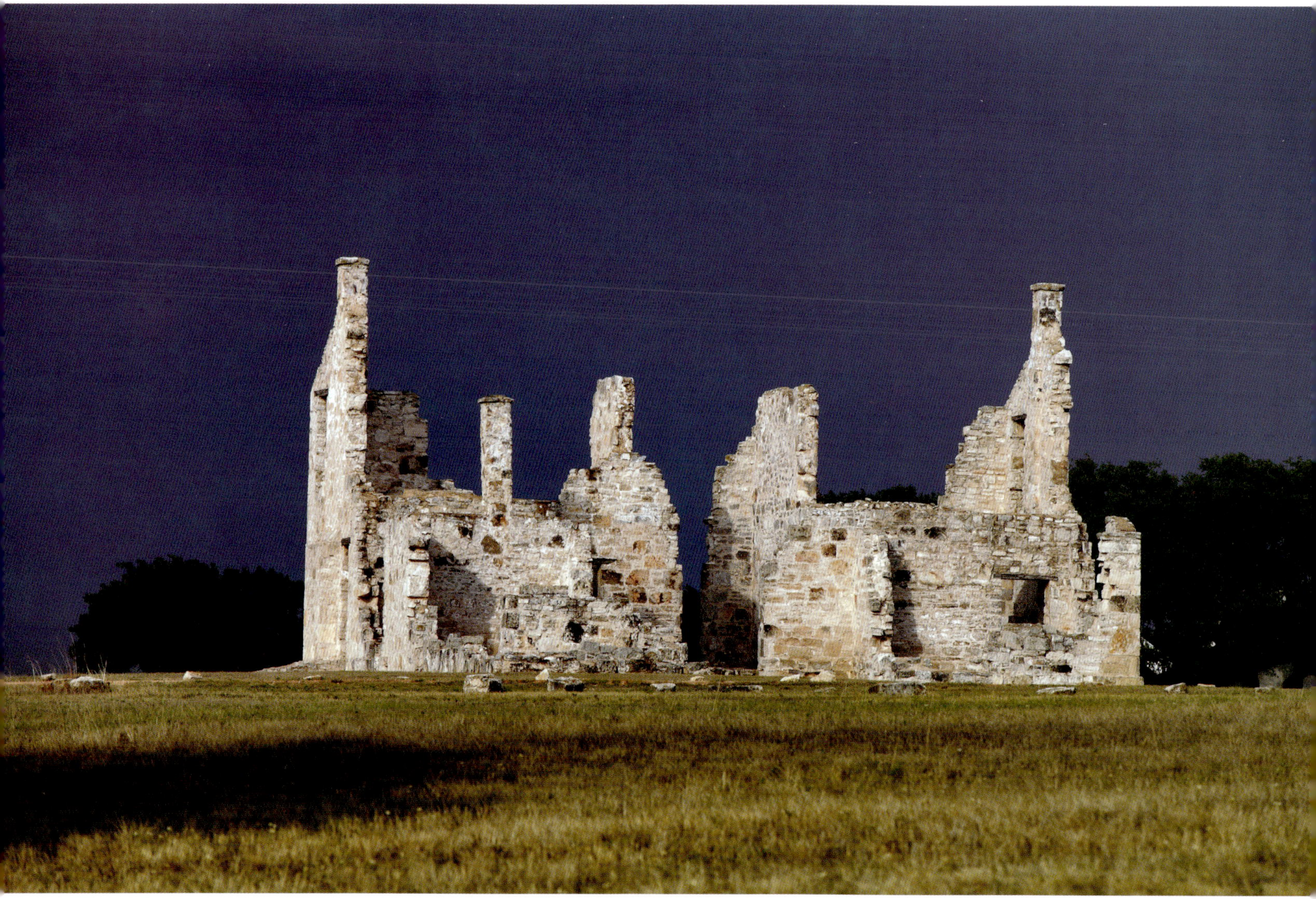

▲▶ On the far western edge of the Hill Country, Fort McKavett State Historic Site encompasses the grounds of a former US military post. Built in 1852 as Camp San Saba to protect settlers from Indians, in 1868 it was renamed Fort McKavett. Today the park's eighty-two acres house a variety of ruins and dozens of restored buildings and exhibits that preserve the history of Texas' frontier era.

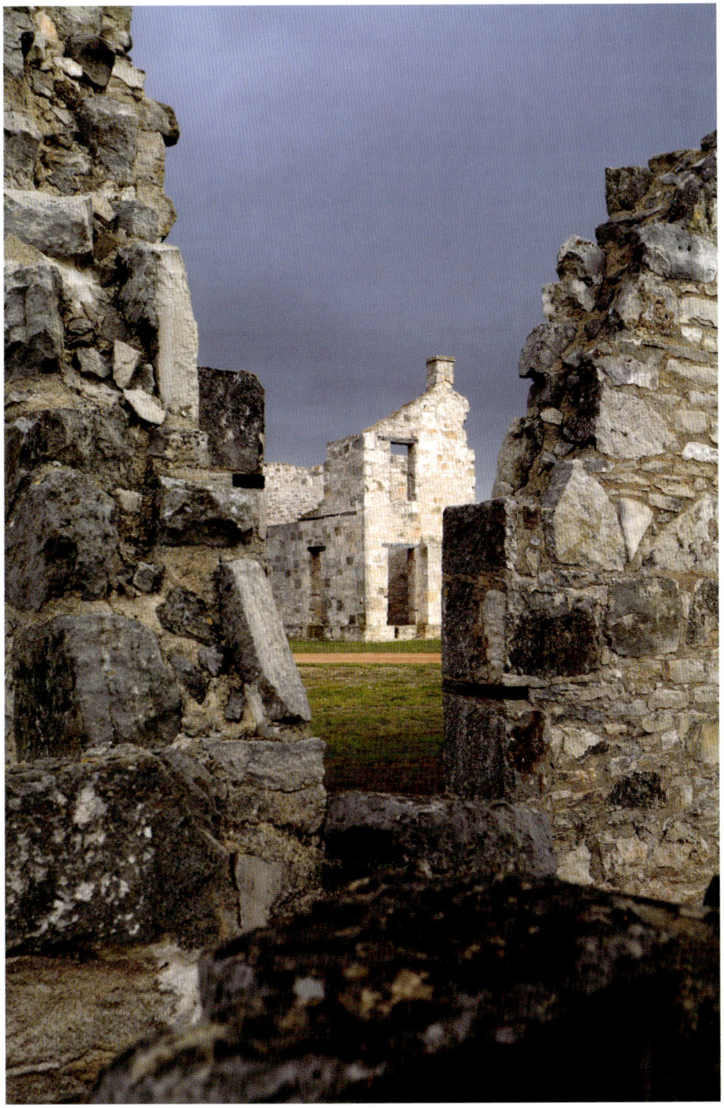

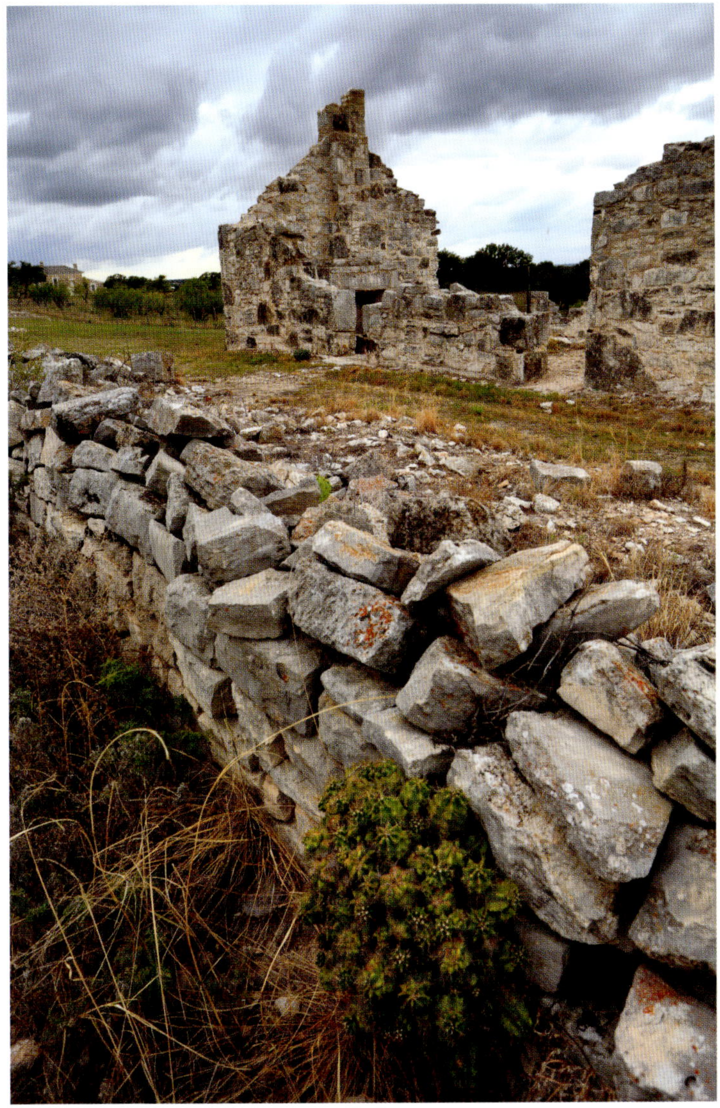

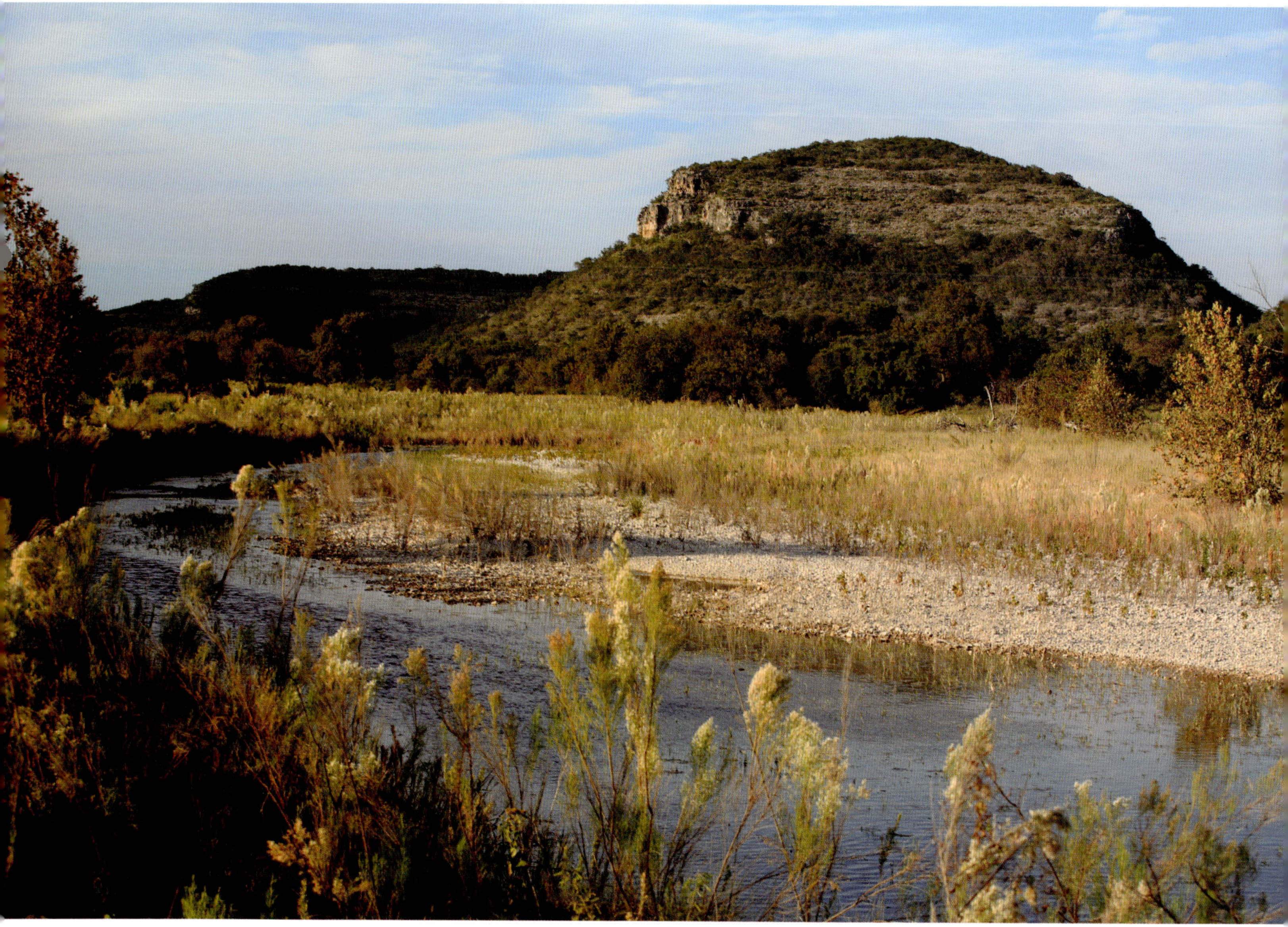

▲ Rugged topography and semi-arid flora typify the Neuces River bottom near the confluence of Bullhead Creek. The Nueces River rises from headwaters in Edwards and Real counties and then snakes through the steep-walled canyons and across shallow flood plains of the Hill Country.

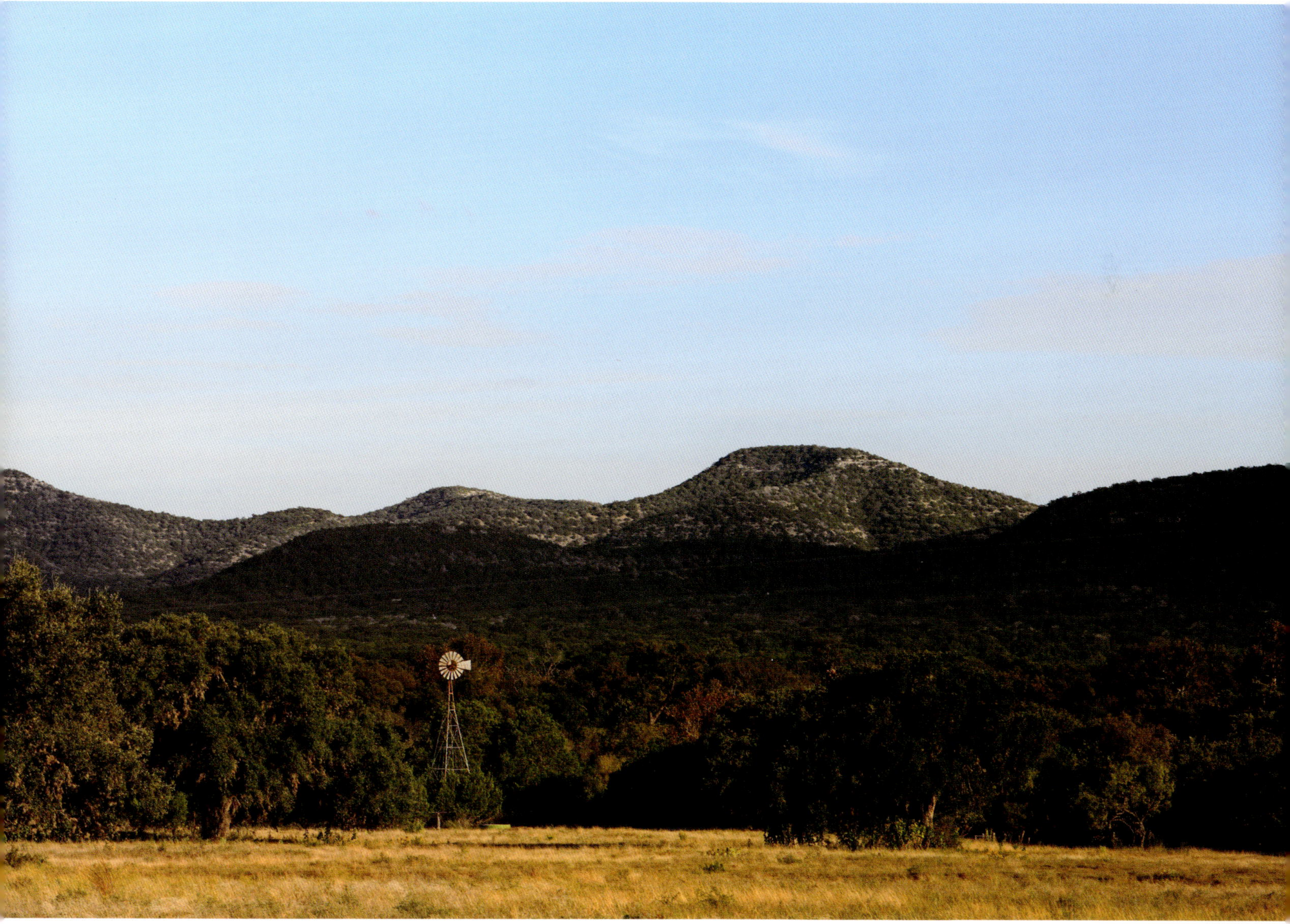

▲ Nueces Canyon is known for the winding Nueces River, crisscrossing streams, breathtaking hills, and scenic drives like this scene near Vance on Farm-to-Market Road 335. Alonso De León named the canyon's river Río de las Nueces ("River of Nuts") after the abundant pecan trees growing along its banks.

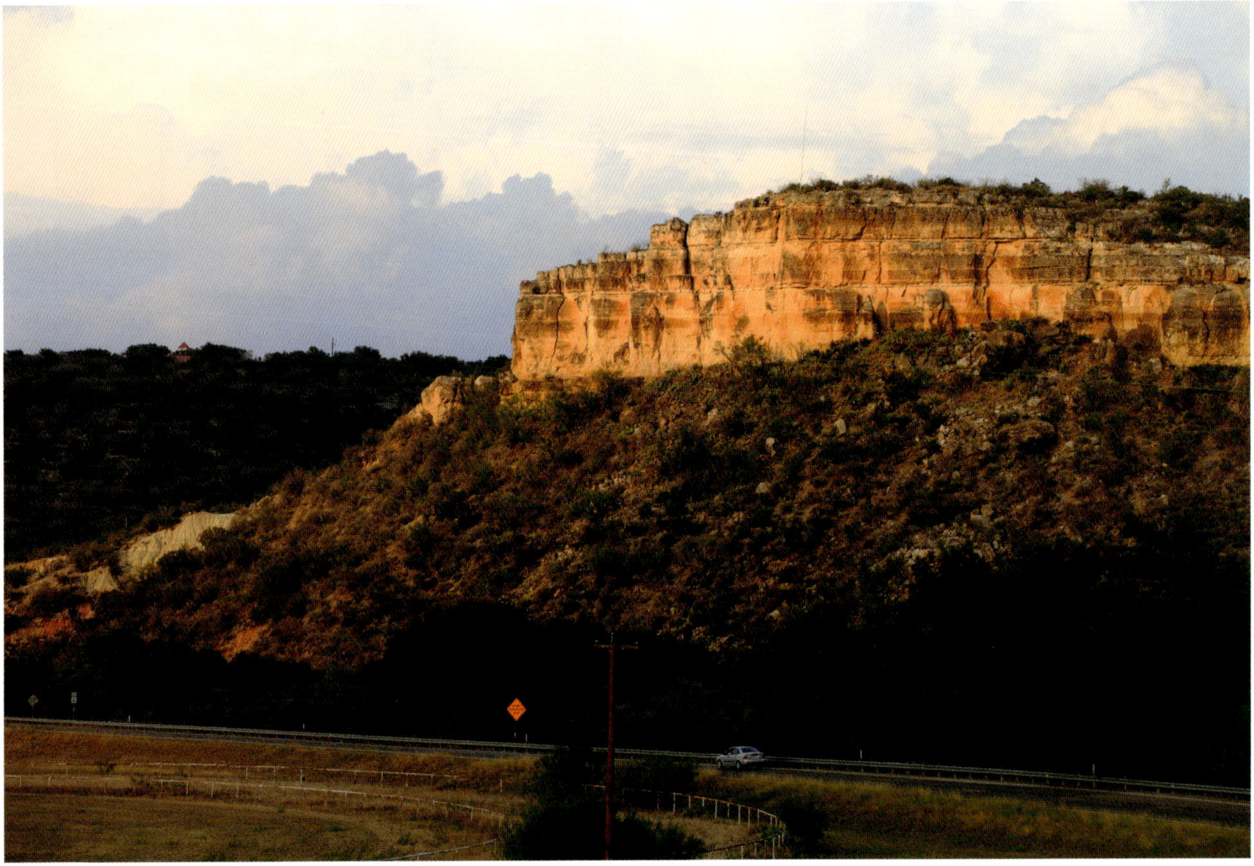

▲ Just south of Junction, a hilltop known as Lover's Leap rises more than 200 feet above Cedar Creek, a tributary of the Llano River. Although many versions of the legend of Lover's Leap have been passed by oral tradition, the stories similarly involve a young Native American girl who jumped from the top. Today it remains a landmark easily identified by its chalky sheer precipice.

▶ Pedernales Falls State Park showcases a spectacular bed of 300-million-year-old exposed limestone which form a series of pools, channels, and cascading falls that stair-step down in elevation over a distance of 3,000 feet.

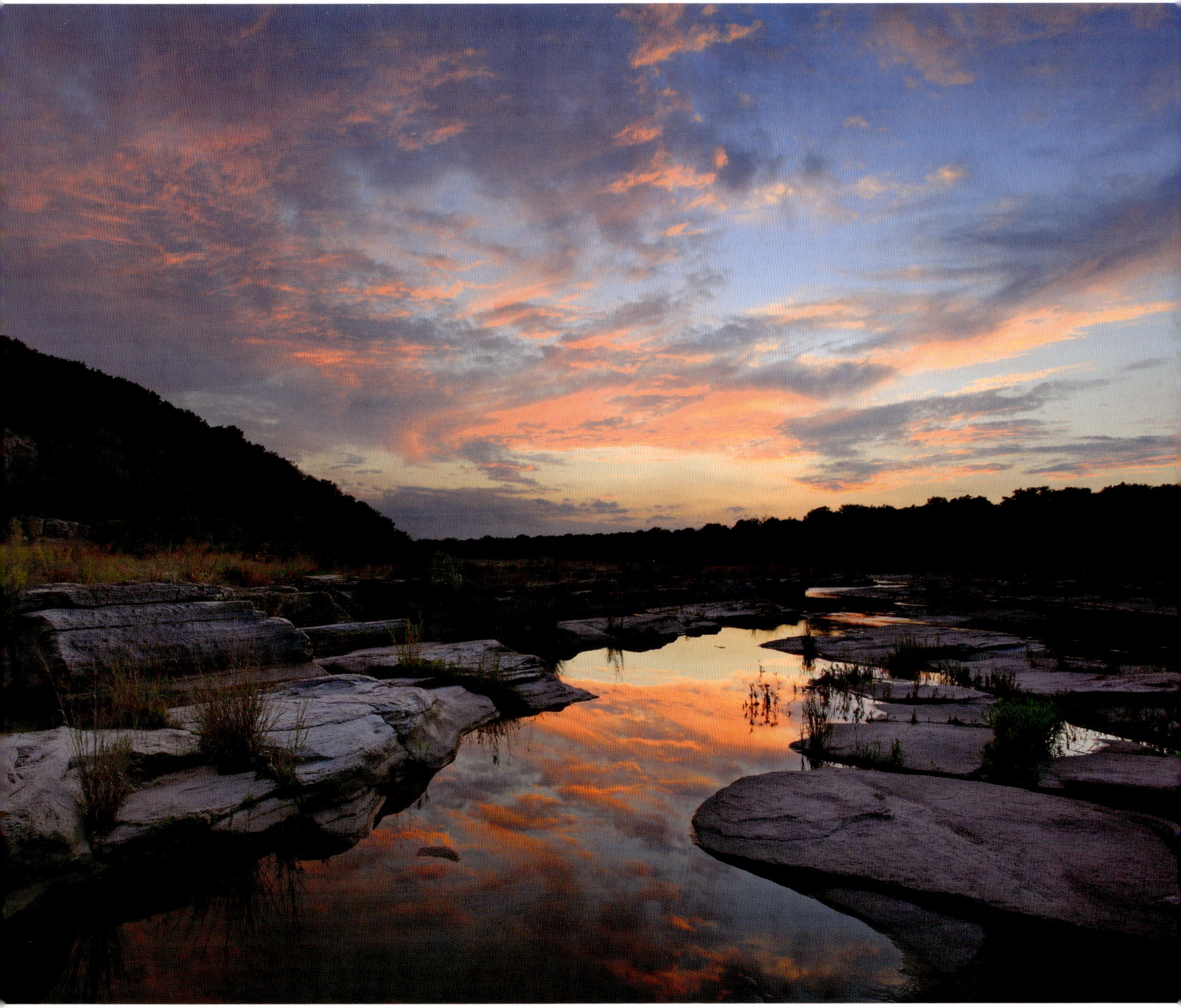

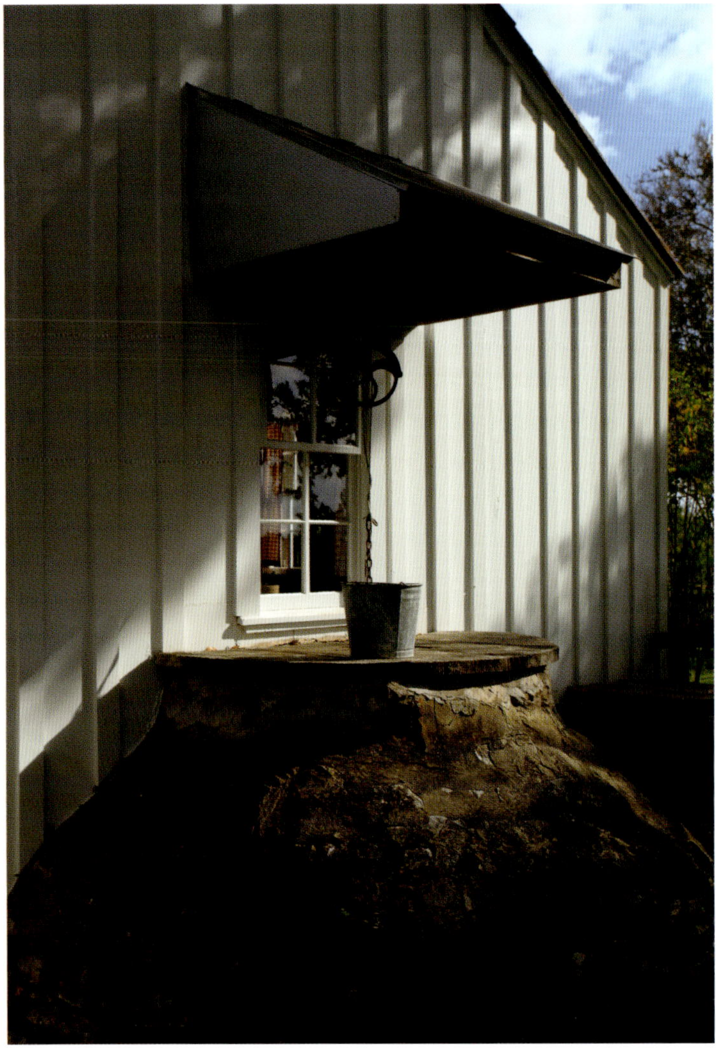

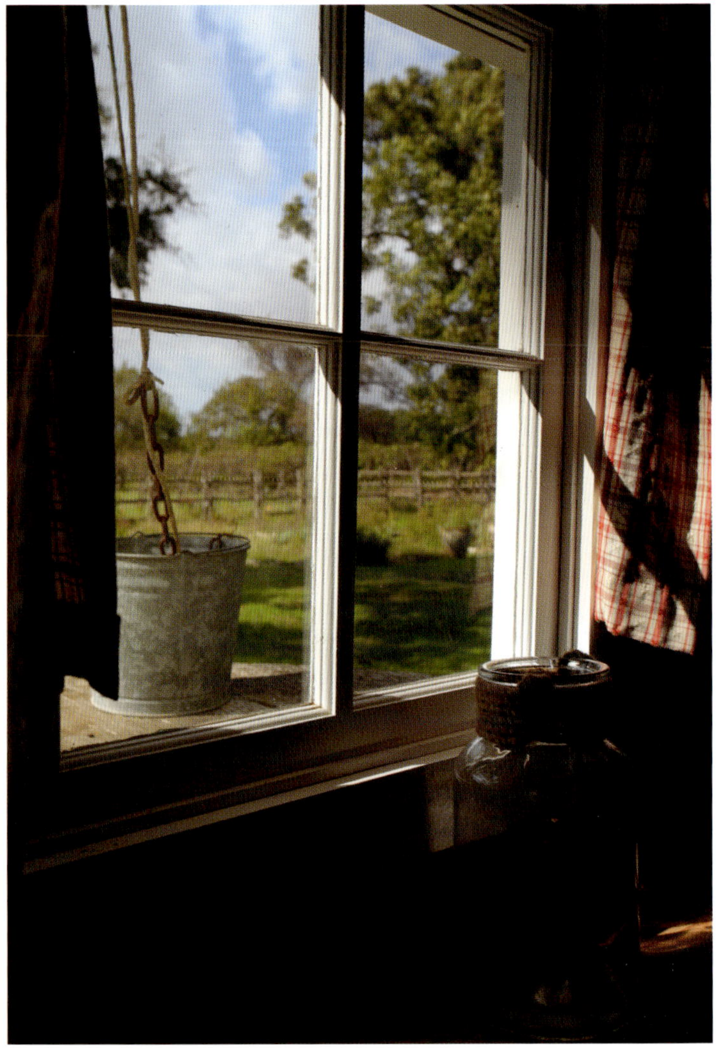

▲◥ In the early 1850s, Sarah and Joseph Pound settled on part of the Texas frontier that would later become Dripping Springs. Today the Pound family's dogtrot home stands as a museum, including the twenty-two foot hand-dug limestone cistern built into the dining room/kitchen. Water could be drawn by opening the window and lowering the bucket.

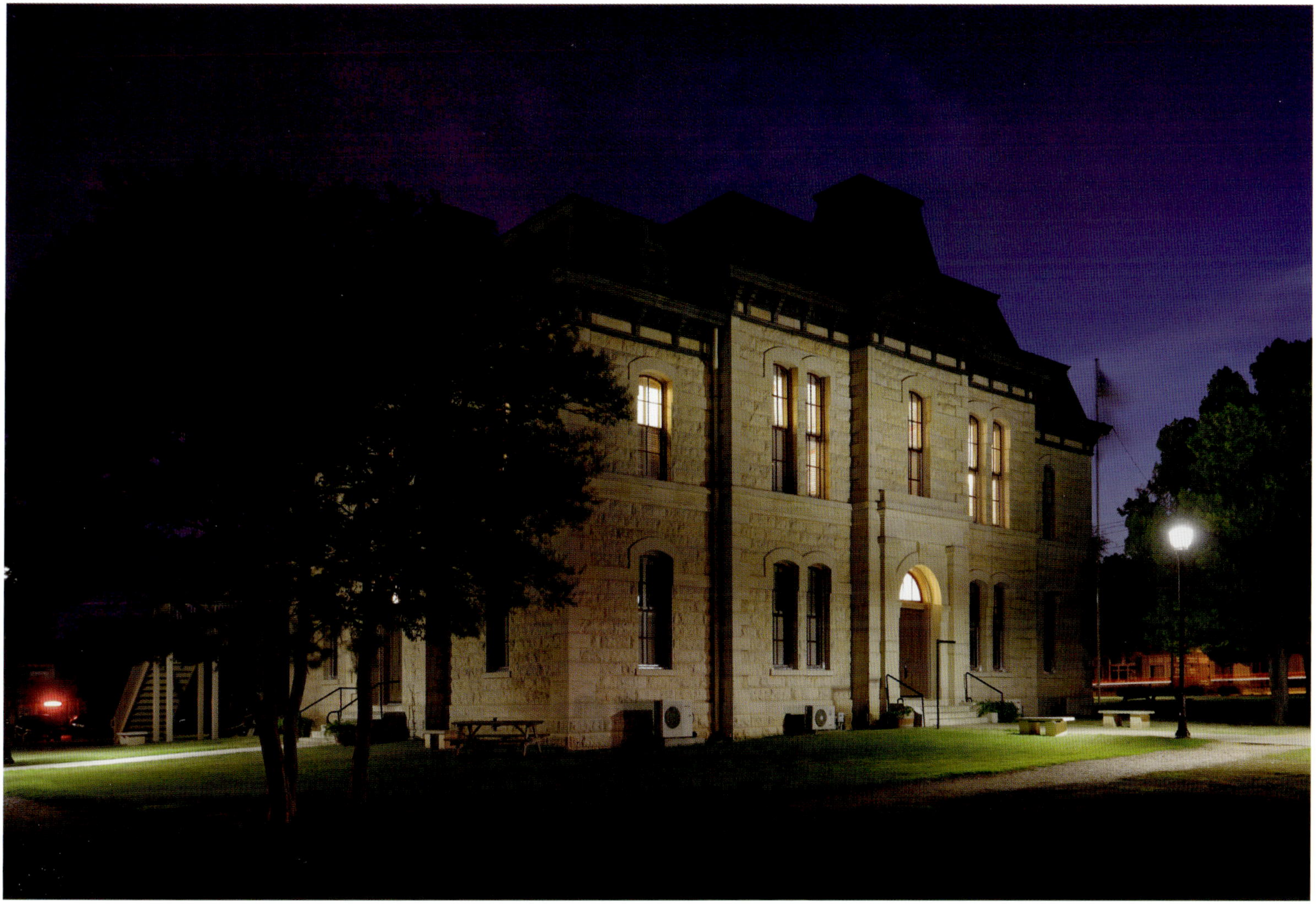

▲ Completed in 1886, the old Blanco County Courthouse only served for four years before the county seat was moved to Johnson City. The old courthouse continued serving the Blanco community as office space, a school, a bank, and operated as a hospital from 1937–1961. Today the restored building can be rented for events and houses the Blanco Welcome Center.

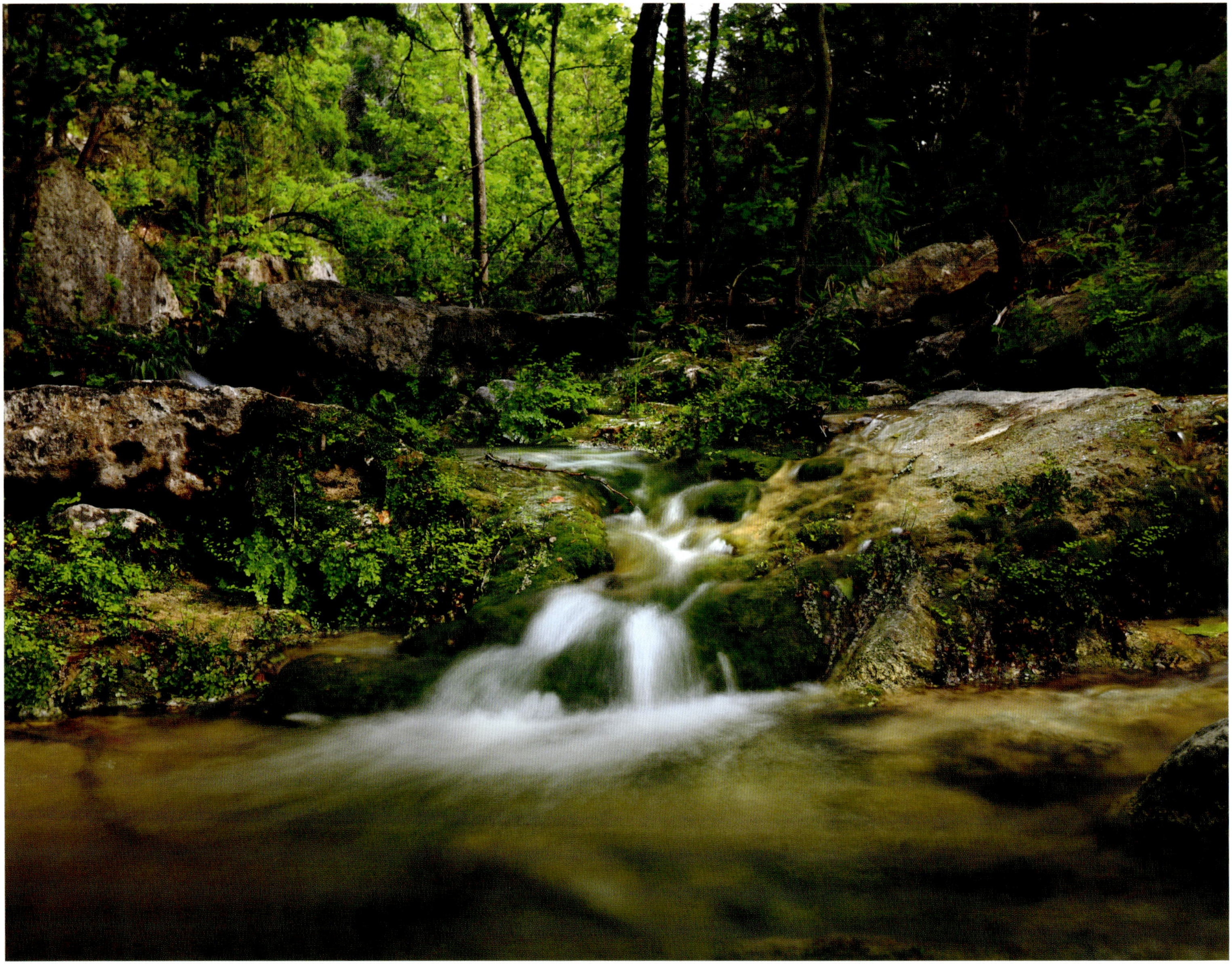

▲ In Pedernales Falls State Park intermittent sunlight trickles through a canopy of hardwoods on to the babbling waters of Bee Creek, one of several spring-fed streams that flow through the park.

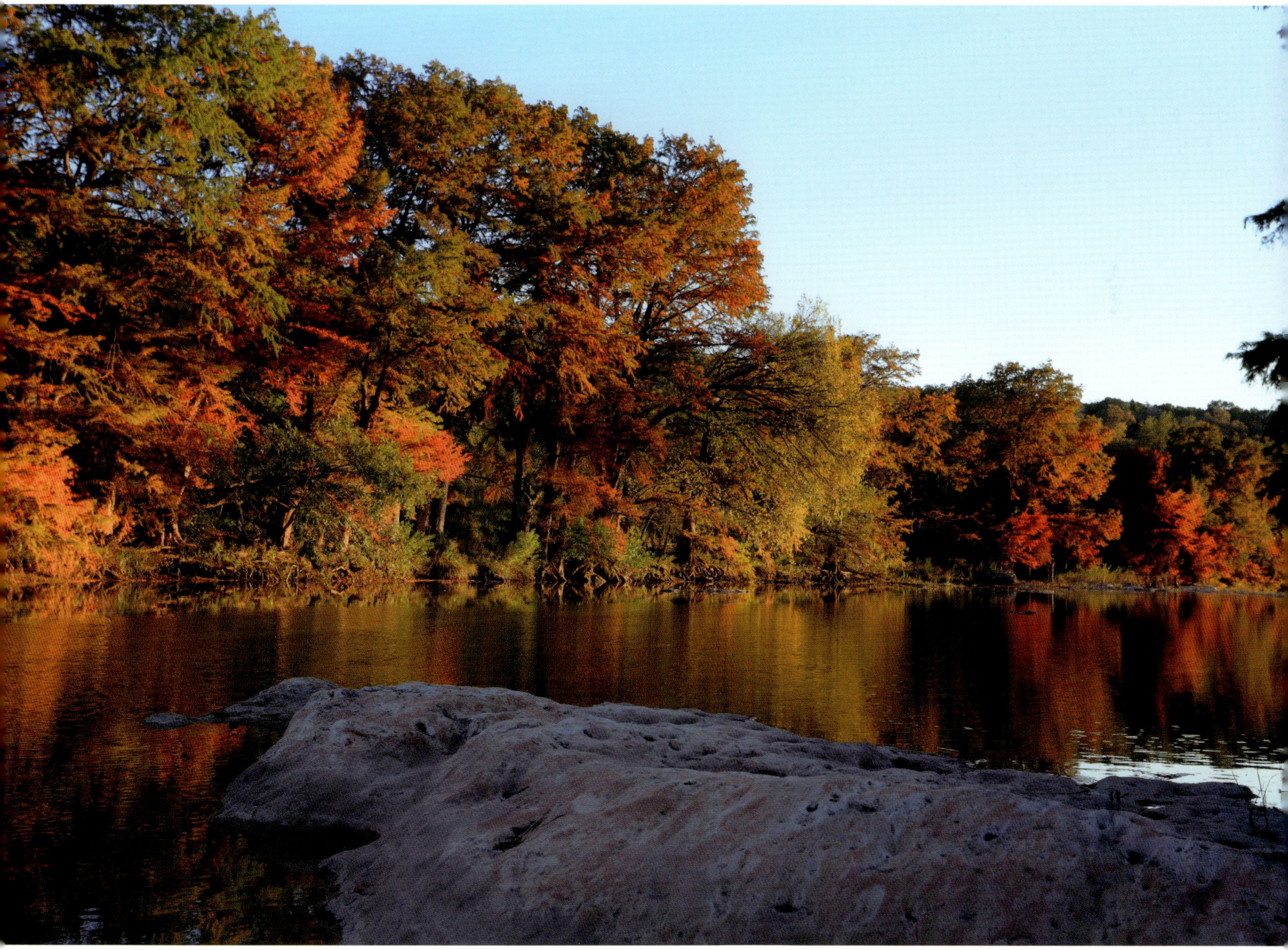

▲ A medley of autumn hues reflects the changing of the seasons, as the banks of the Pedernales River are ablaze with vivid yellow hardwoods and splashes of burnt orange from bald cypress trees.

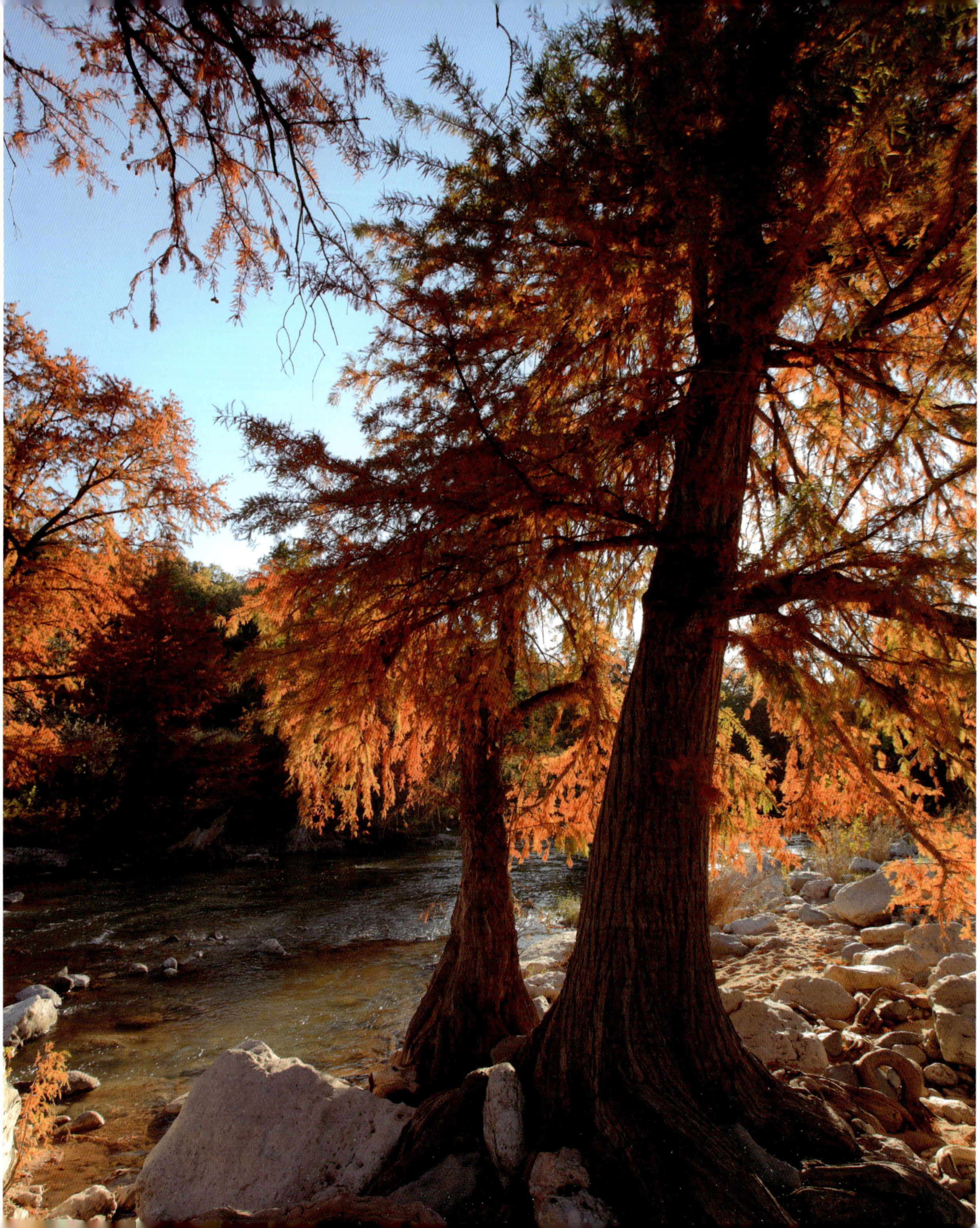

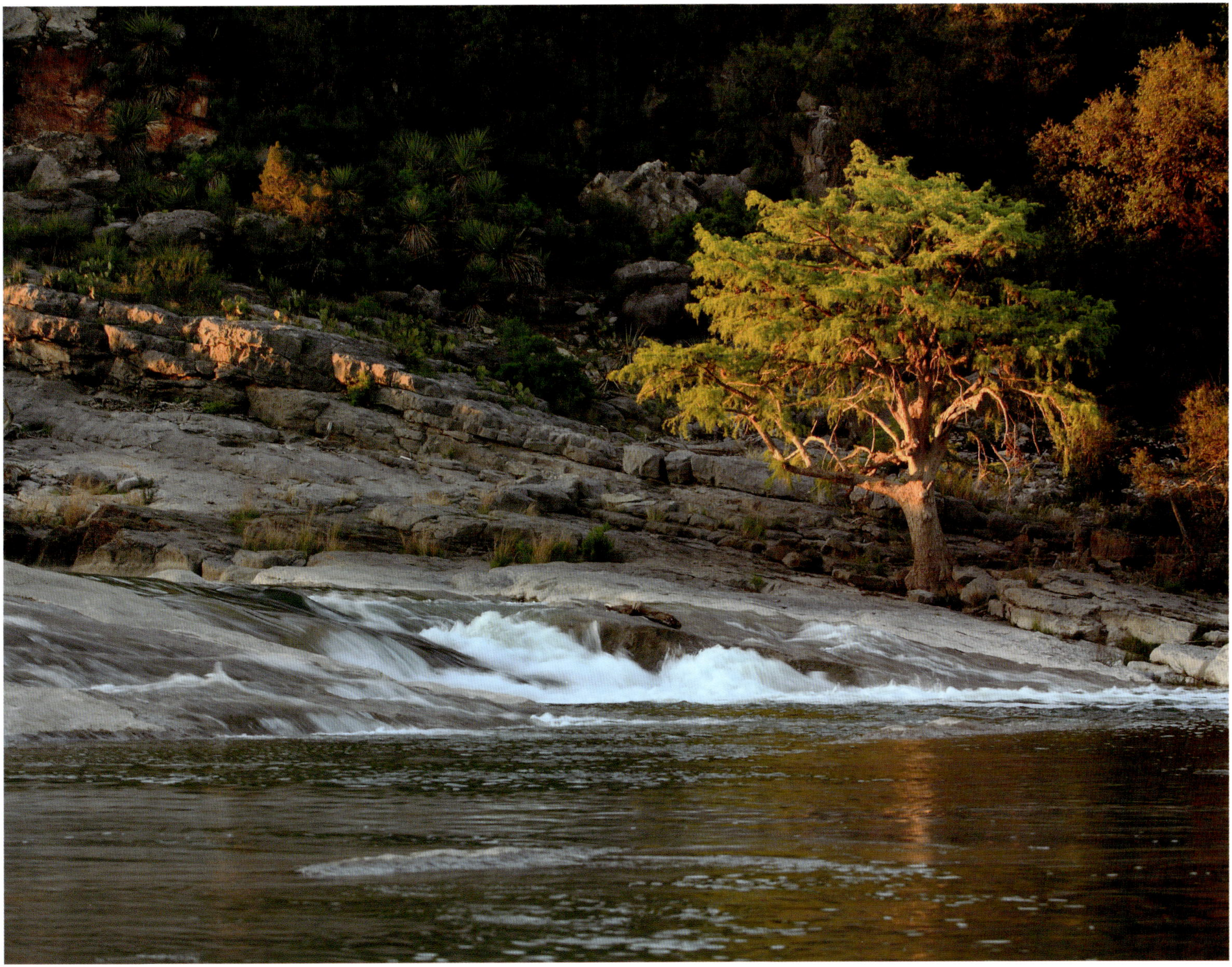

◀ Common along the banks of many Hill Country rivers like the Pedernales, bald cypress trees' shady bows turn a dramatic rust color in the fall.

▲ Amid the sharply uplifted strata at the edge of Pedernales Falls the last light into the canyon highlights a single bald cypress tree at Cypress Pool.

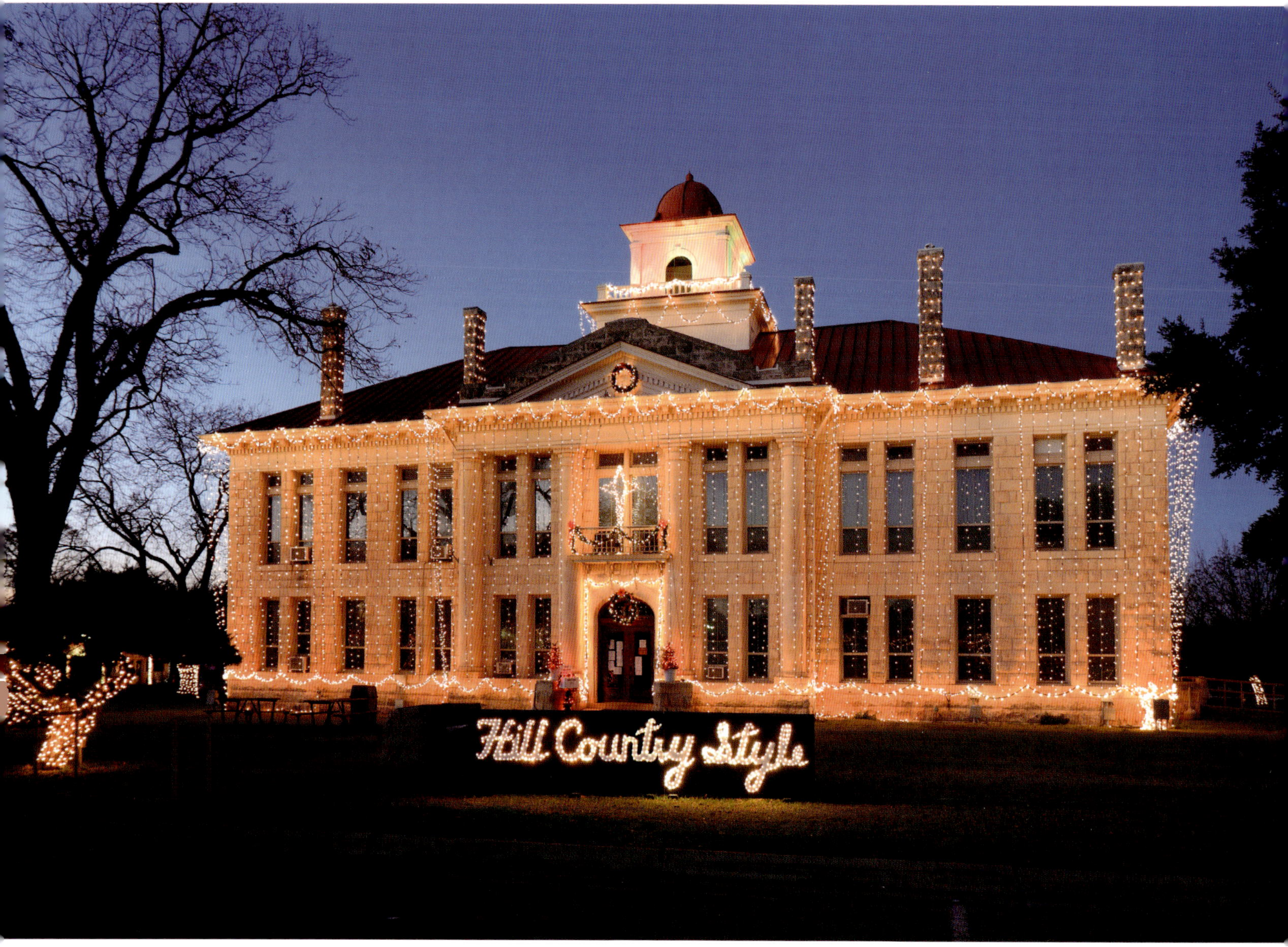

▲ The 1916 Blanco County Courthouse in Johnson City is known for its holiday lighting each year following Thanksgiving. The limestone and red-roofed courthouse shines like a beacon bathed in 100,000 twinkling holiday lights.

▶ Pedernales Electric Cooperative, headquartered in Johnson City, is famous for their annual holiday display featuring dozens of live oak trunks and canopies decked out in more than 1 million white and blue lights.

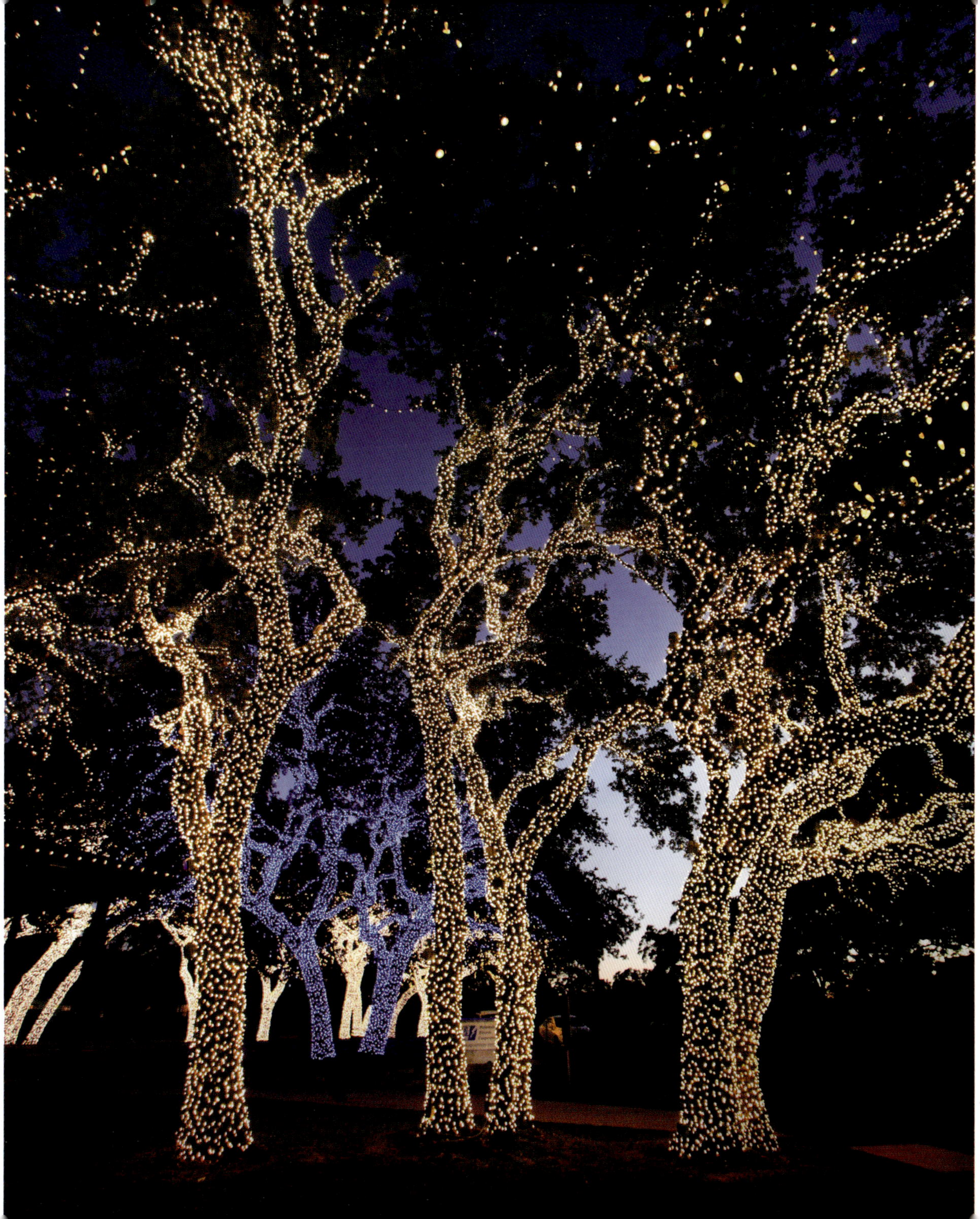

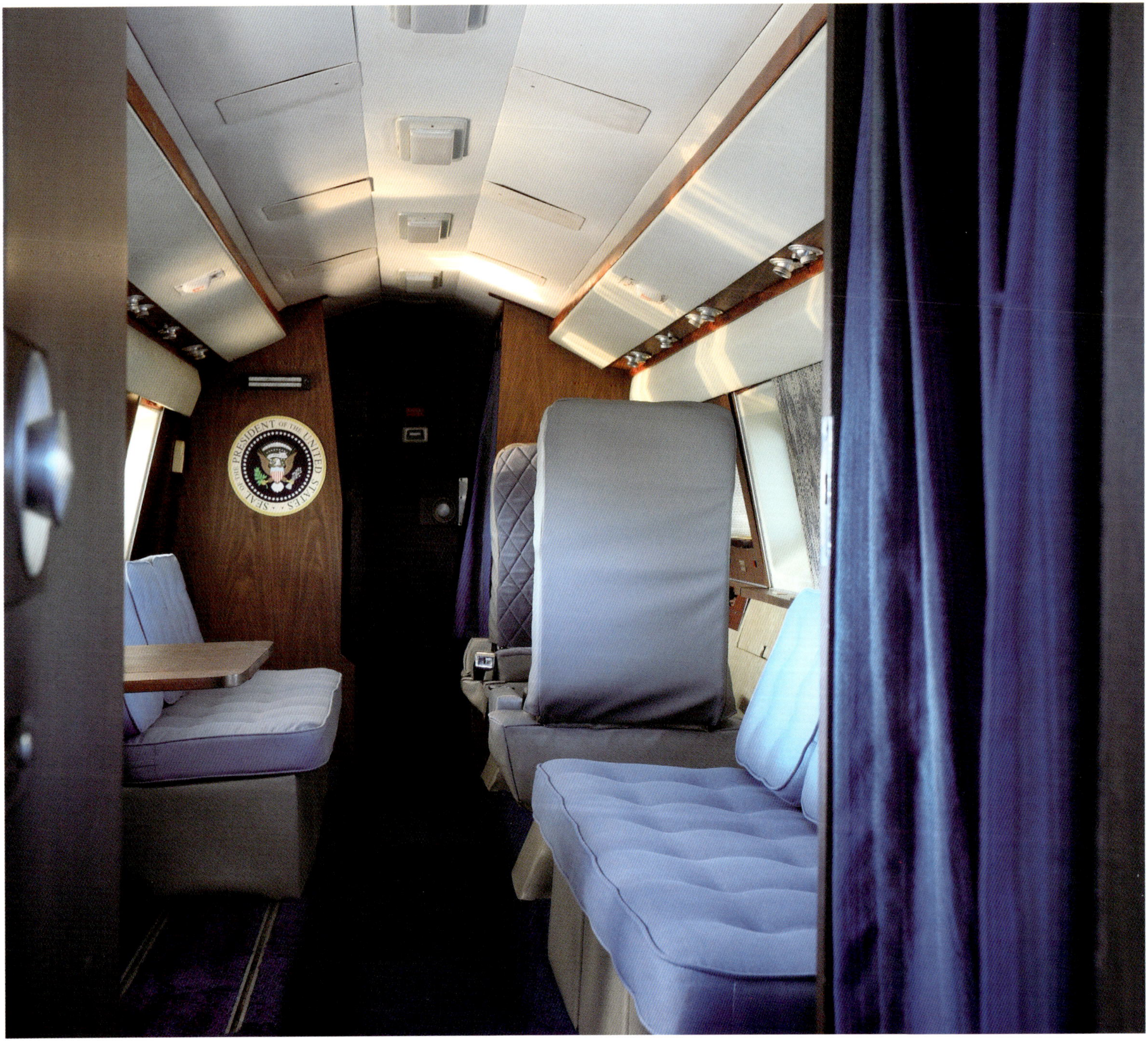
SEAL OF THE PRESIDENT OF THE UNITED STATES

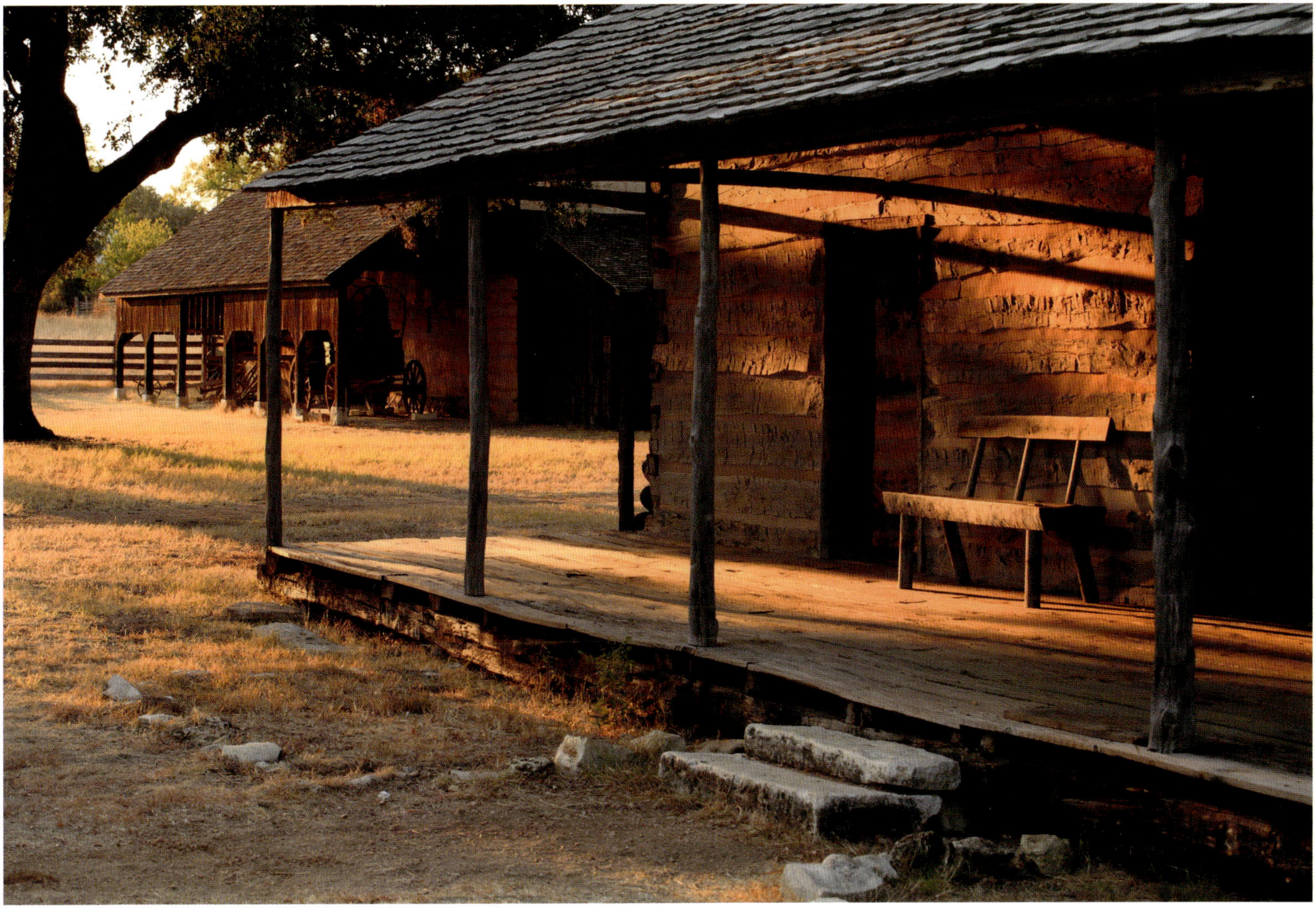

◀ At Lyndon B. Johnson National Historic Park, amid the historic buildings of the former LBJ Ranch sits the presidential Lockheed Jetstar VC-140. The Jetstar was smaller than Airforce One and could land directly at the ranch.

▲ The last golden light of the afternoon punctuates long shadows cast across the Johnson Cabin and Bruckner Barn amid the pastoral grounds of the Johnson Settlement—part of Lyndon B. Johnson National Historical Park. In picturesque Johnson City, the park offers trails and beautifully restored buildings once belonging to the grandfather of former President Johnson.

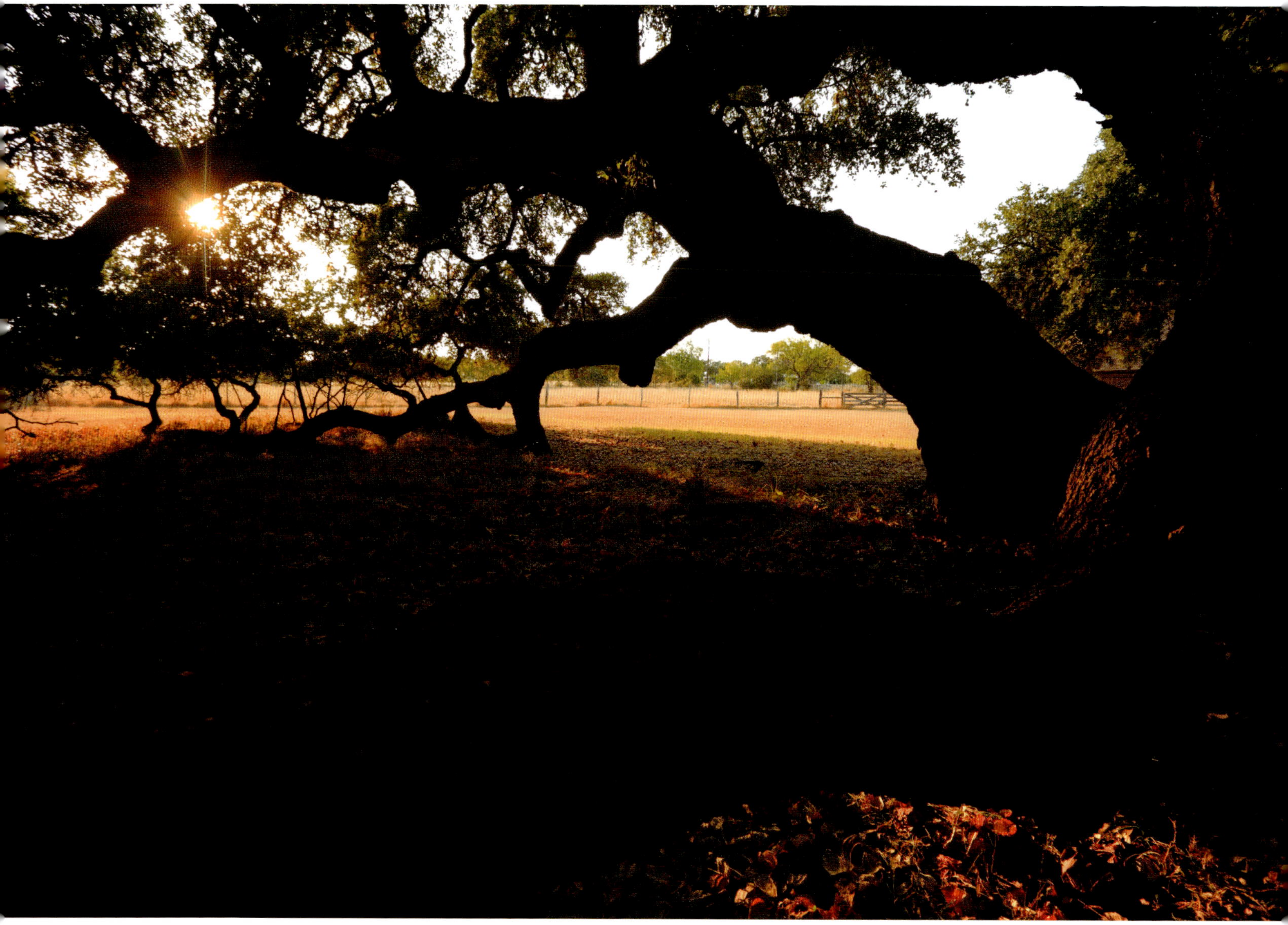

▲ The sprawling branches of a massive live oak tree gracefully spill out across an old farmstead at Lyndon B. Johnson National Historical Park.

▶ A fairly uncommon evergreen tree, the Texas madrone is endemic to the Trans-Pecos and Edwards Plateau regions of Texas, including the Hill Country. It is especially known for its characteristic exfoliating bark that sloughs off to reveal a new velvety-smooth exterior.

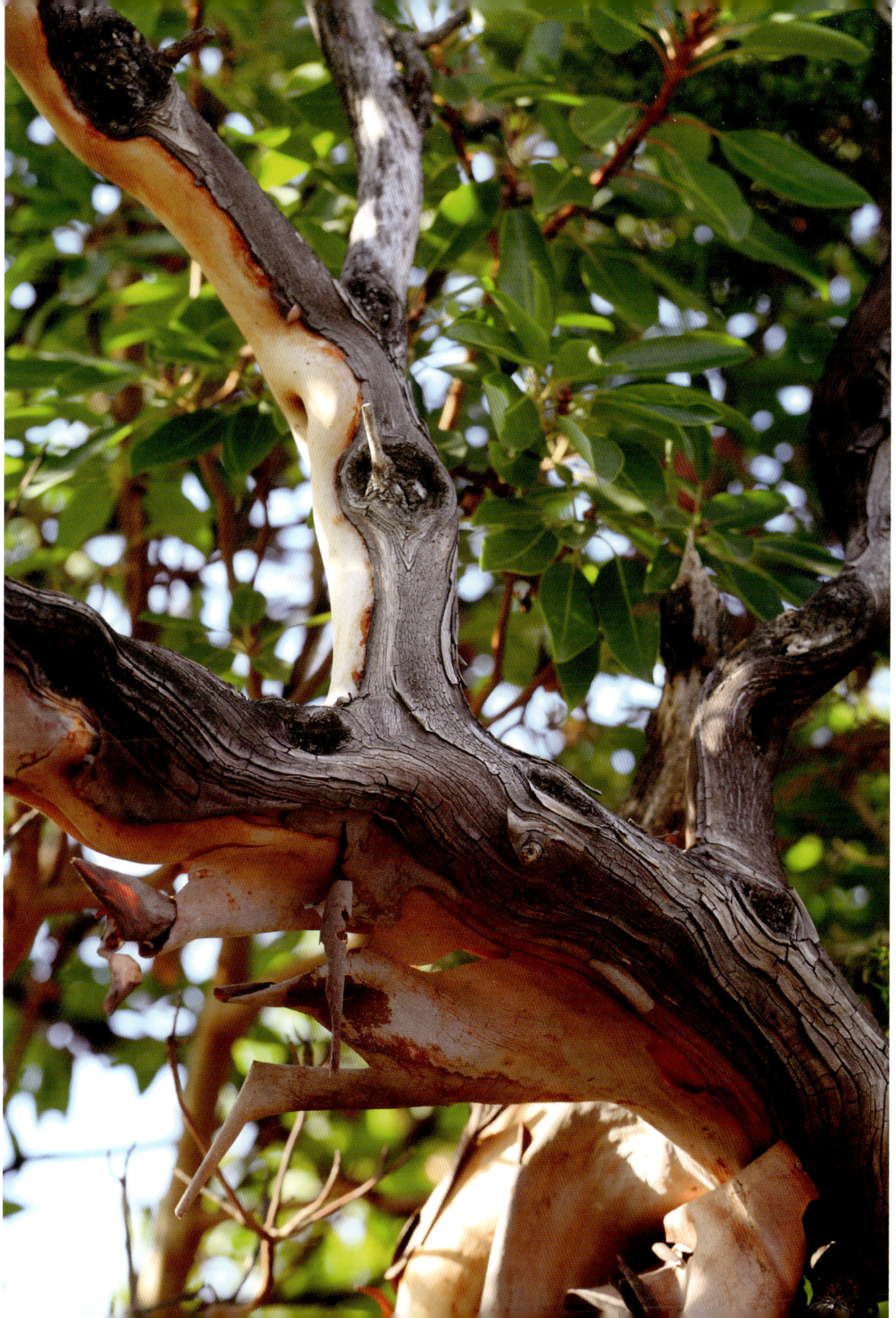

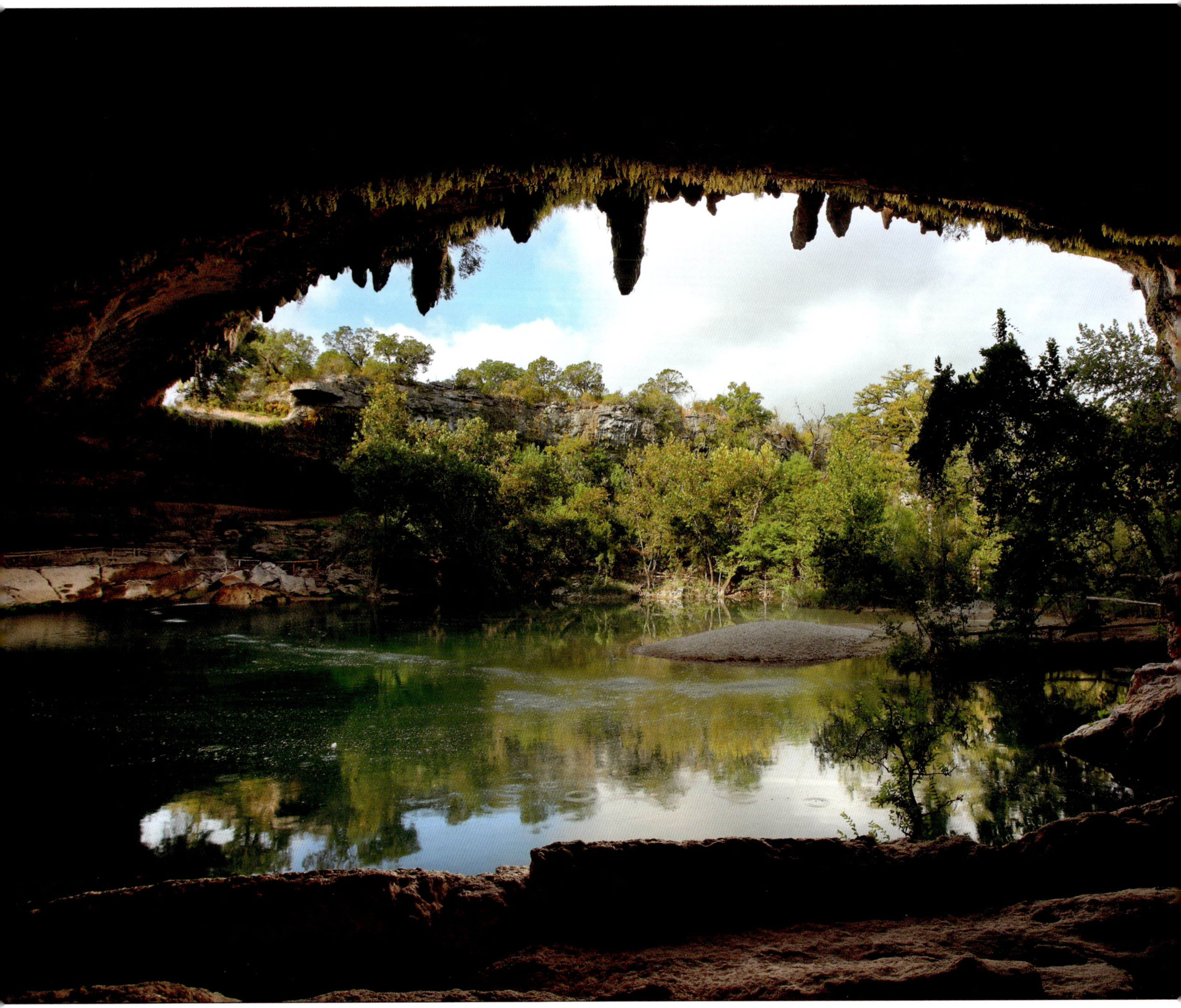

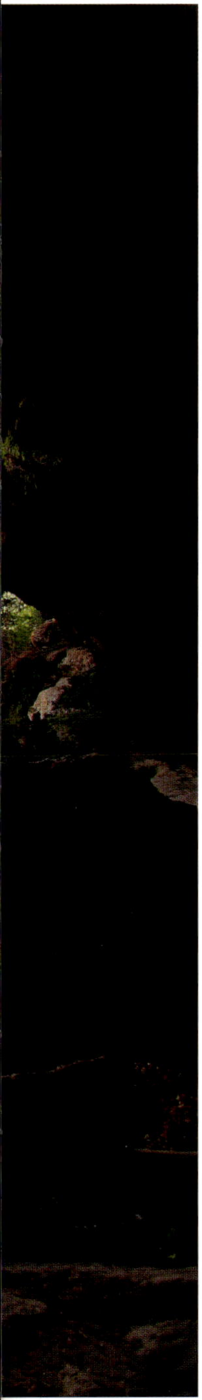

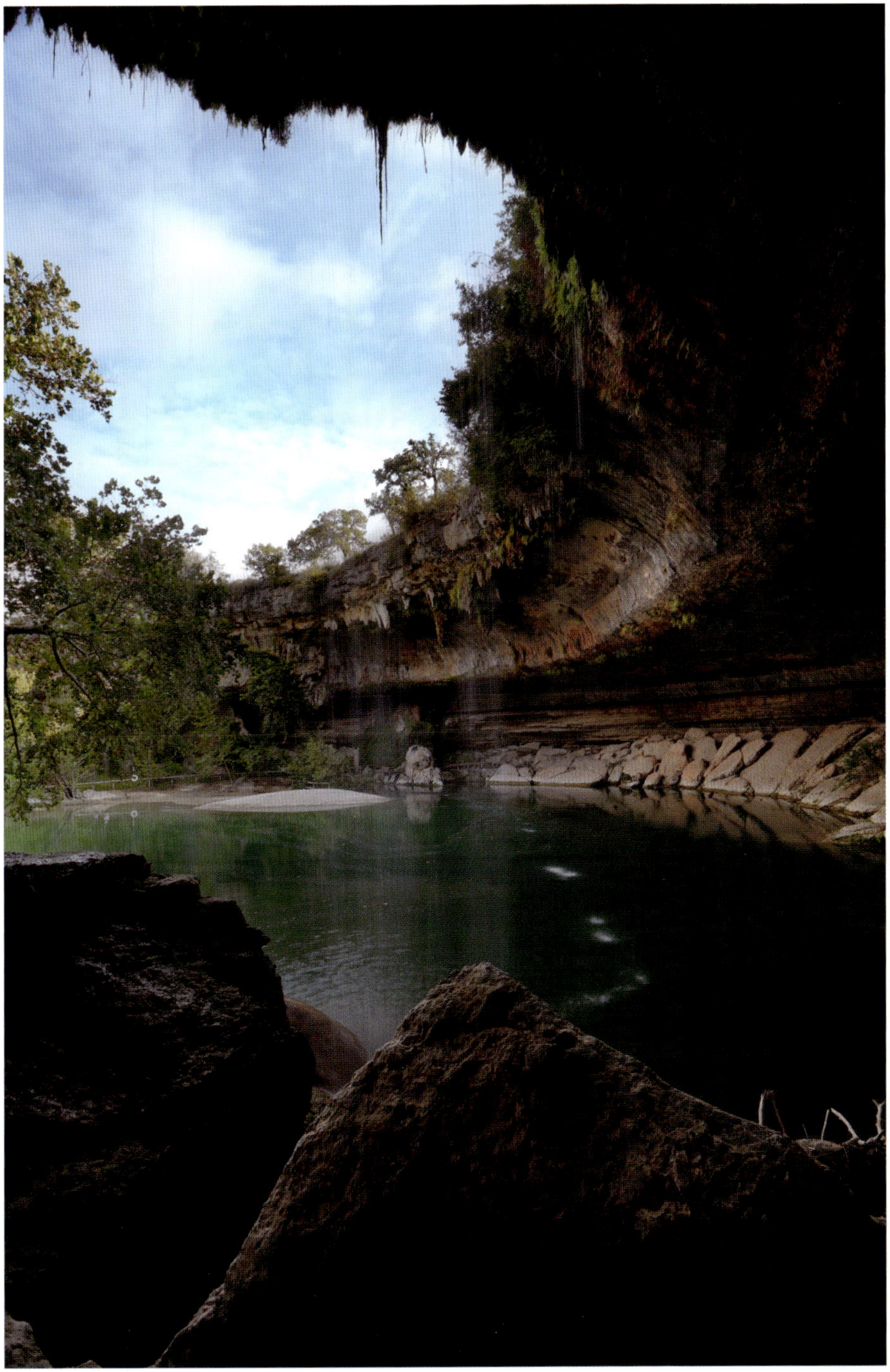

◀ Hamilton Creek tumbles forty-five feet into a collapsed limestone grotto, forming a swimming hole known as Hamilton Pool. The circular emerald pool is flanked by large boulders and cavernous walls at the end of a scenic box canyon in western Travis County.

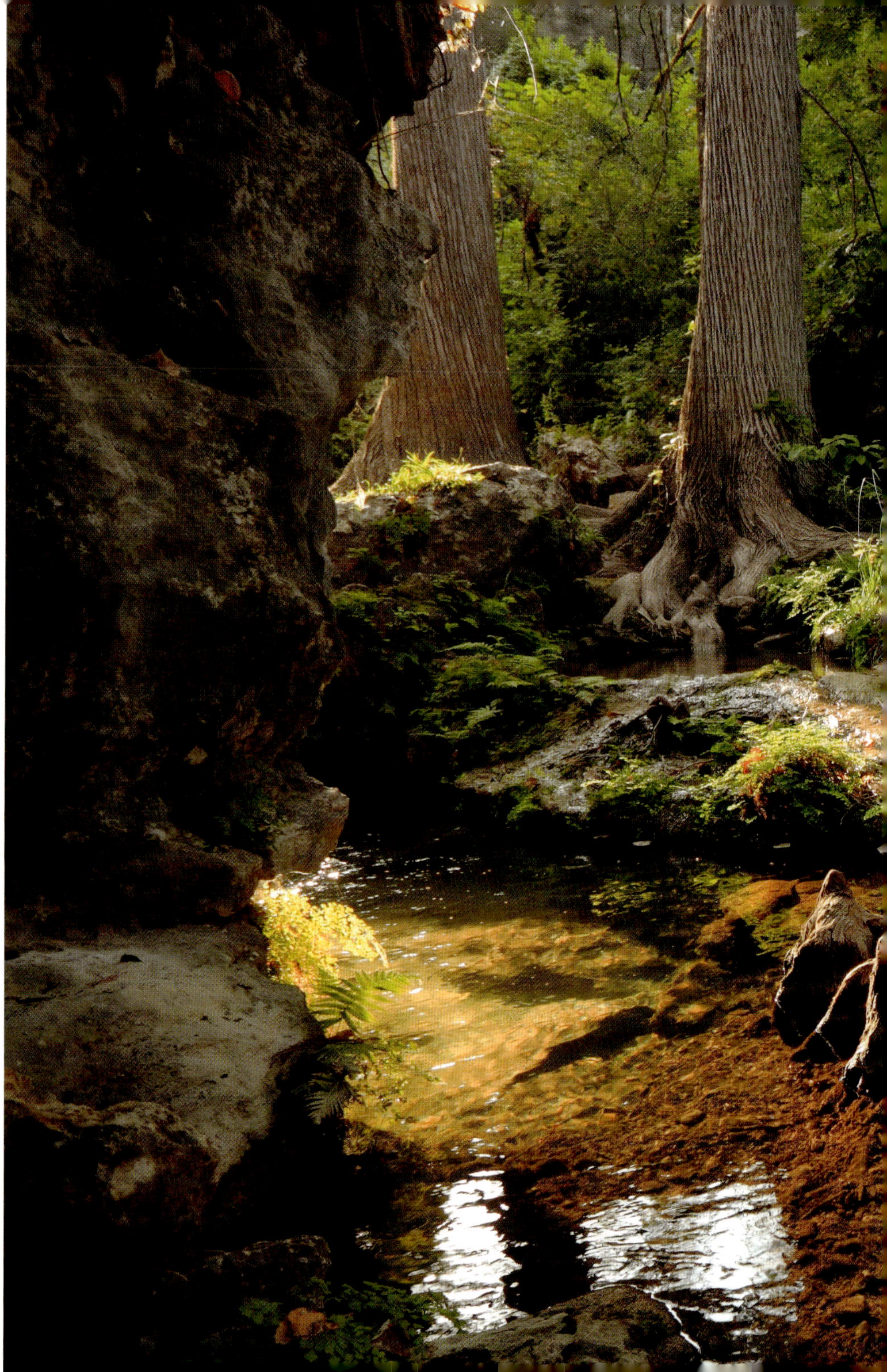

▶ An array of riparian flora thrives along a flowing spring-fed stream in a sheltered ravine called Climbers Canyon in Milton Reimers Ranch Park, a 2,400-acre nature park west of Austin.

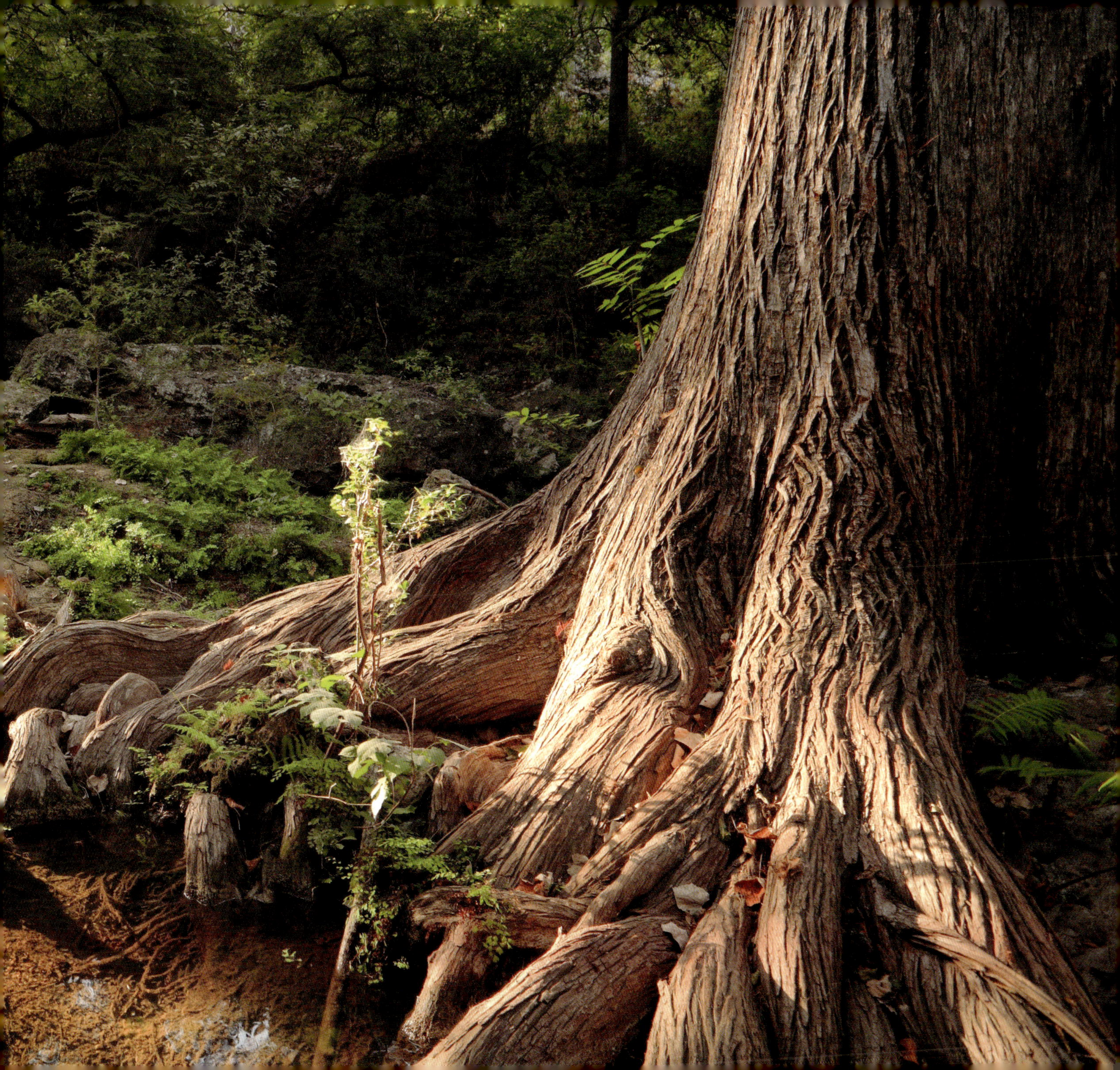

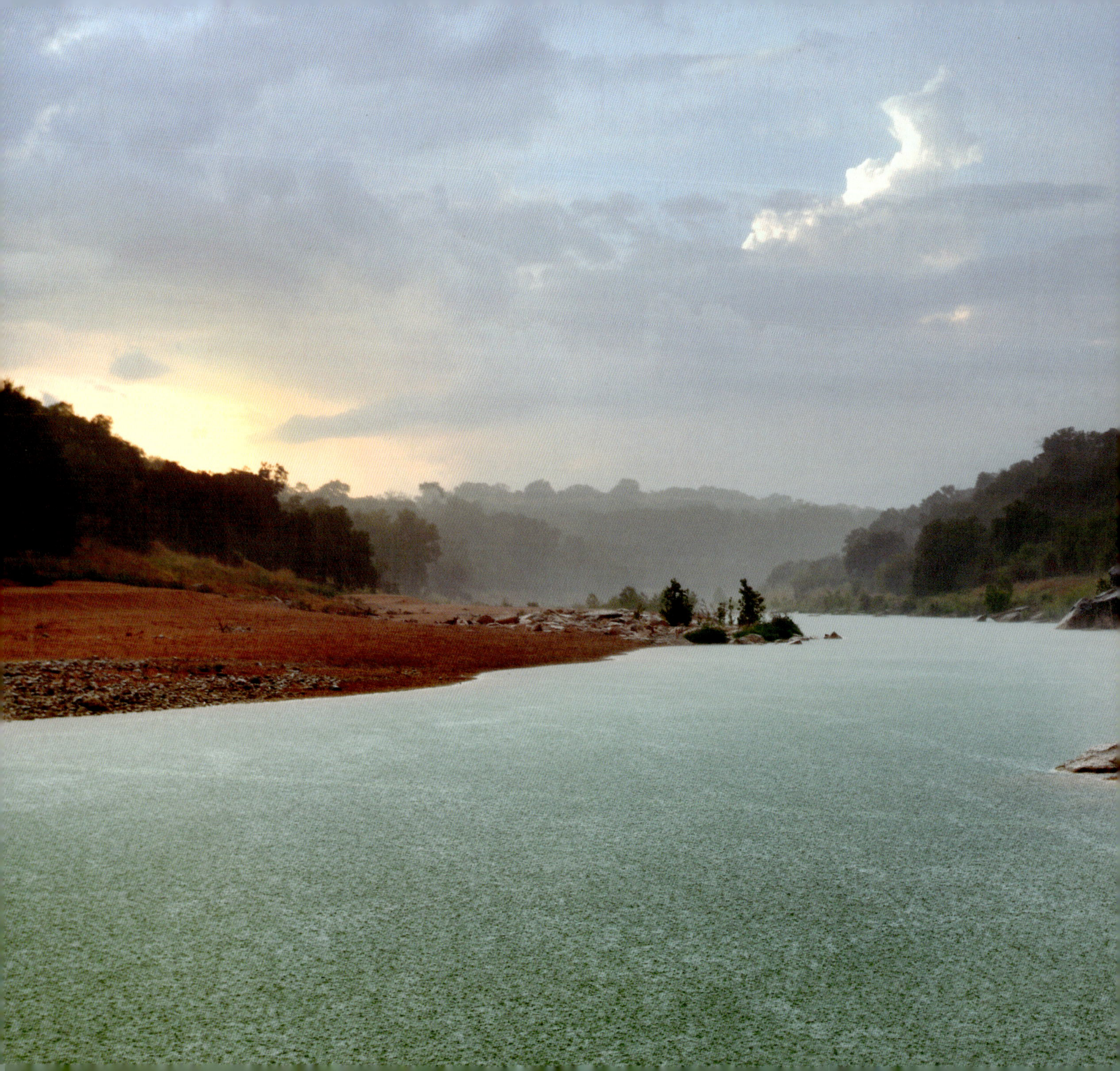

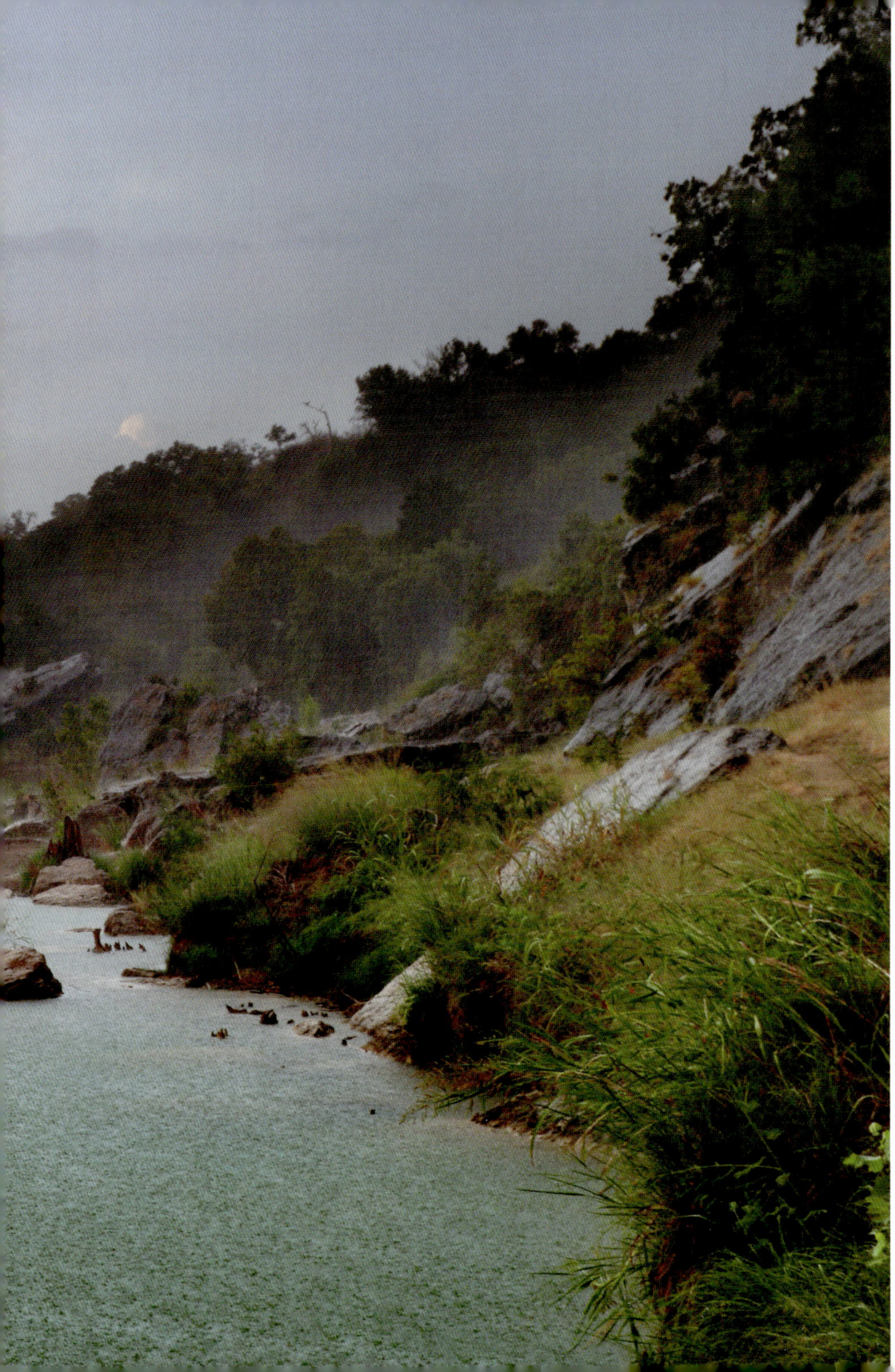

◀ A brief rainstorm passes over the Pedernales River as it winds through Milton Reimers Ranch Park. The Pedernales—named after the Spanish word for flint rocks common in the riverbed—winds through 105 miles of varying Hill Country terrain before emptying into the Colorado River.

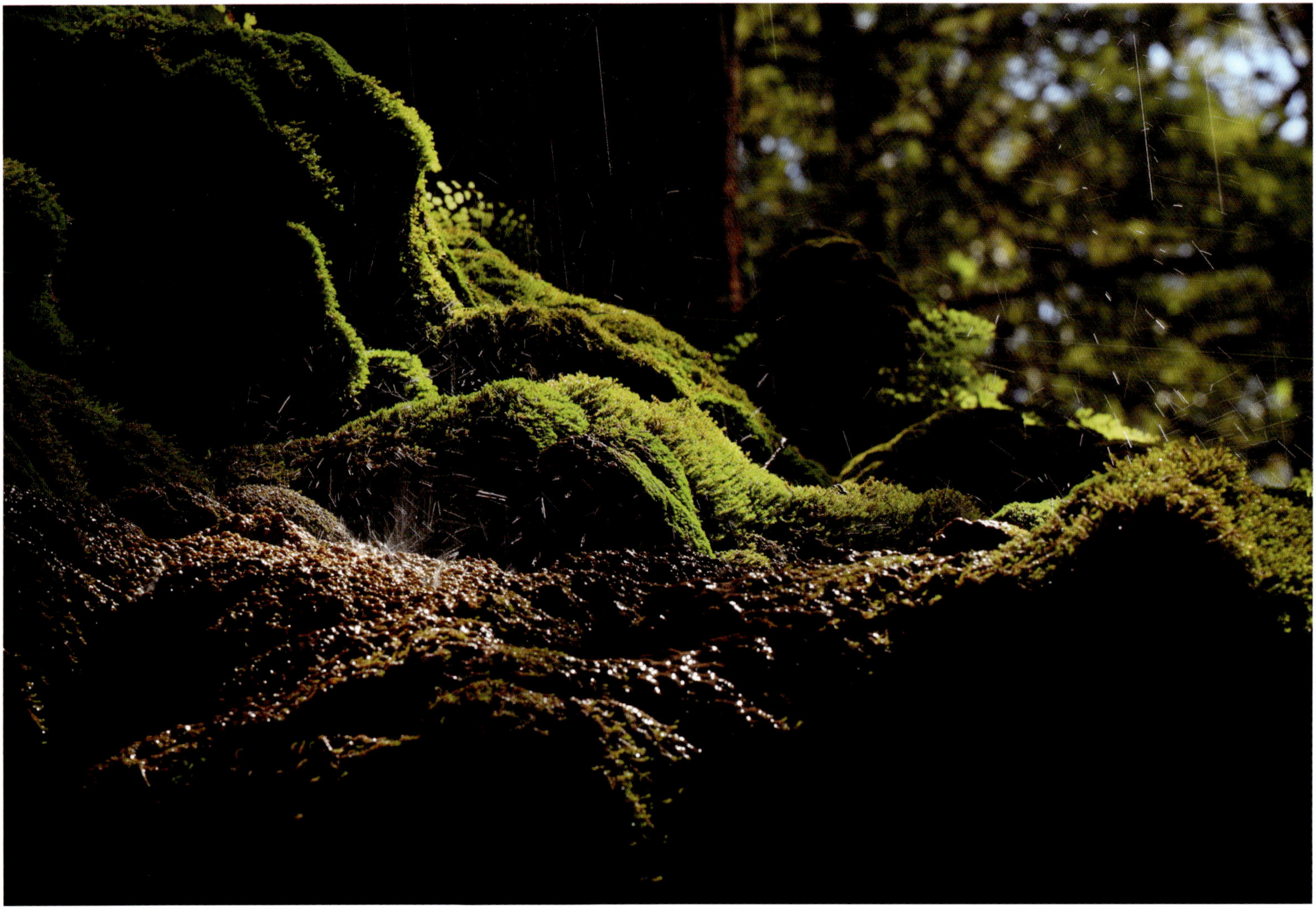

▲▶ A living cave and an impressive collapsed grotto brimming with verdant ferns and moss, natural spring-fed pools, and waterfalls make up the gem of the seventy-six-acre Westcave Preserve in western Travis County.

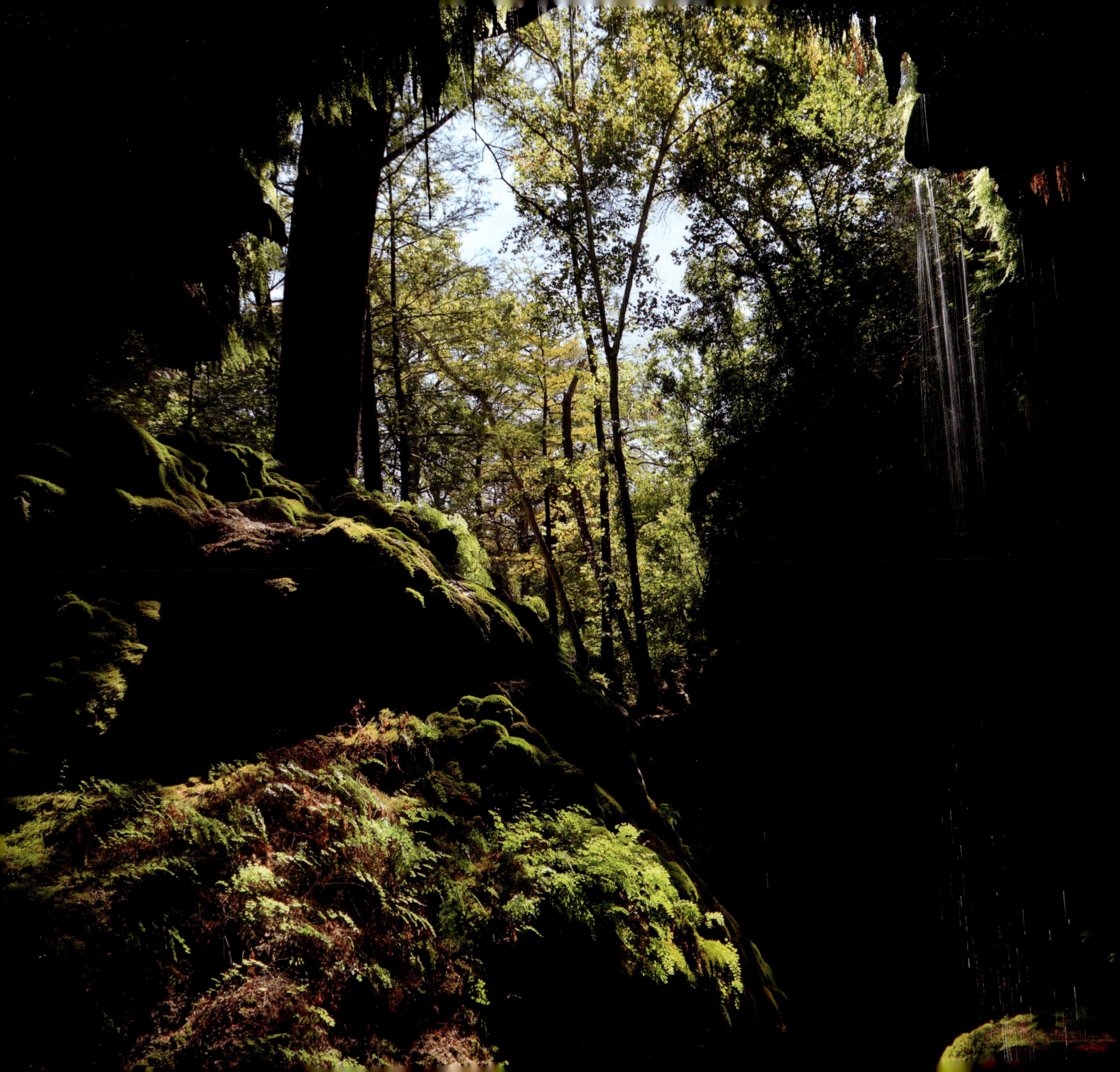

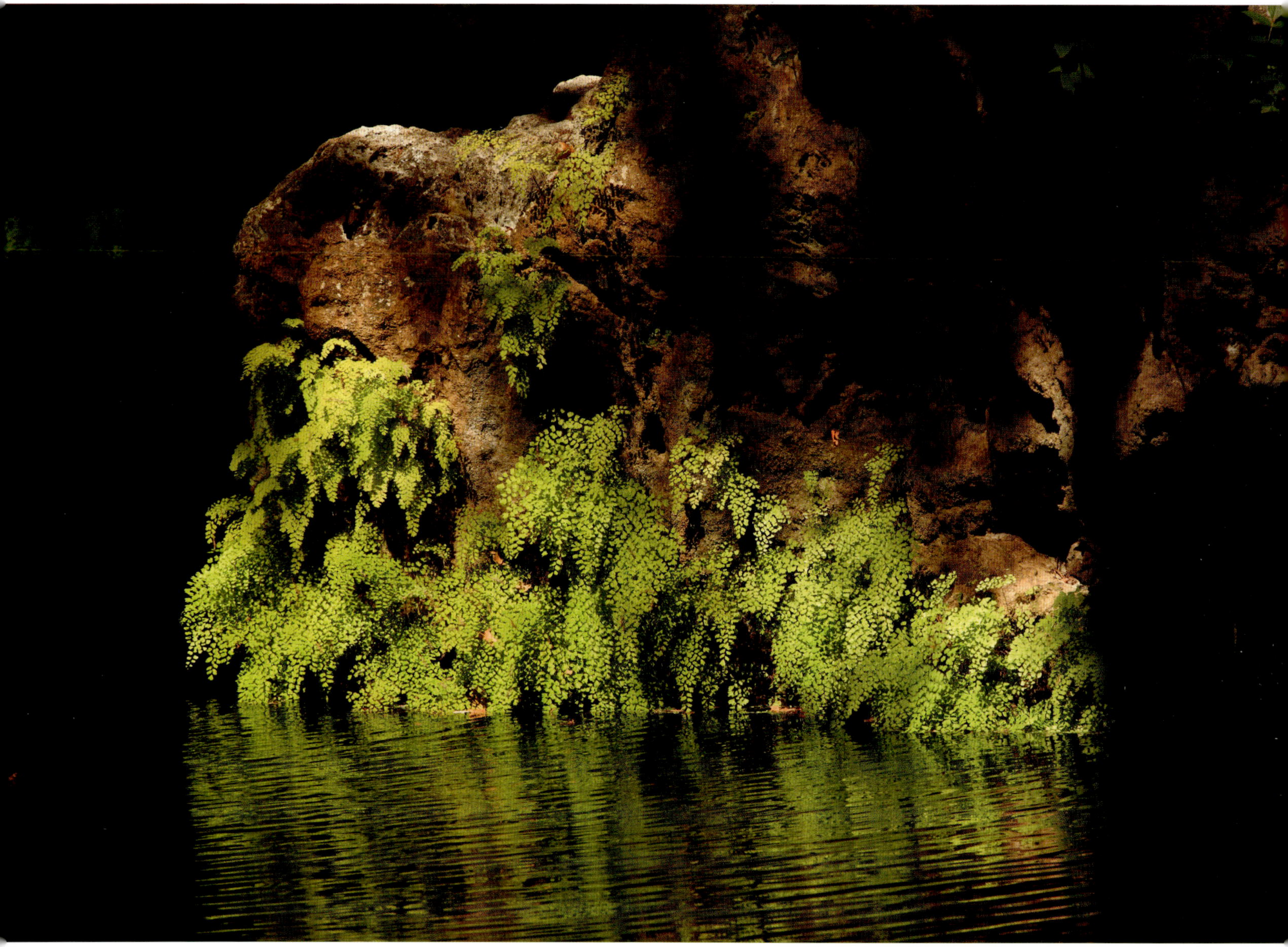

▲ Dappled sunlight highlights the delicate fronds of maidenhair fern clinging to a limestone island in Westcave Preserve.

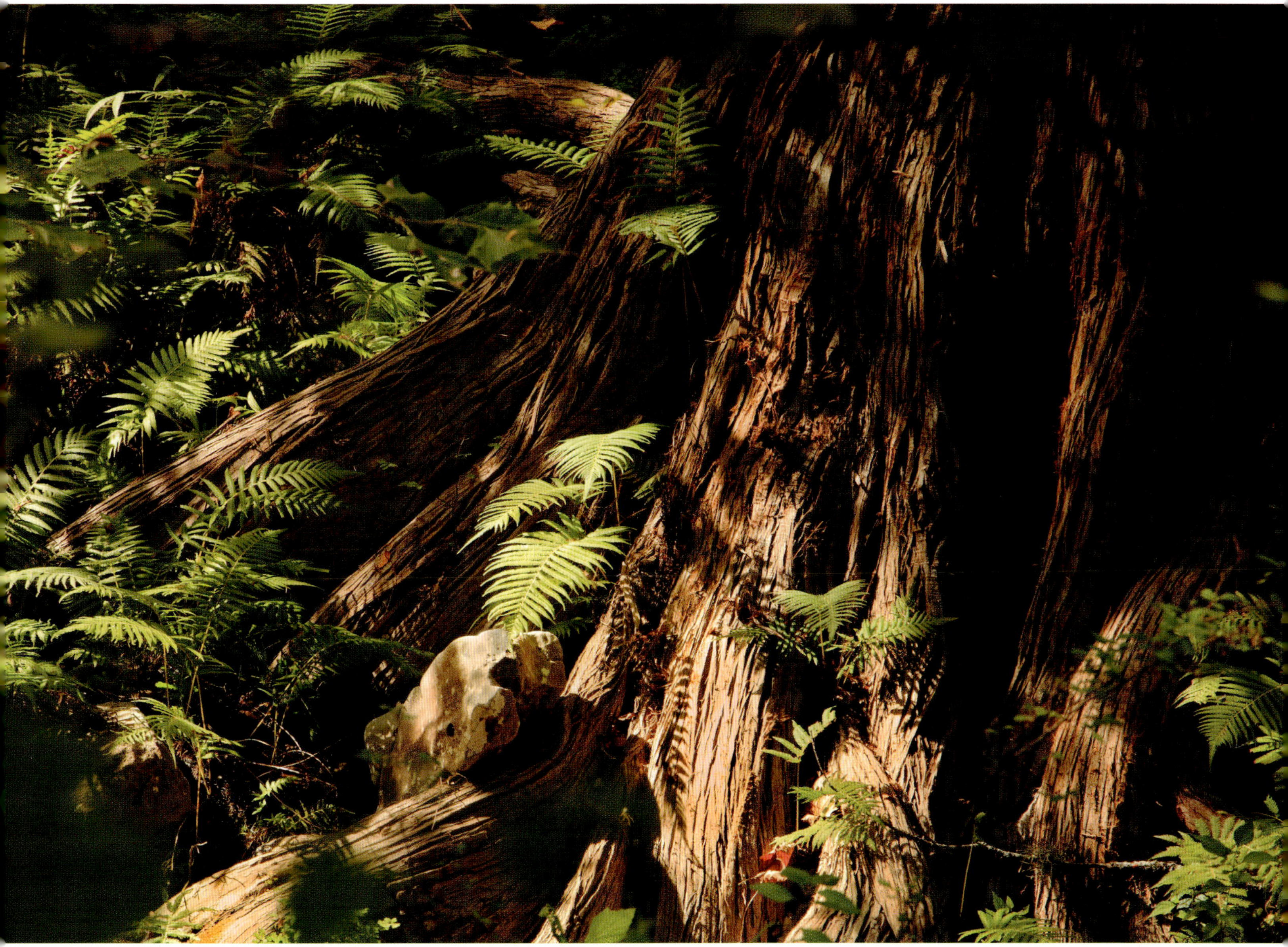

▲ Amid the riparian woodlands of Westcave Preserve, shield fern surrounds the base of an old bald cypress tree along Heinz Branch, a small stream that empties into the Pedernales River.

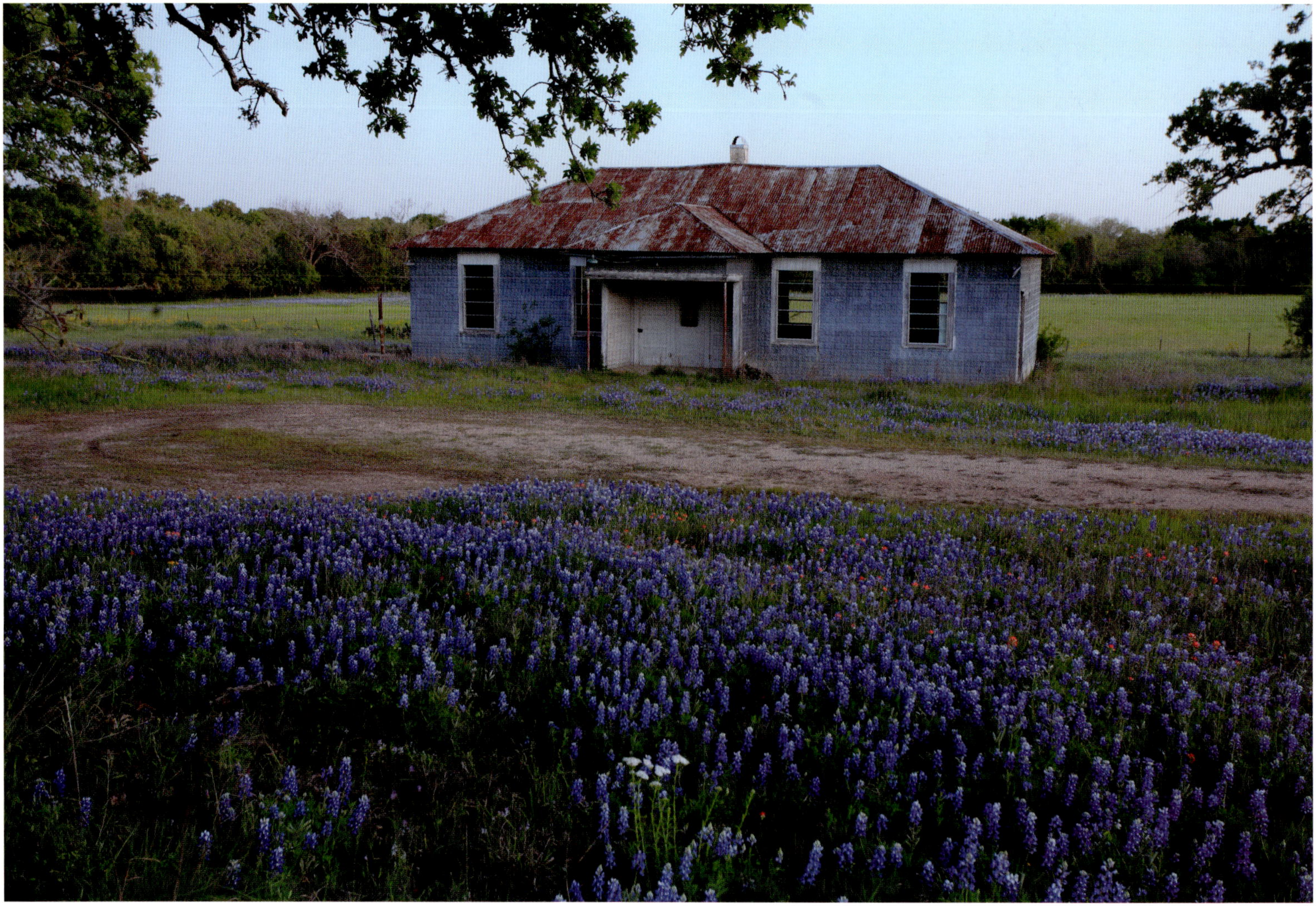

▲ An abandoned relic of the 1920s, the old Sandy school house in Blanco County creates a quaint backdrop for bluebonnets that carpet the grounds in the spring. The one-room building served the community of Sandy and neighboring communities as a consolidated school with two teachers.

▶ Peppered among indigo spires of Texas bluebonnets are the occasional rare white bluebonnets, a natural mutation that grows as a white strain.

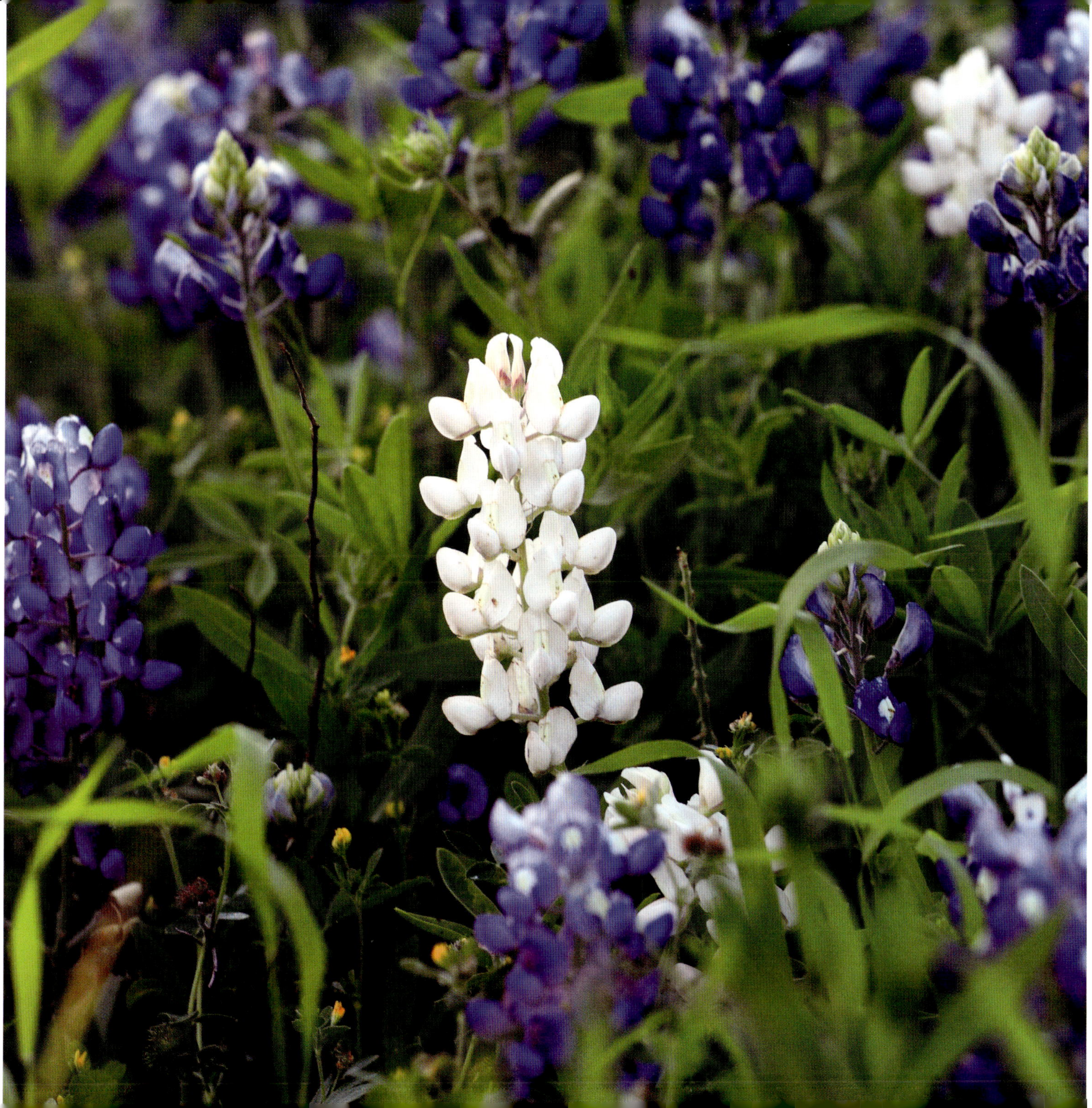

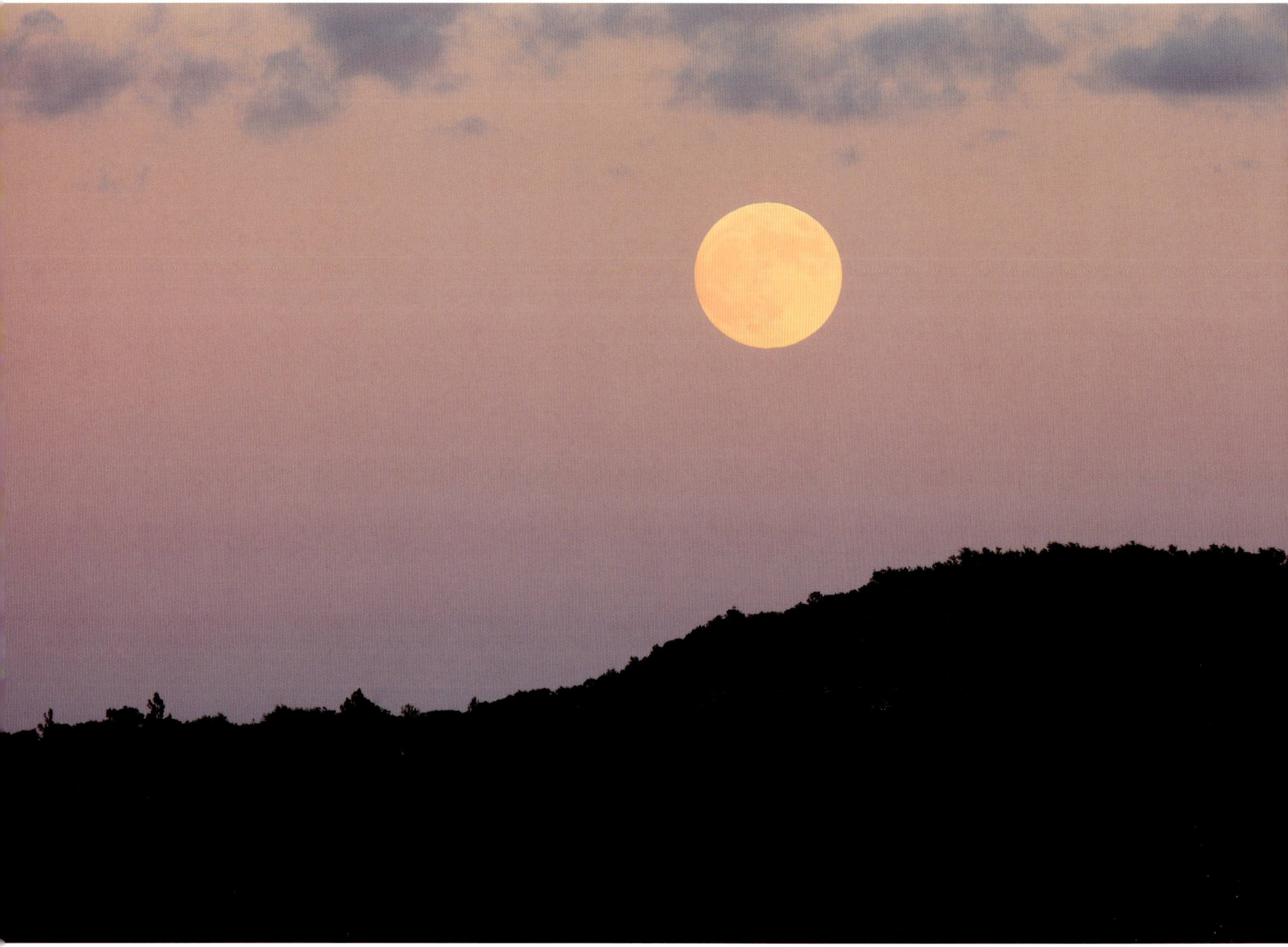

▲ Against the soft purple glow of a twilight sky, a full moon rises over a hilltop in Hays County. On moonless nights, stargazers enjoy the exceptionally dark night skies of the Hill Country region.

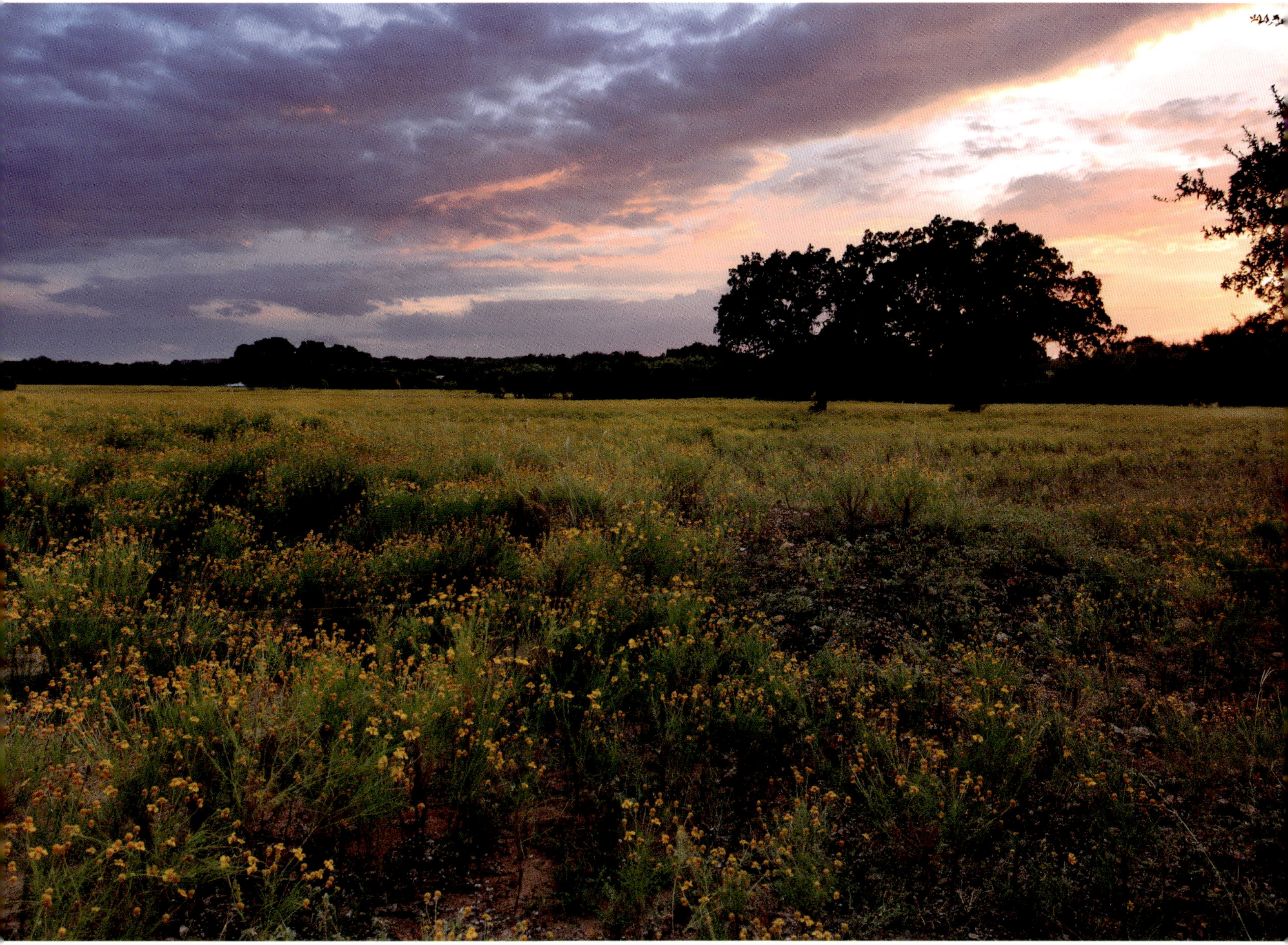

▲ The setting sun paints a pastel sky over a prairie of yellow basin sneezeweed near Johnson City.

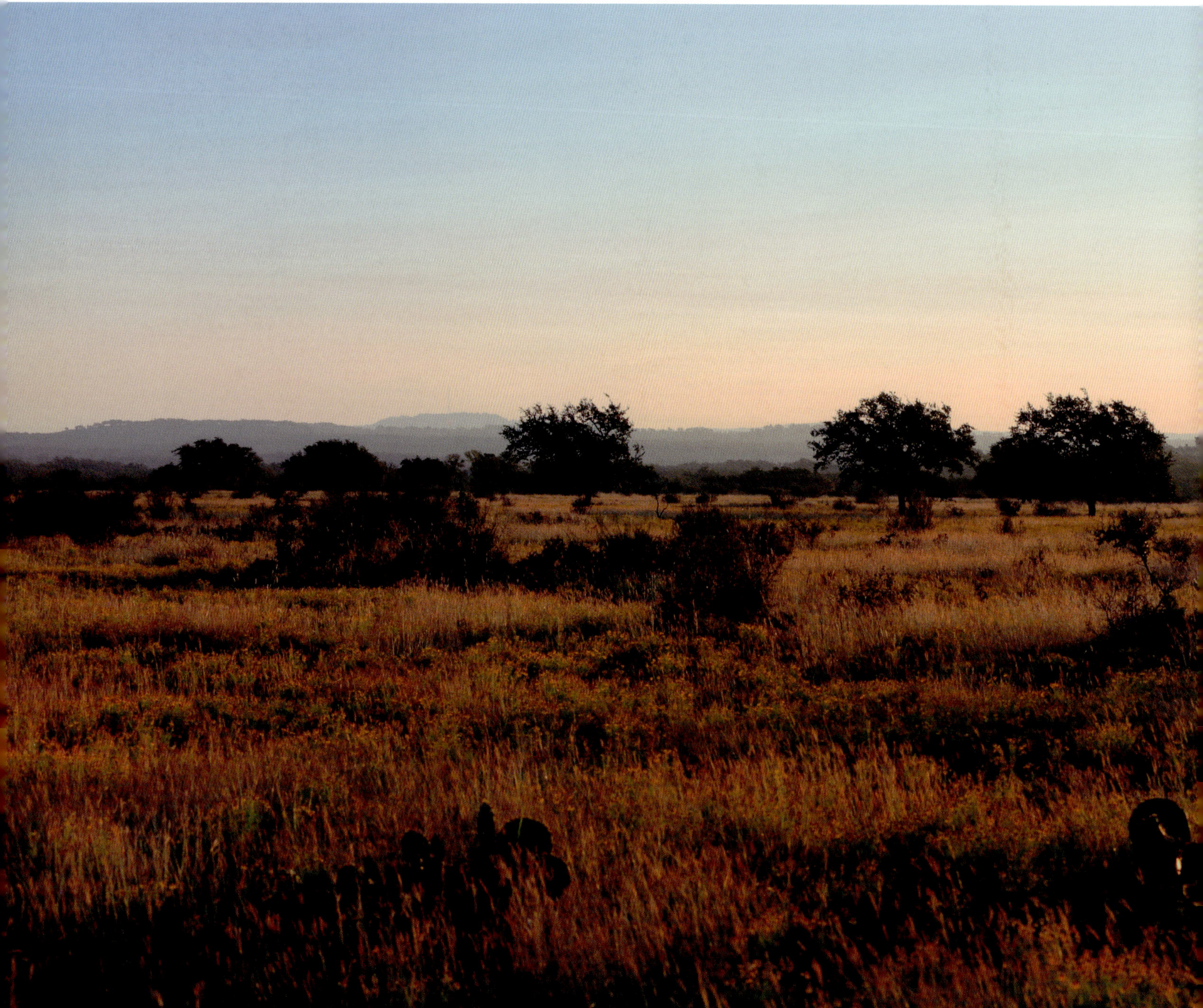

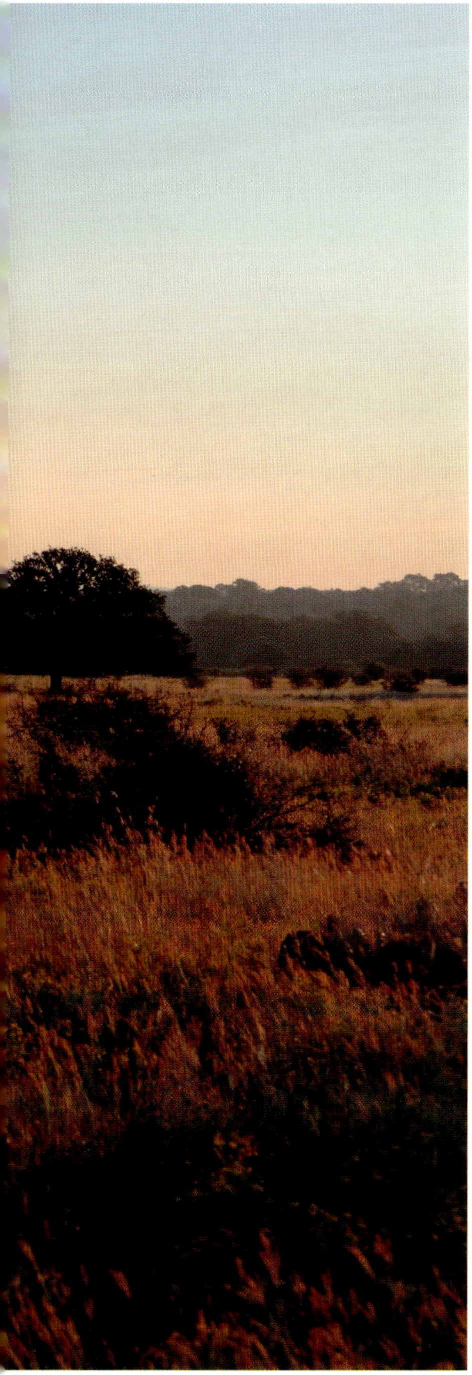

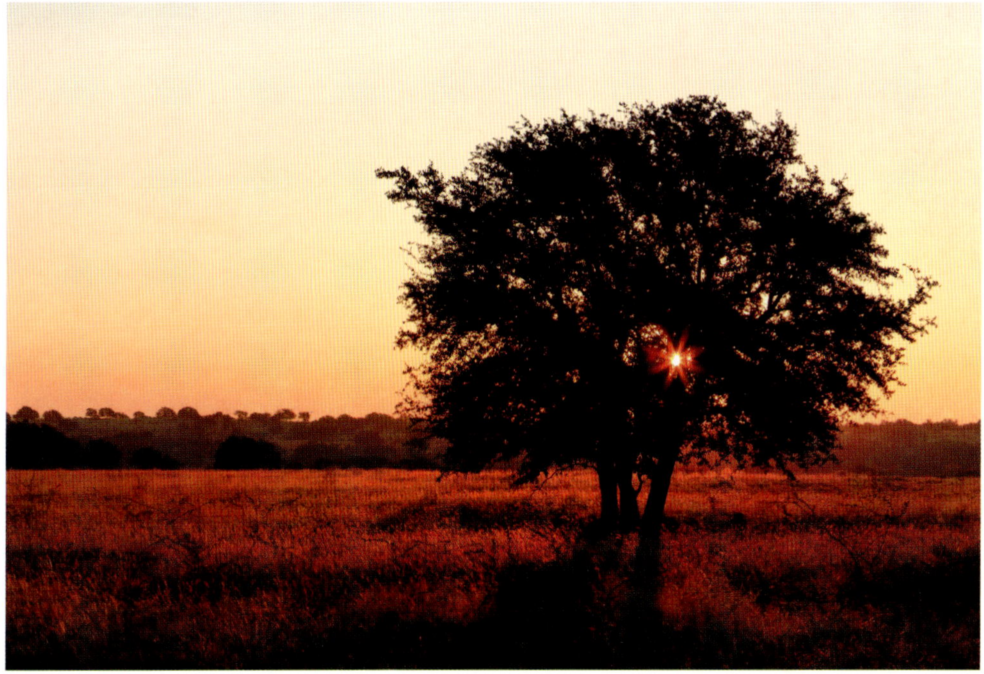

▲ The morning light shimmers through the leaves and branches of escarpment live oak trees near Round Mountain. This hardier cousin of the southern live oak grows in clusters or "mottes" along the grassy hilltops and rocky outcroppings of the Hill Country.

◀ Distant layers of upland terrain hint at the drastic change in elevation compared to this live oak savanna near Round Mountain. A peppering of prickly pear cactus and hardy shrubs such as agarita break up the sea of grasses.

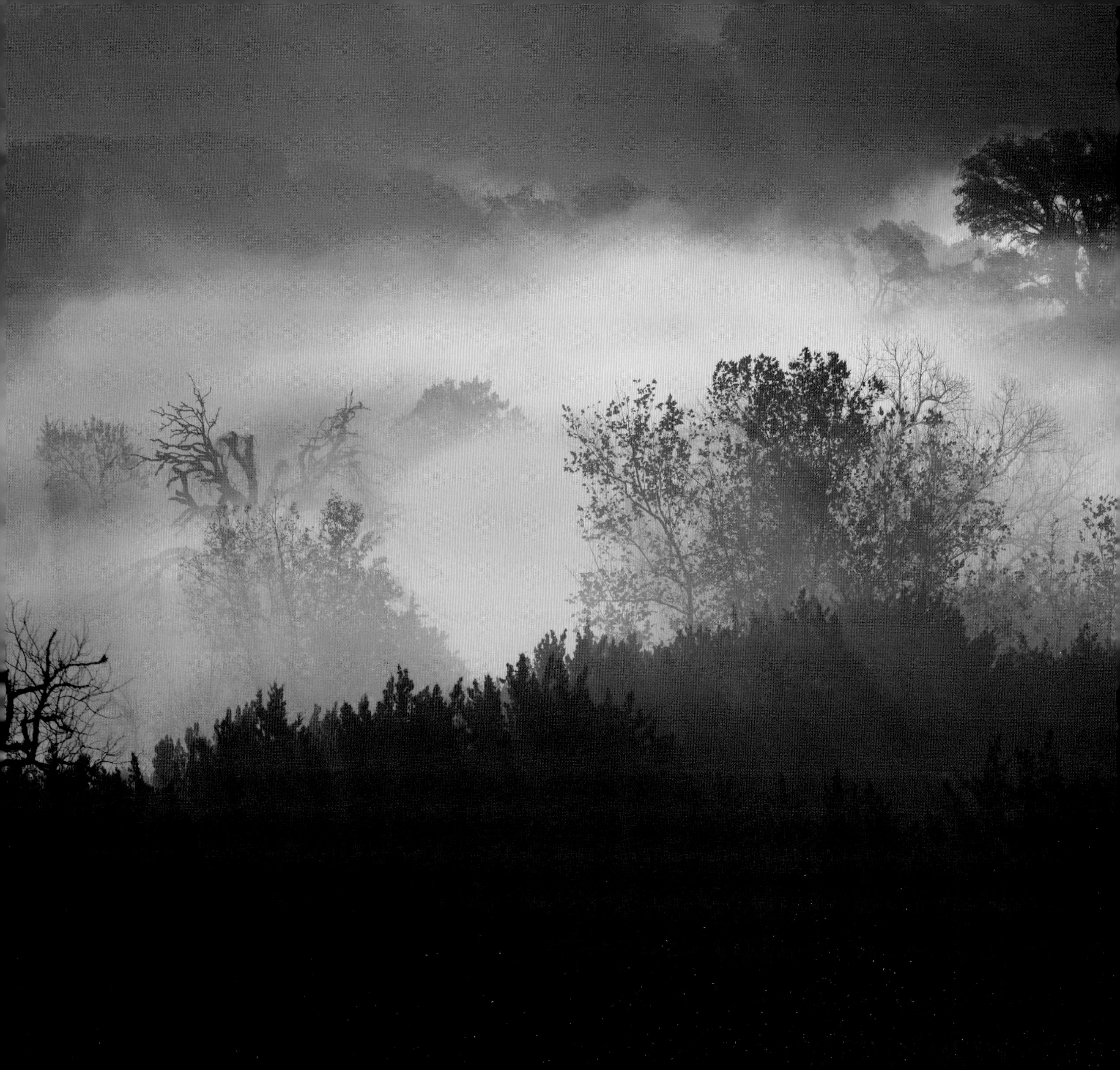

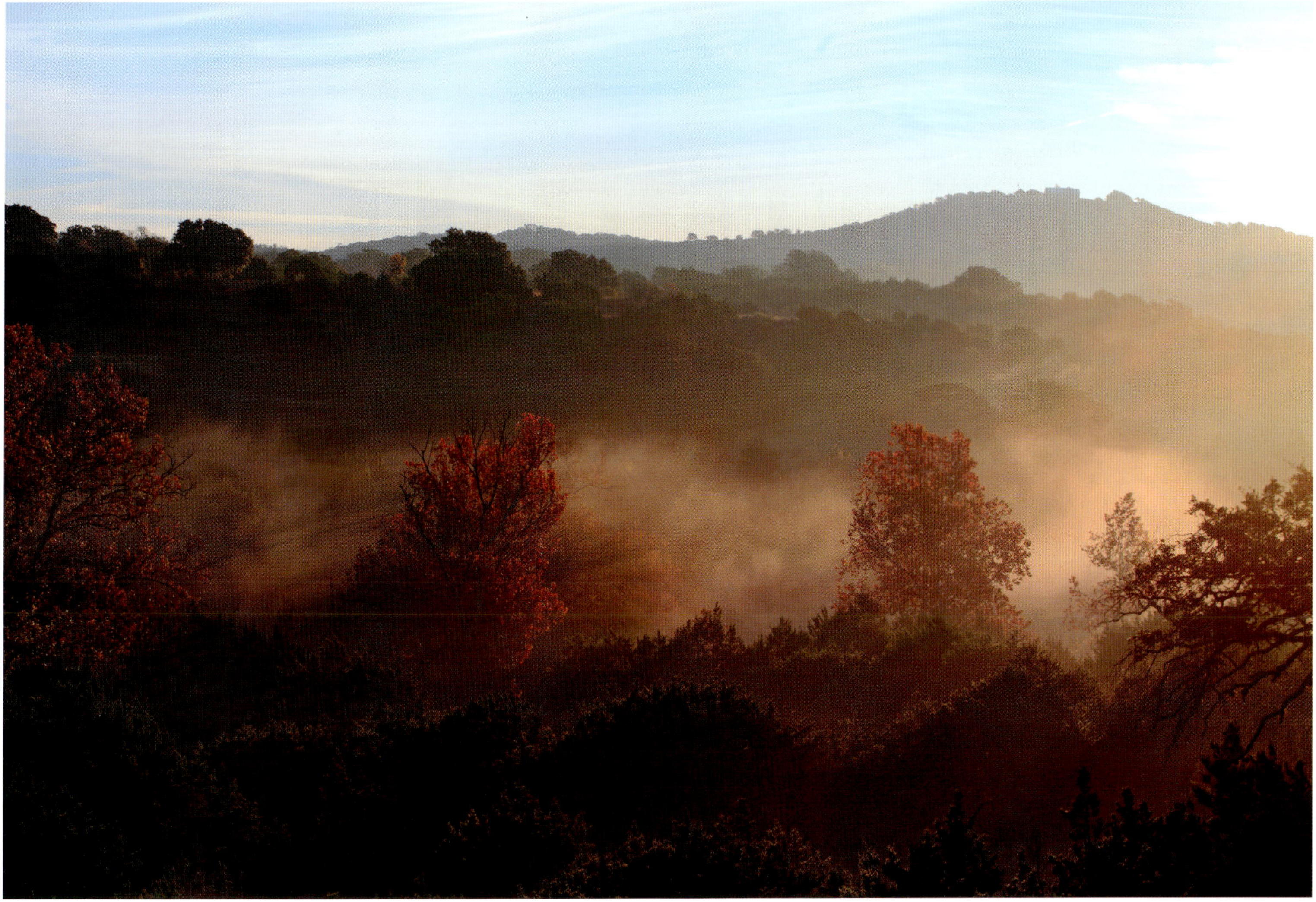

◀▲ Cold autumn air sinks along the slopes of Calohan Creek Valley, condensing into fog and enveloping the cottonwoods and junipers along the creek bottom.

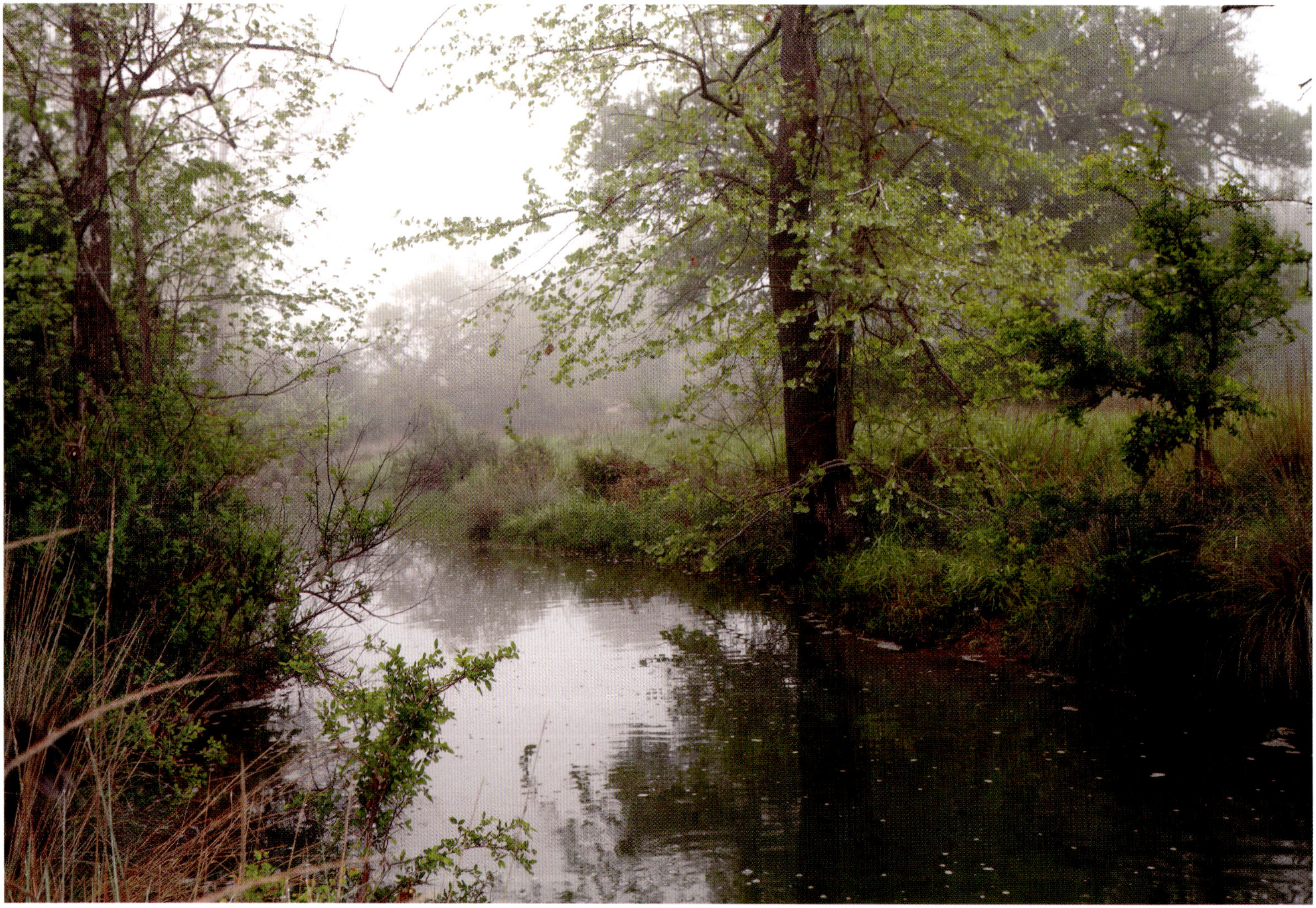

▲ A quiet foggy spring morning reveals newly budded foliage and grasses along the banks of Calohan Creek, a small spring-fed stream in the Pedernales watershed.

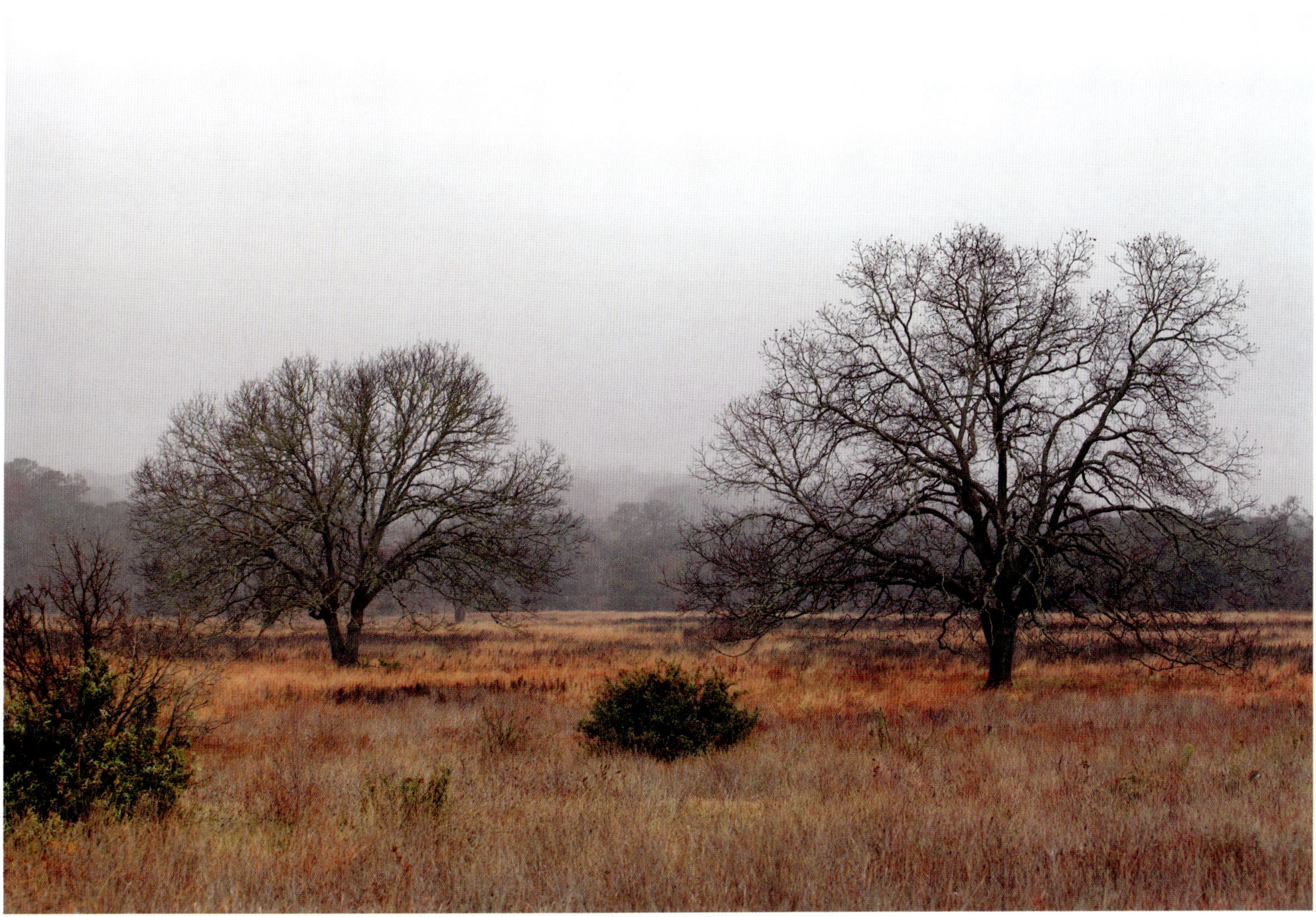

▲ The sprawling bare bows of hardwoods contrast against the yellows and oranges of native grasses on a foggy winter day in northwestern Hays County.

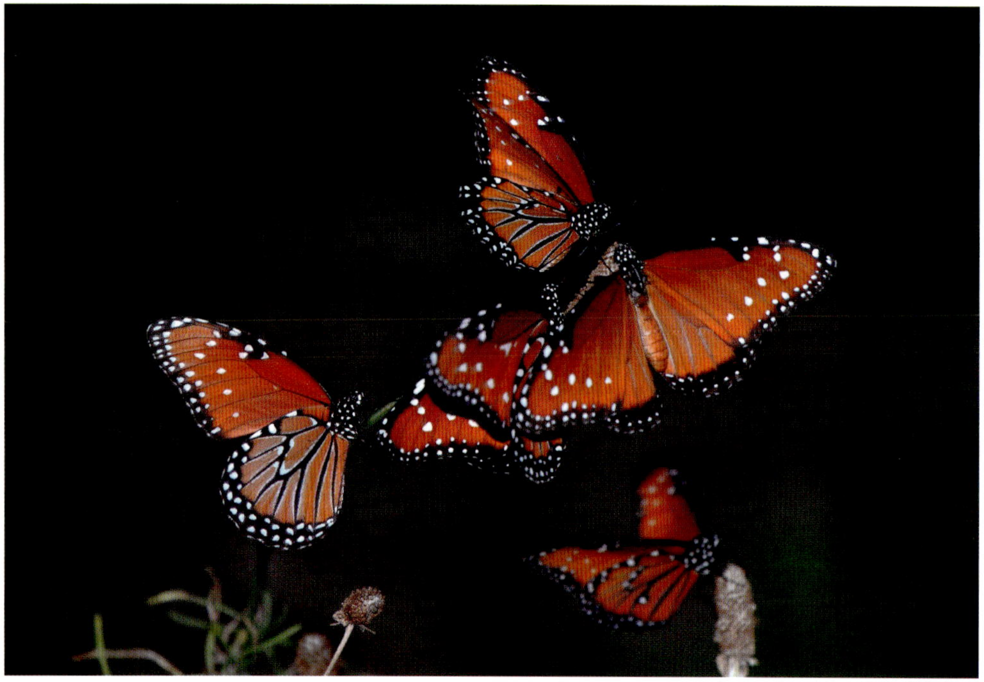

▲ A common seasonal sight throughout the Hill Country, queen butterflies congregate and roost along the valleys and creek bottoms.

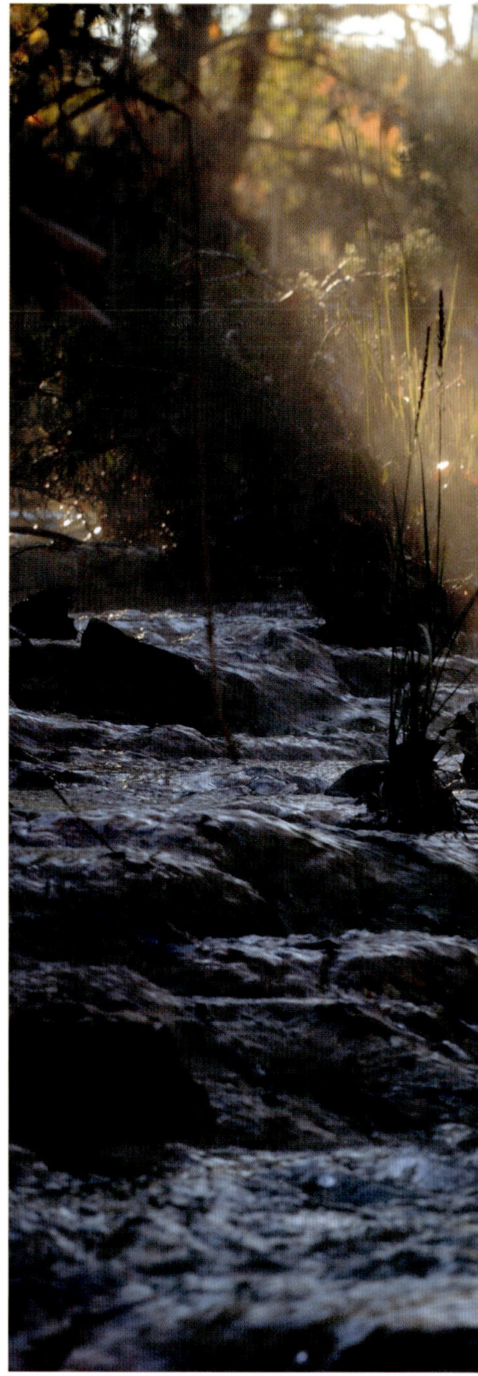

▶ On a cold fall morning shafts of light break through the riparian canopy, illuminating steam fog rising from Calohan Creek.

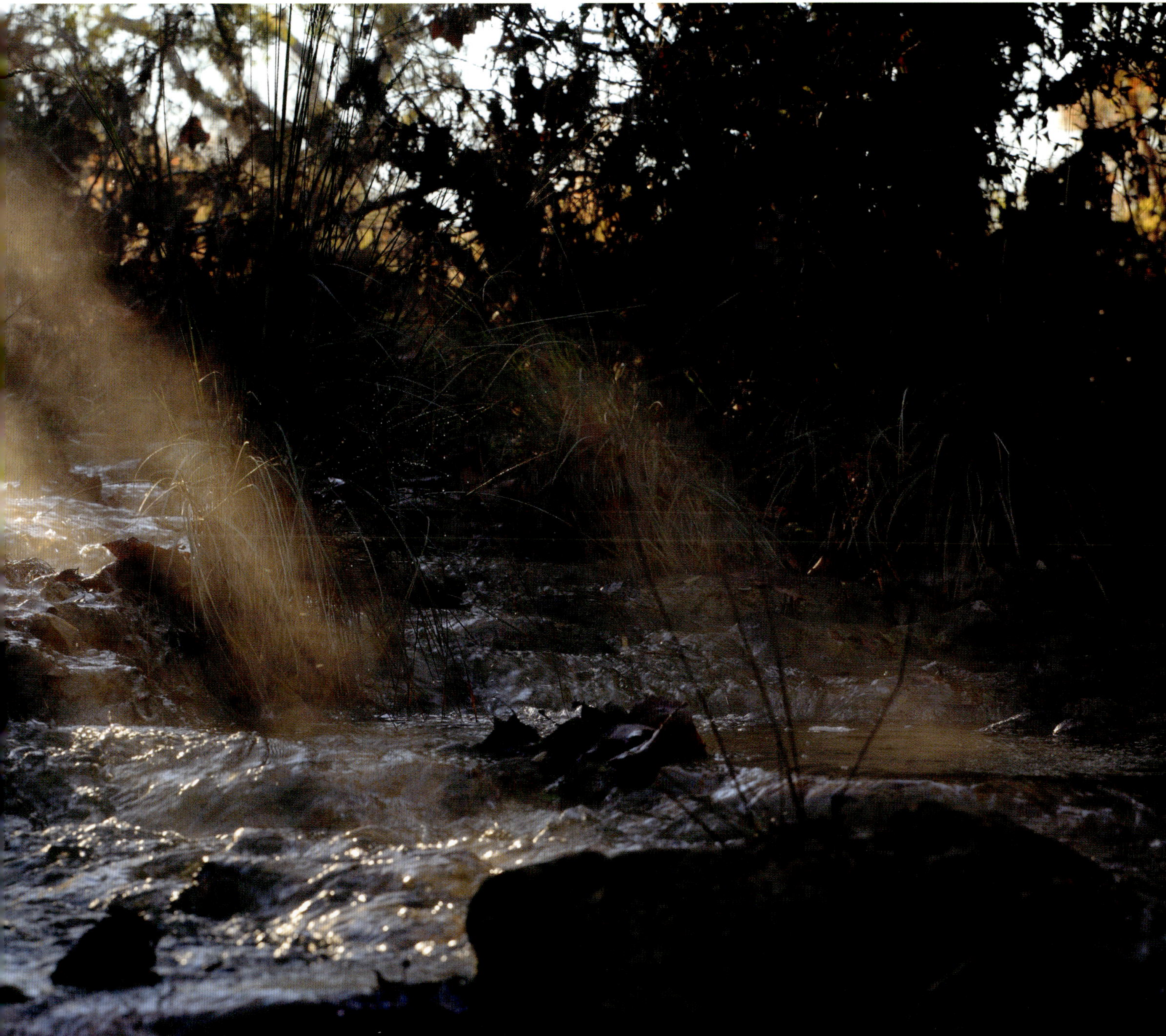

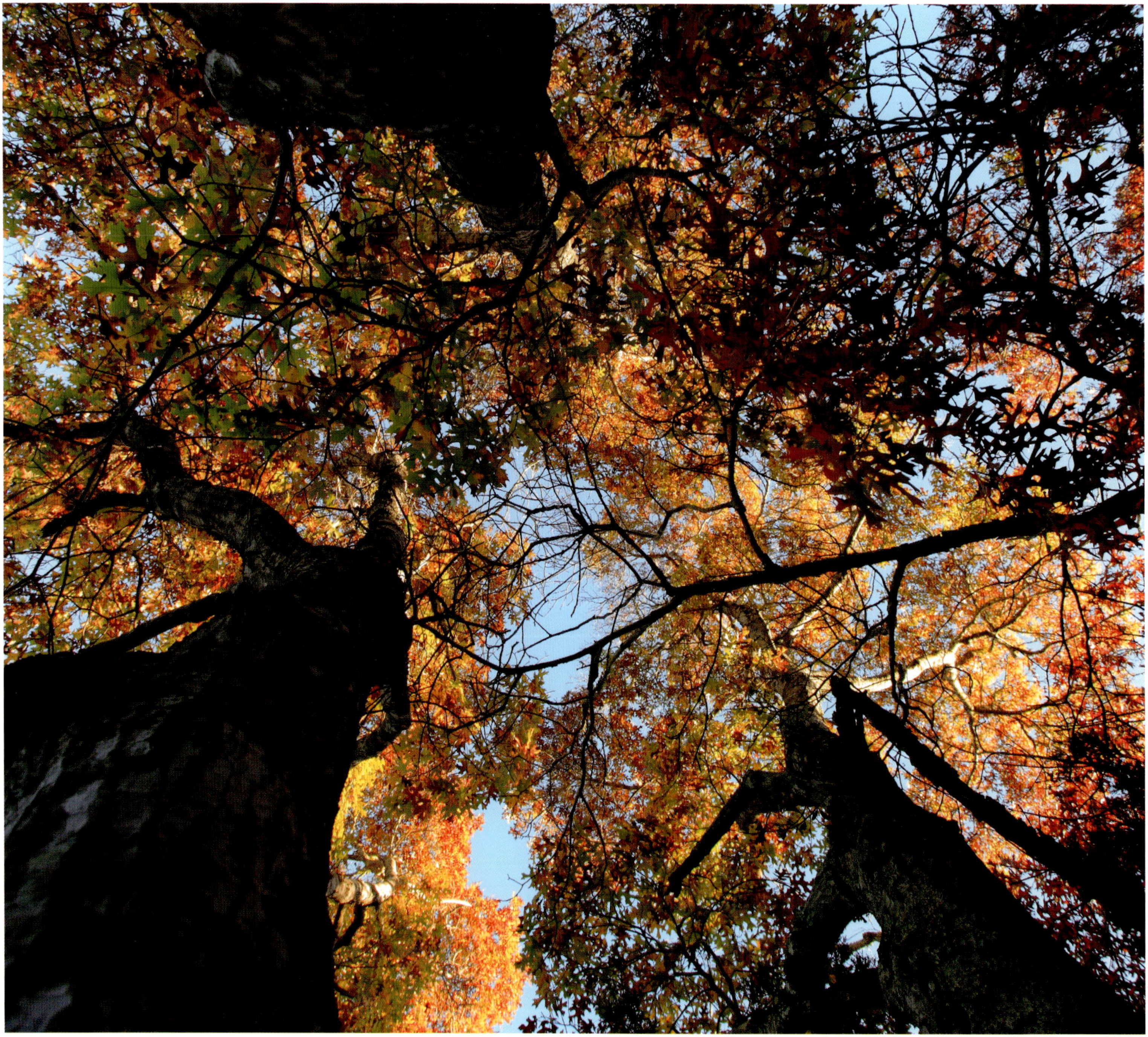

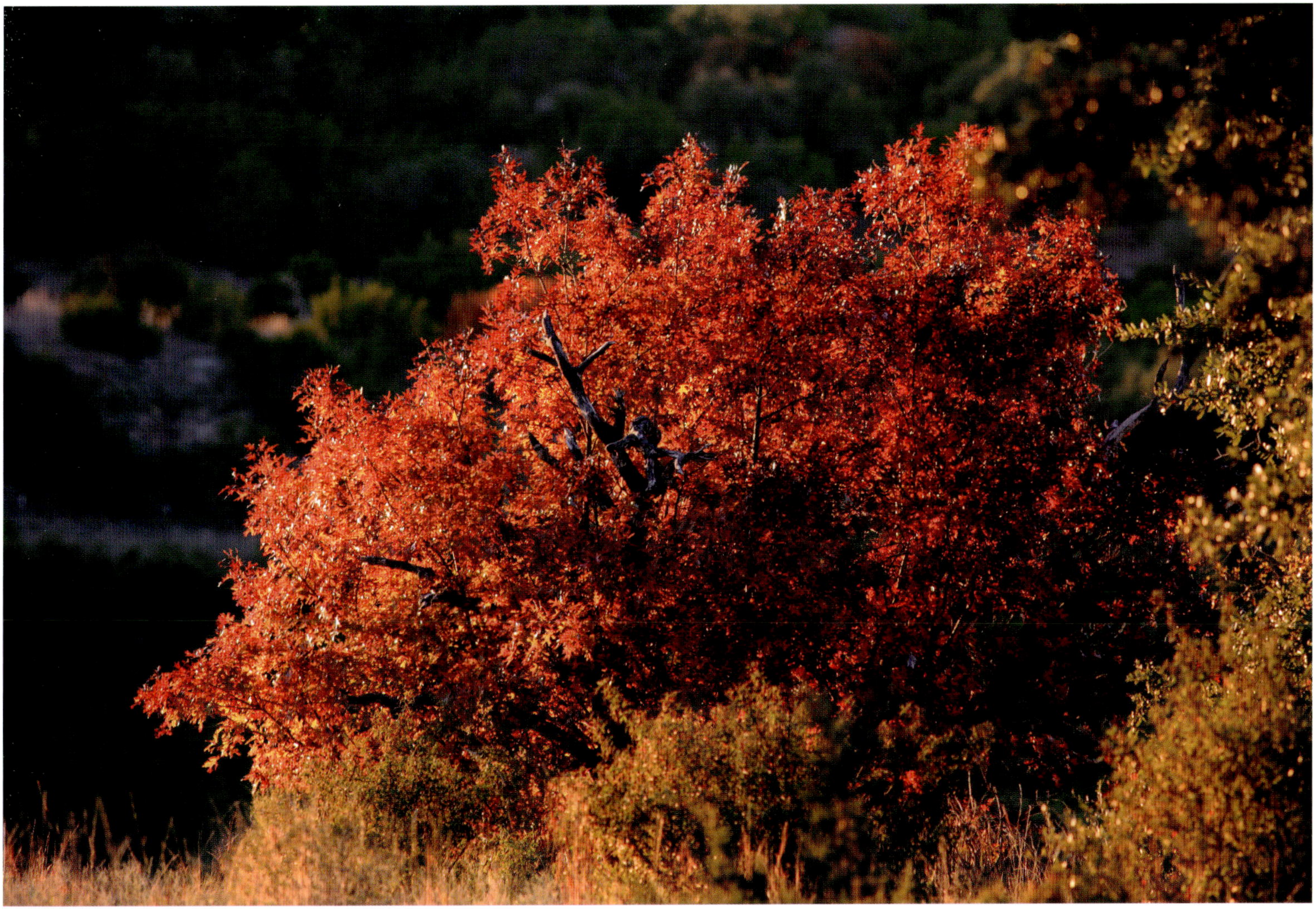

◀ Cradled along rocky slopes, ridges, and ravines, Texas red oaks add bursts of vivid autumn reds, yellows, and oranges to the Hill Country offset by their distinctive mottled silver bark.

▲ A small hardy tree, the prairie flameleaf sumac explodes with brilliant red and orange fall foliage from rocky hillsides and grasslands across Central Texas.

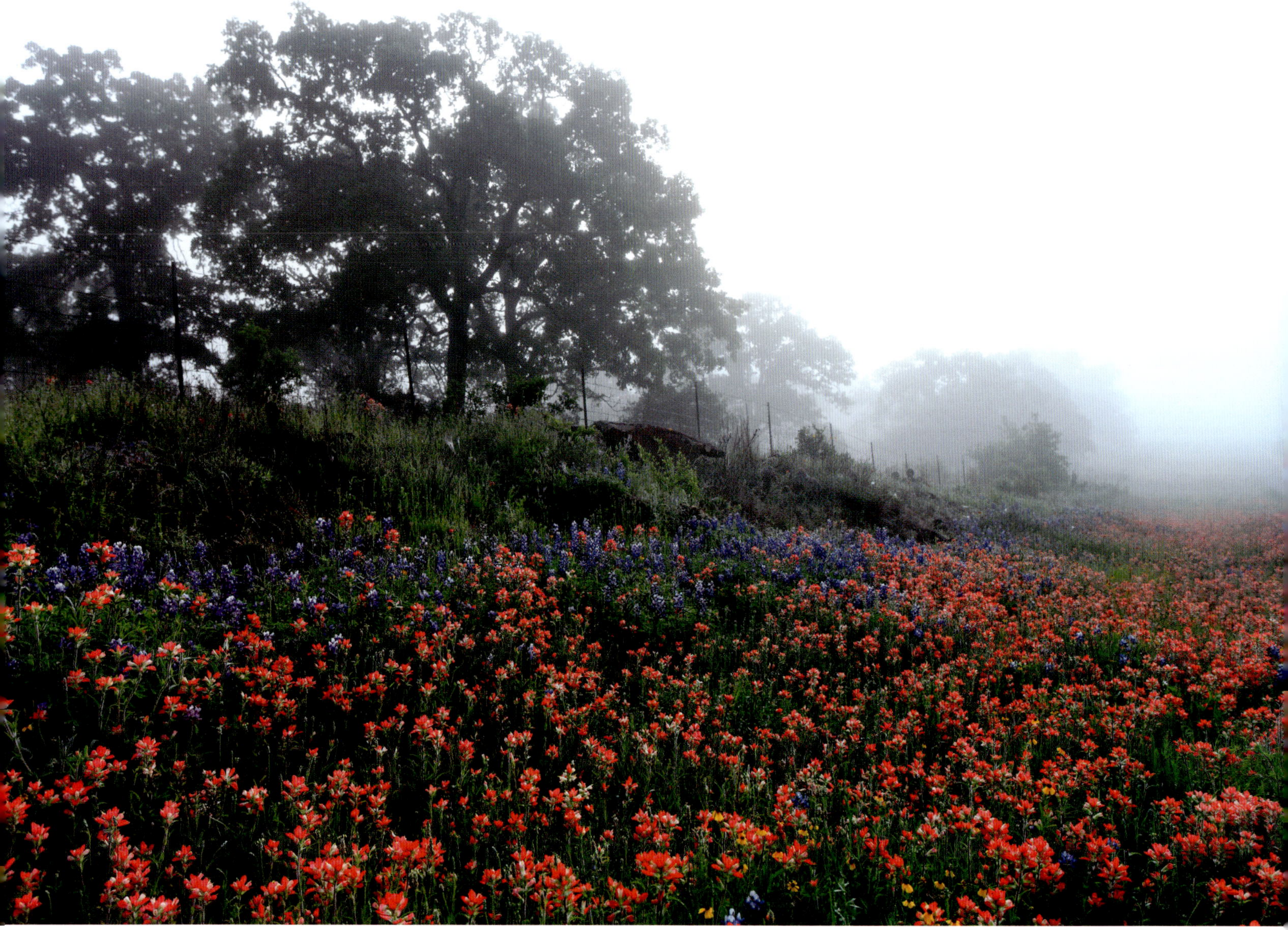

▲ Beneath a veil of thick fog and towering live oaks, vibrant Indian paintbrush and bluebonnets line a hillside in Blanco County.

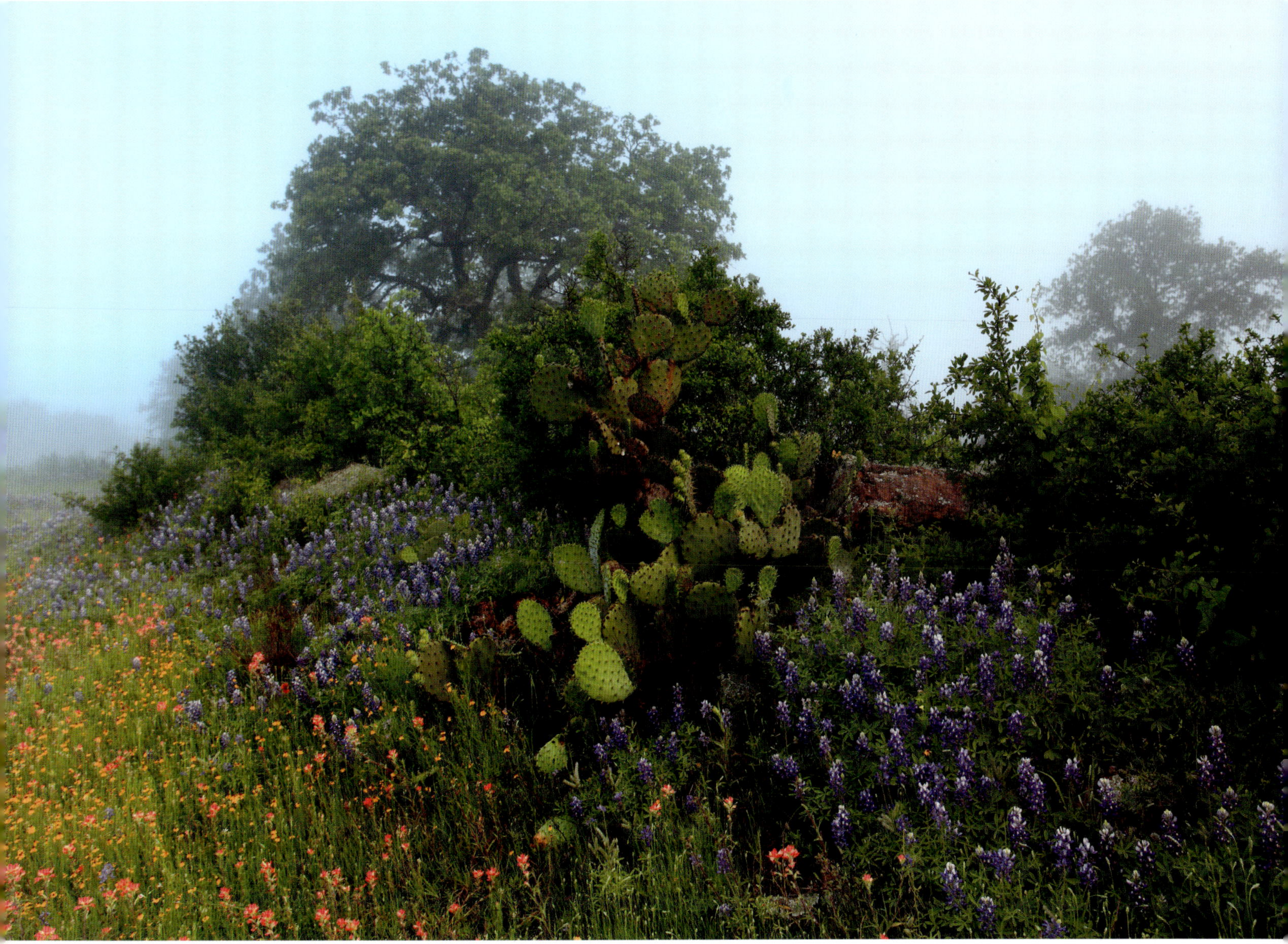

▲ A medley of springtime wildflowers bloom along a rocky mound in the company of prickly pear cactus and Texas persimmons.

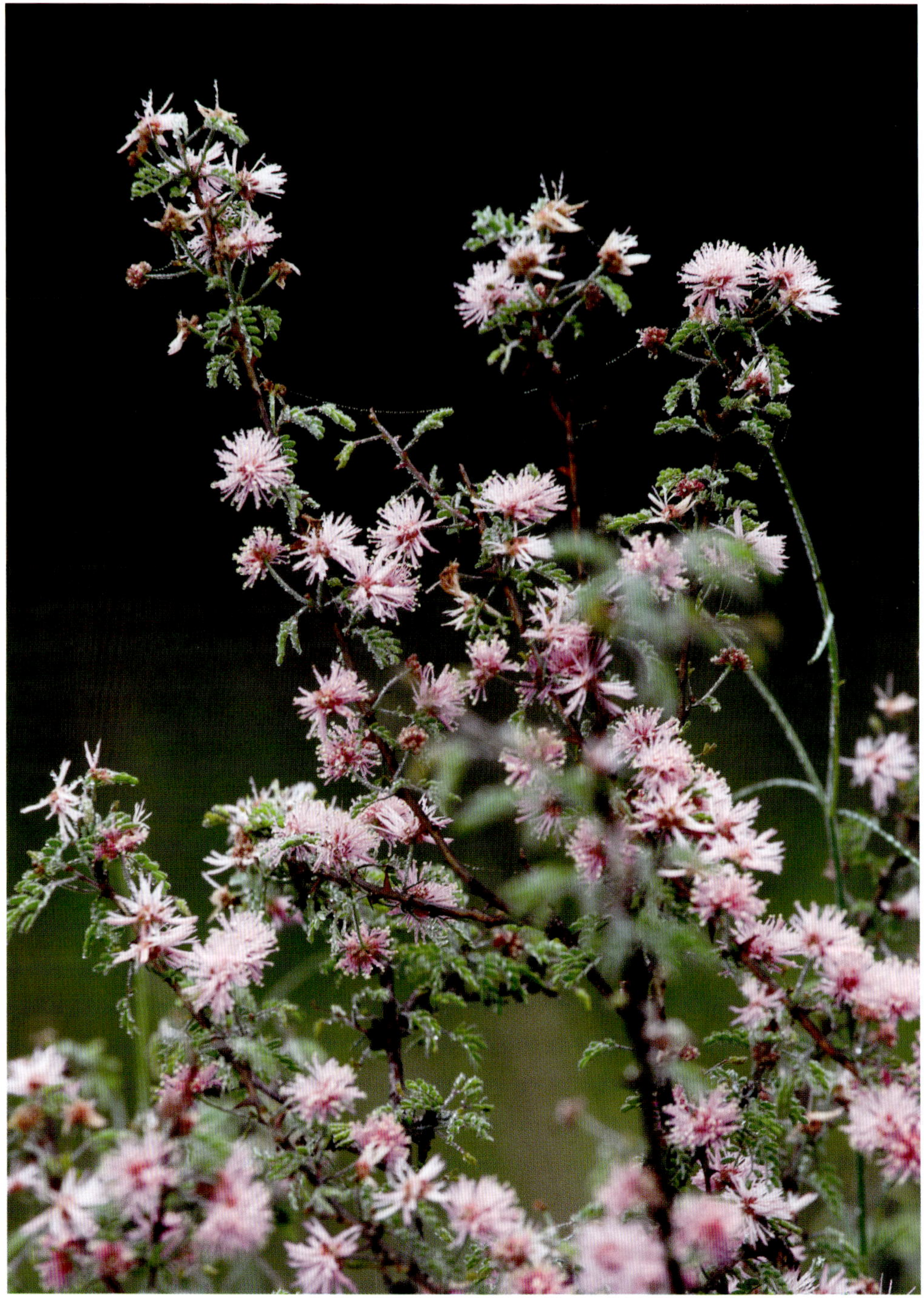

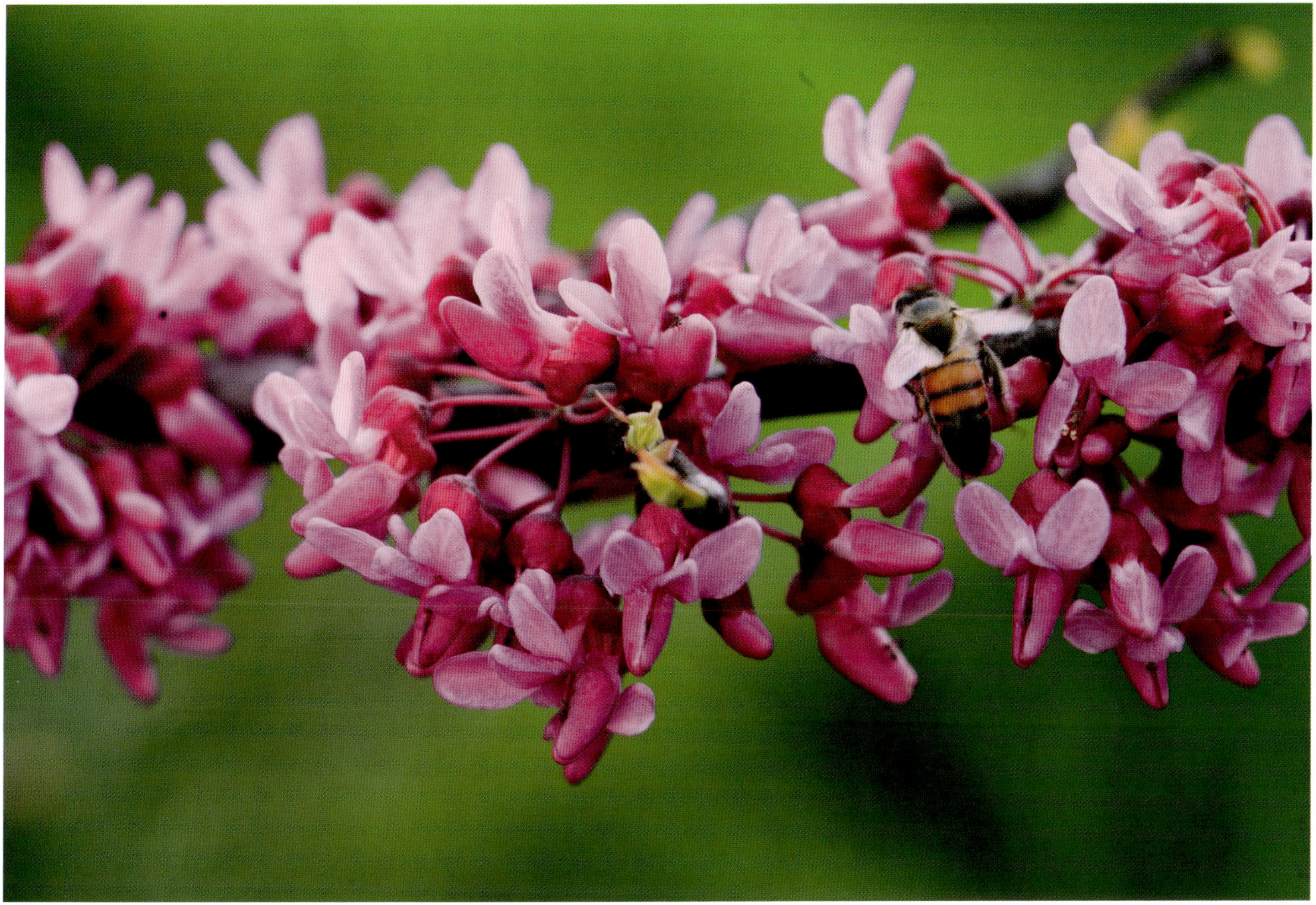

◀ The fragrant mimosa bush, an otherwise unremarkable and thorny shrub, bursts with spring color as pink, puffy, and aromatic flowers fill the air with their sweet scent.

▲ Heralding in the spring season in the Hill Country, Texas redbud trees blossom with clusters of tiny pink-red flowers in early spring, peppering otherwise verdant tree lines and grassy hillsides with intense pockets of color.

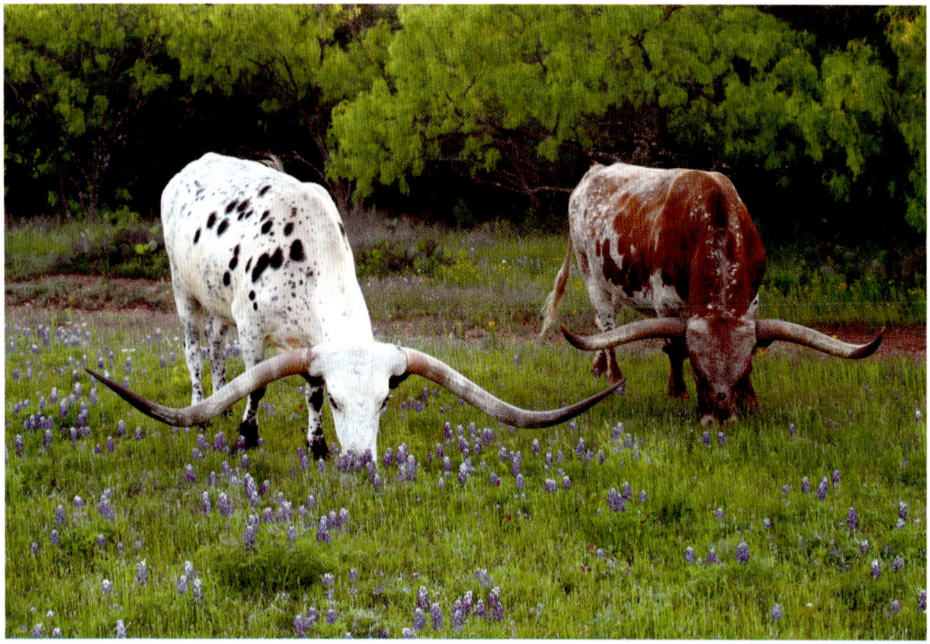

◀ Long considered a symbol of Texas' ranching heritage, longhorns are a common site among the sprawling ranch lands across the Hill Country. Longhorns are designated the official state large mammal of Texas.

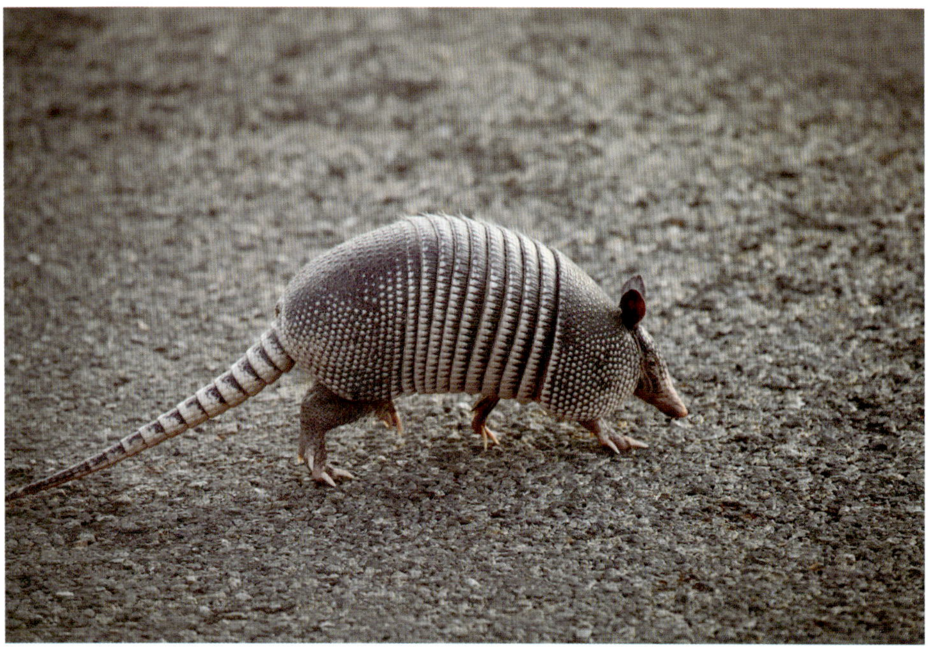

◀ A nine-banded armadillo—the official small mammal of Texas—crosses a blacktop road in Comal County.

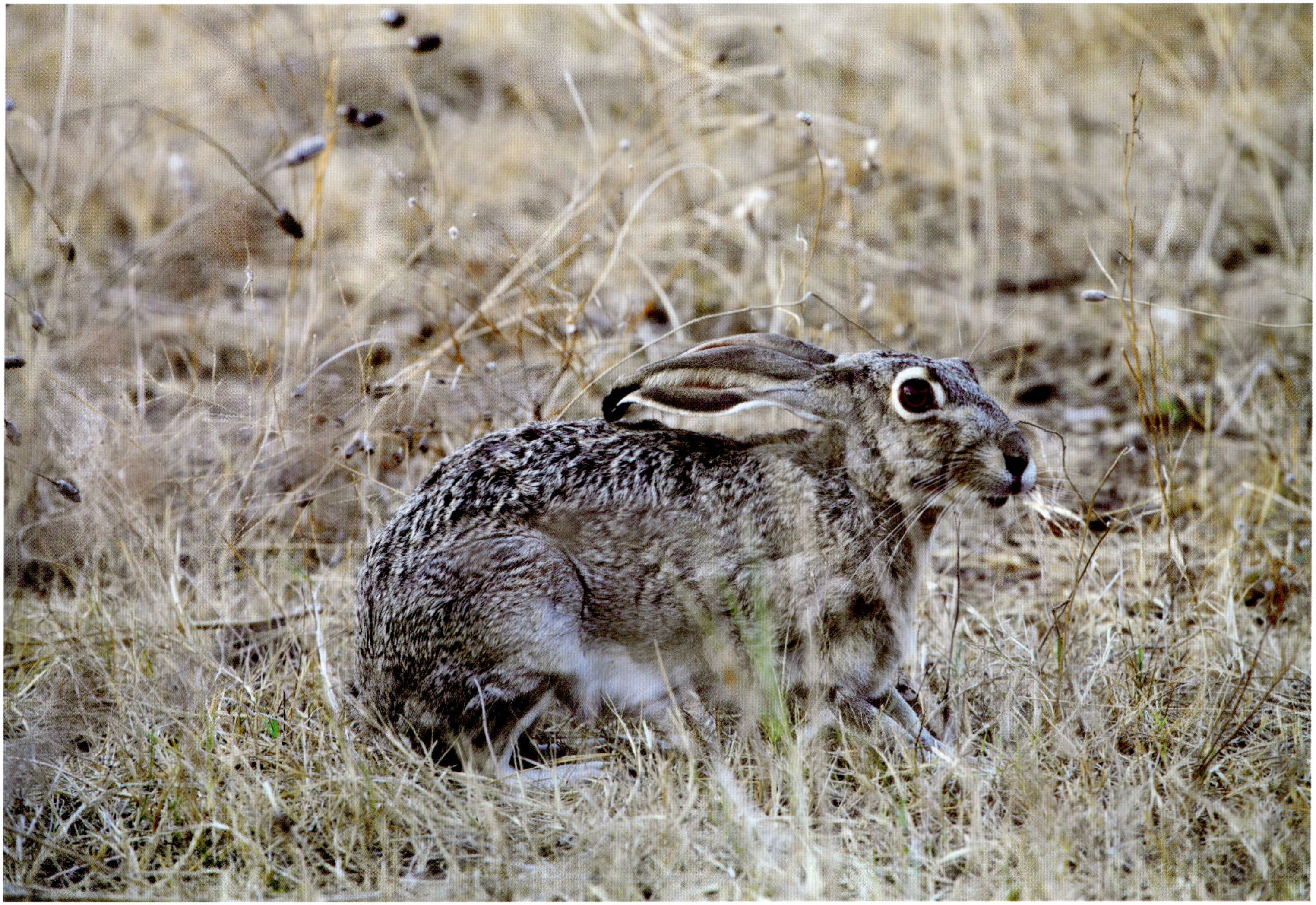

▲ A black-tailed jackrabbit crouches and blends in with dormant winter grasses in Blanco County.

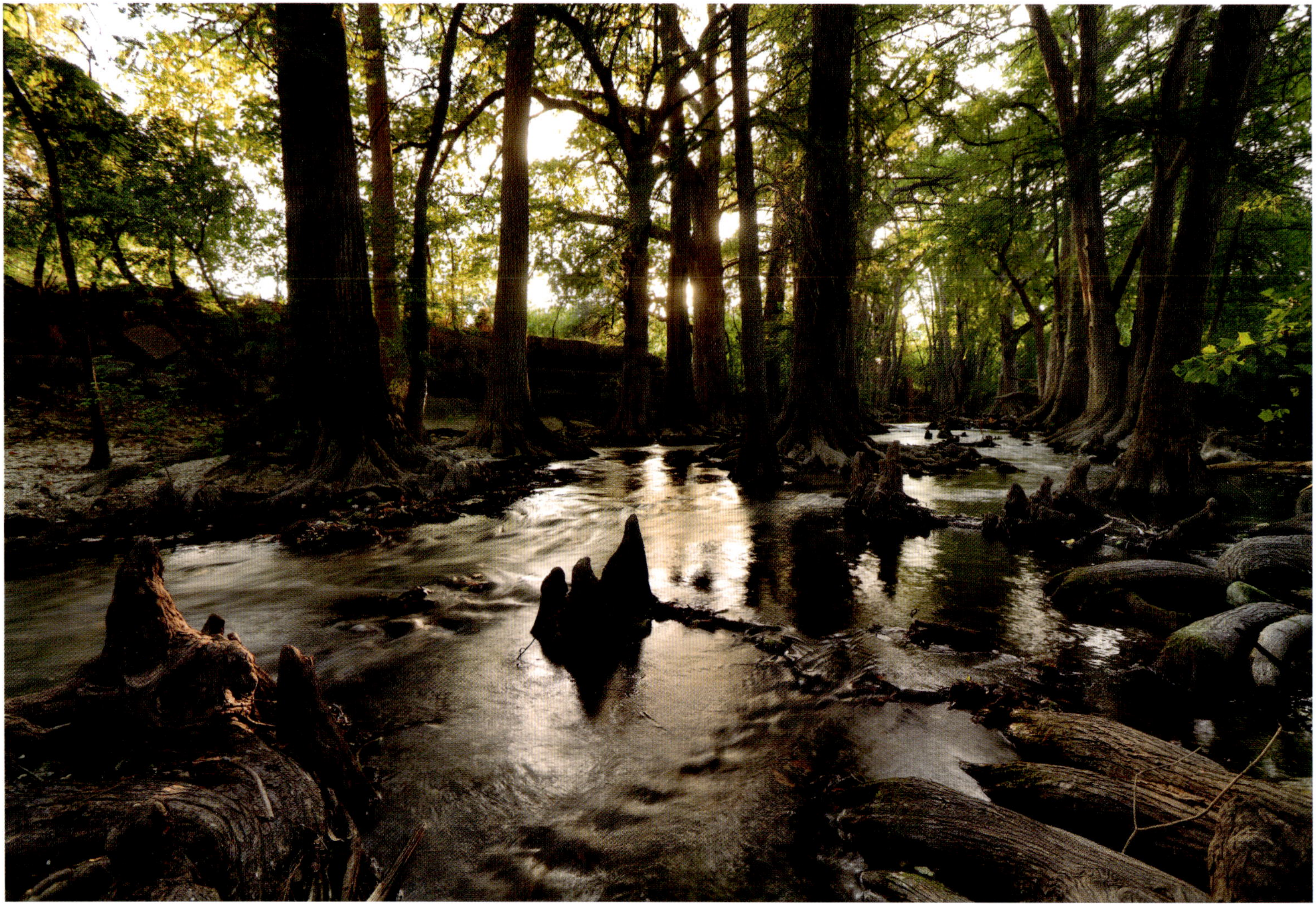

▲▶ Towering bald cypress trees flank Cibolo Creek in the Cibolo Nature Center, a one hundred acre preserve in Boerne encompassing several ecological habitats, including prairie, wetlands, and creek bottom.

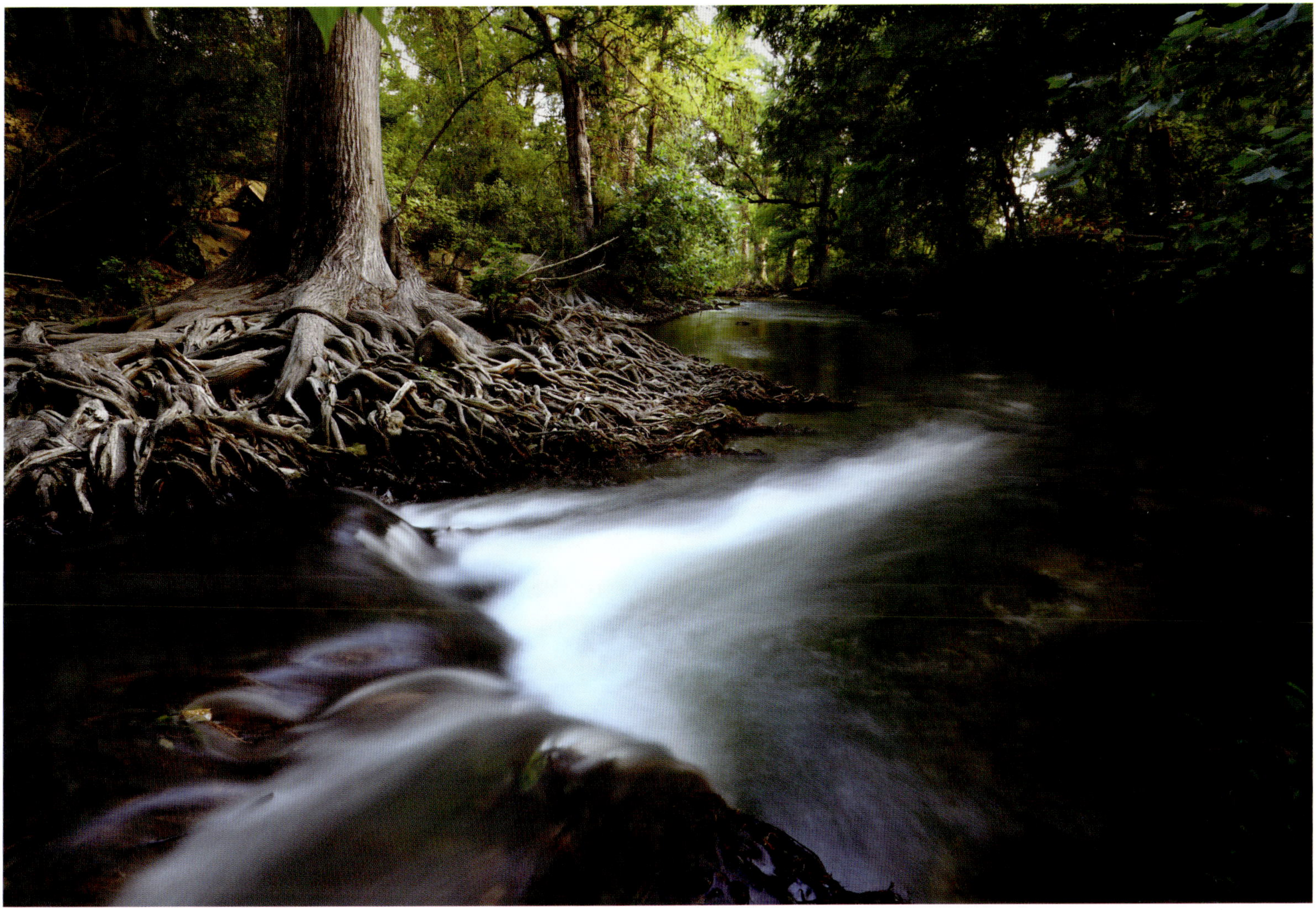

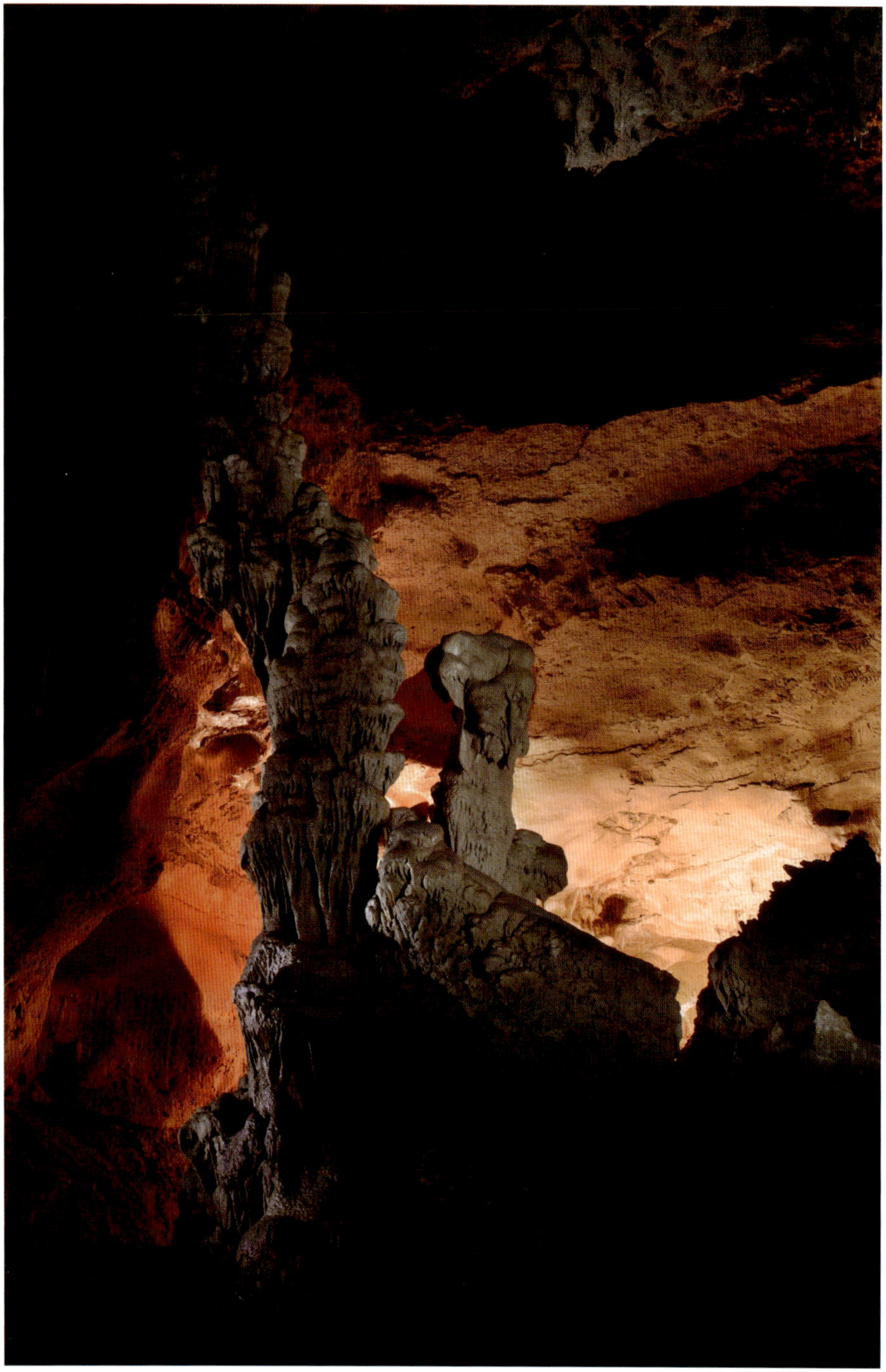

◀▶ Amid the Hill Country's karst topography is a labyrinth of subterranean wonders like Cave Without a Name, northeast of Boerne. The cave was discovered in 1927 and opened to the public in 1939. The cave floor sits one hundred feet below ground and houses a variety of large living formations, cathedral-like chambers, pools, and a flowing underground stream.

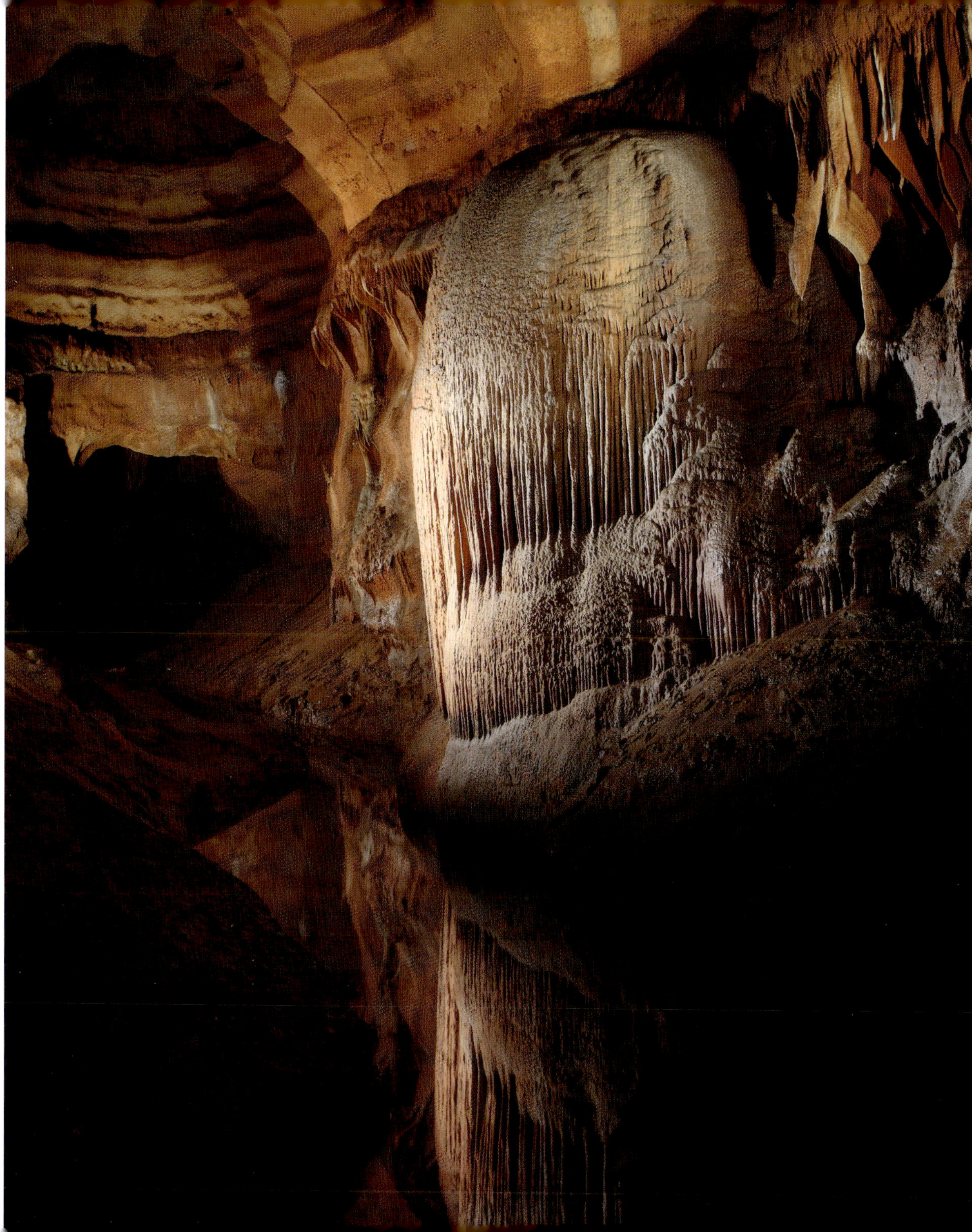

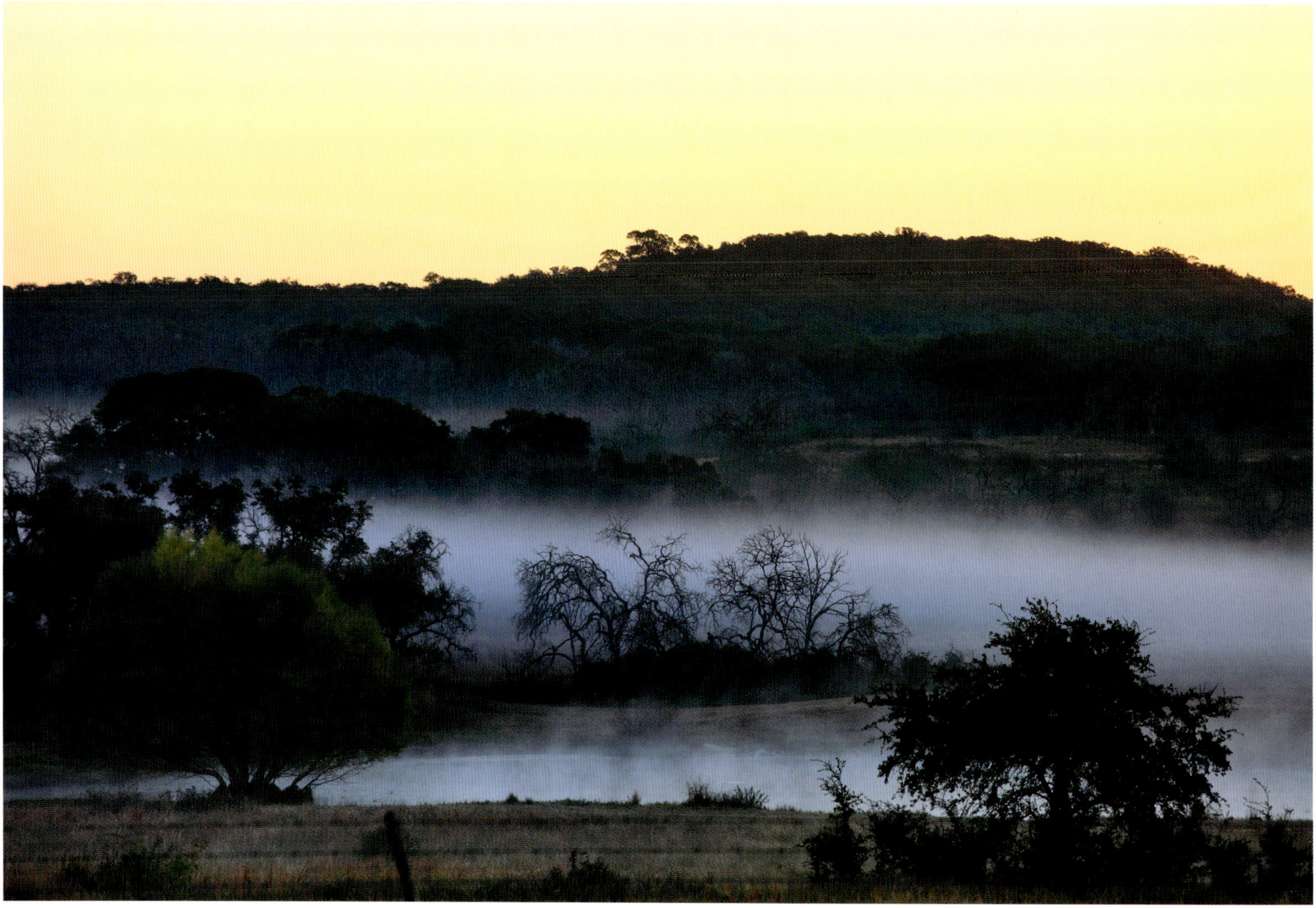

▲ Layers of dense fog contrast against ascending hilltop terraces on a cold fall morning near Boerne.

▶ Just after sunset, vibrant pink clouds rise over the stair-stepped limestone bed and dramatic deep blue pool of Little Edge Falls on Curry Creek near Kendalia.

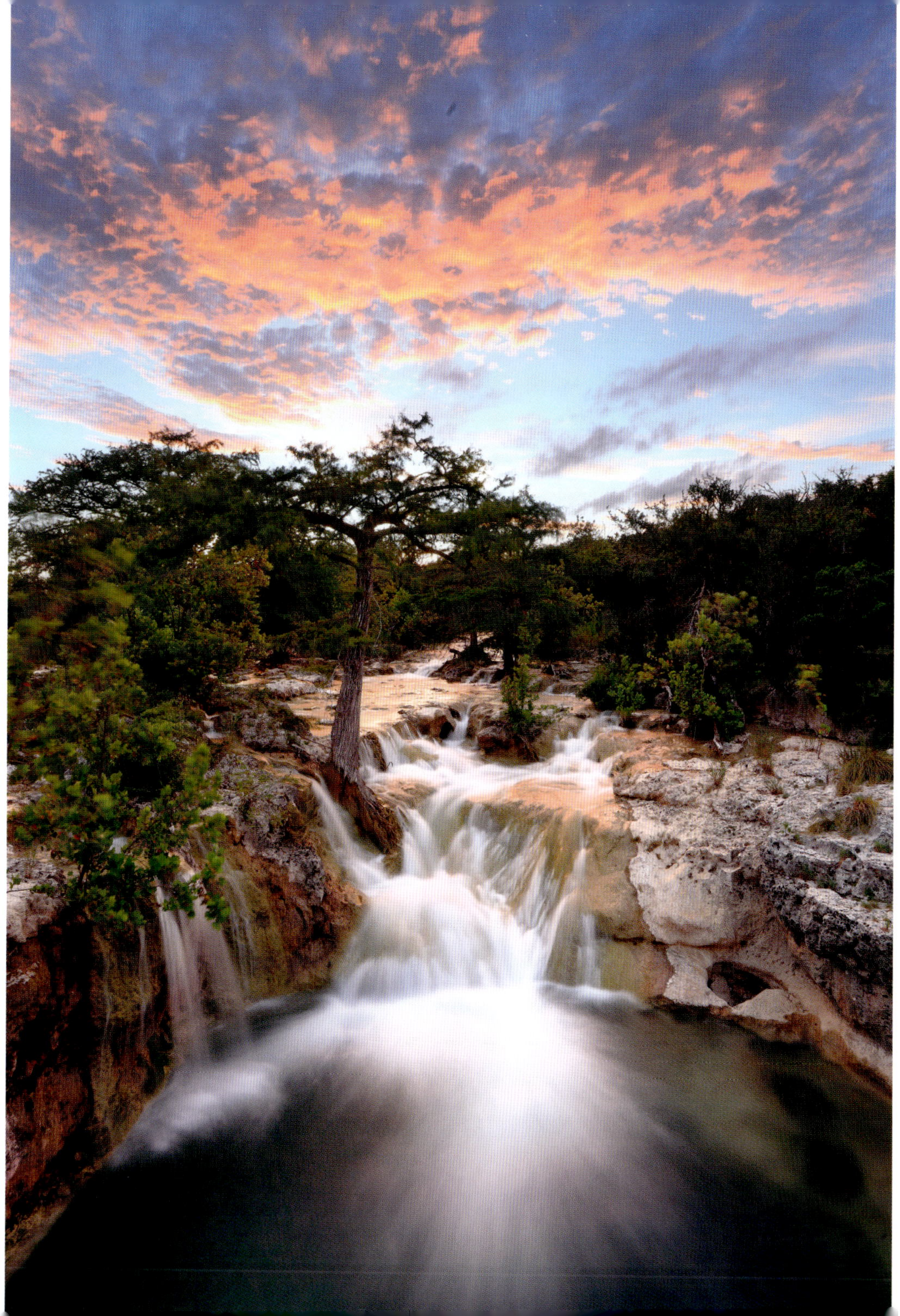

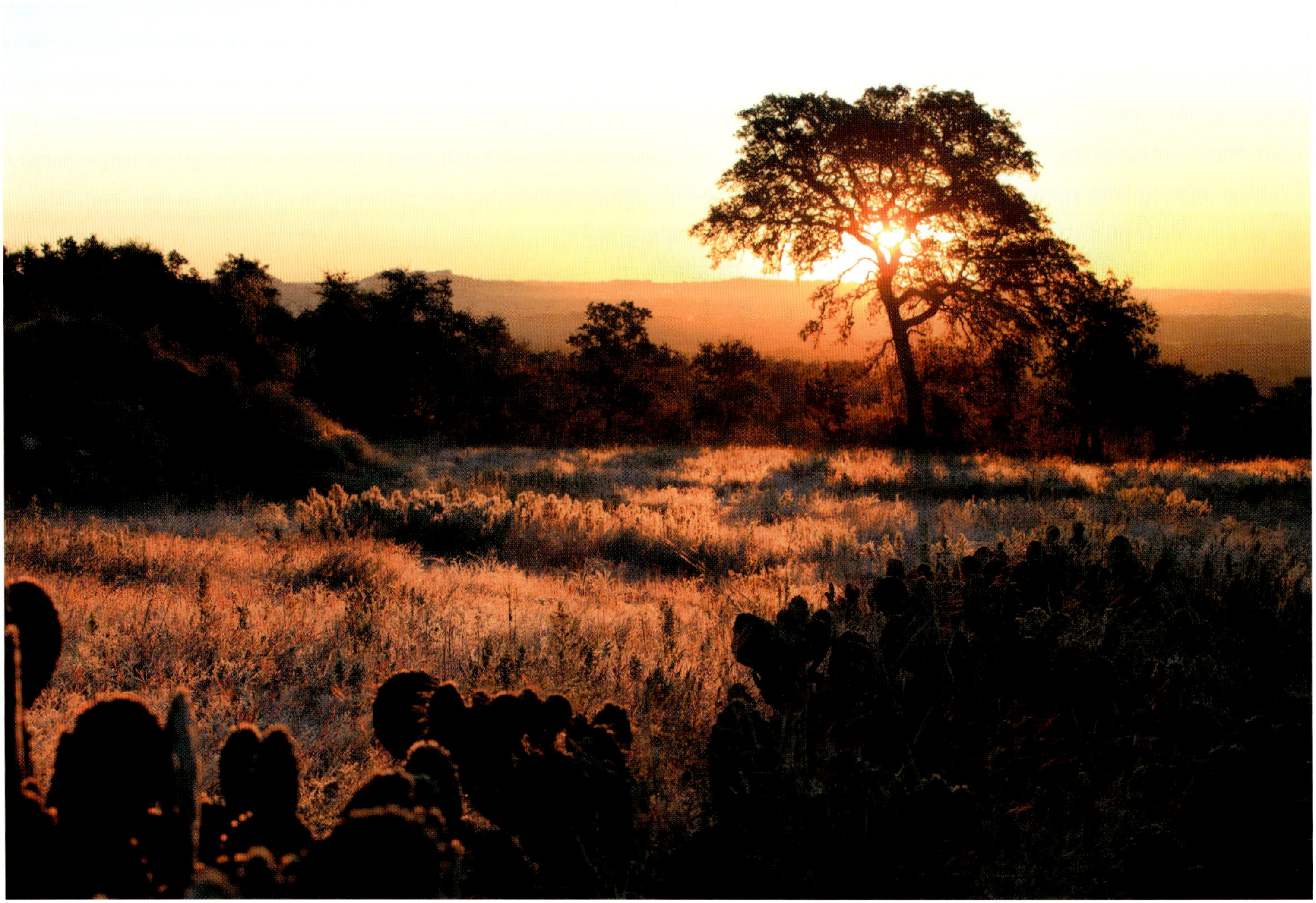

▲▶ A wintry morning landscape is revealed as the first light of day scrapes across frost-covered grasses, cactus, and live oaks in Comal County.

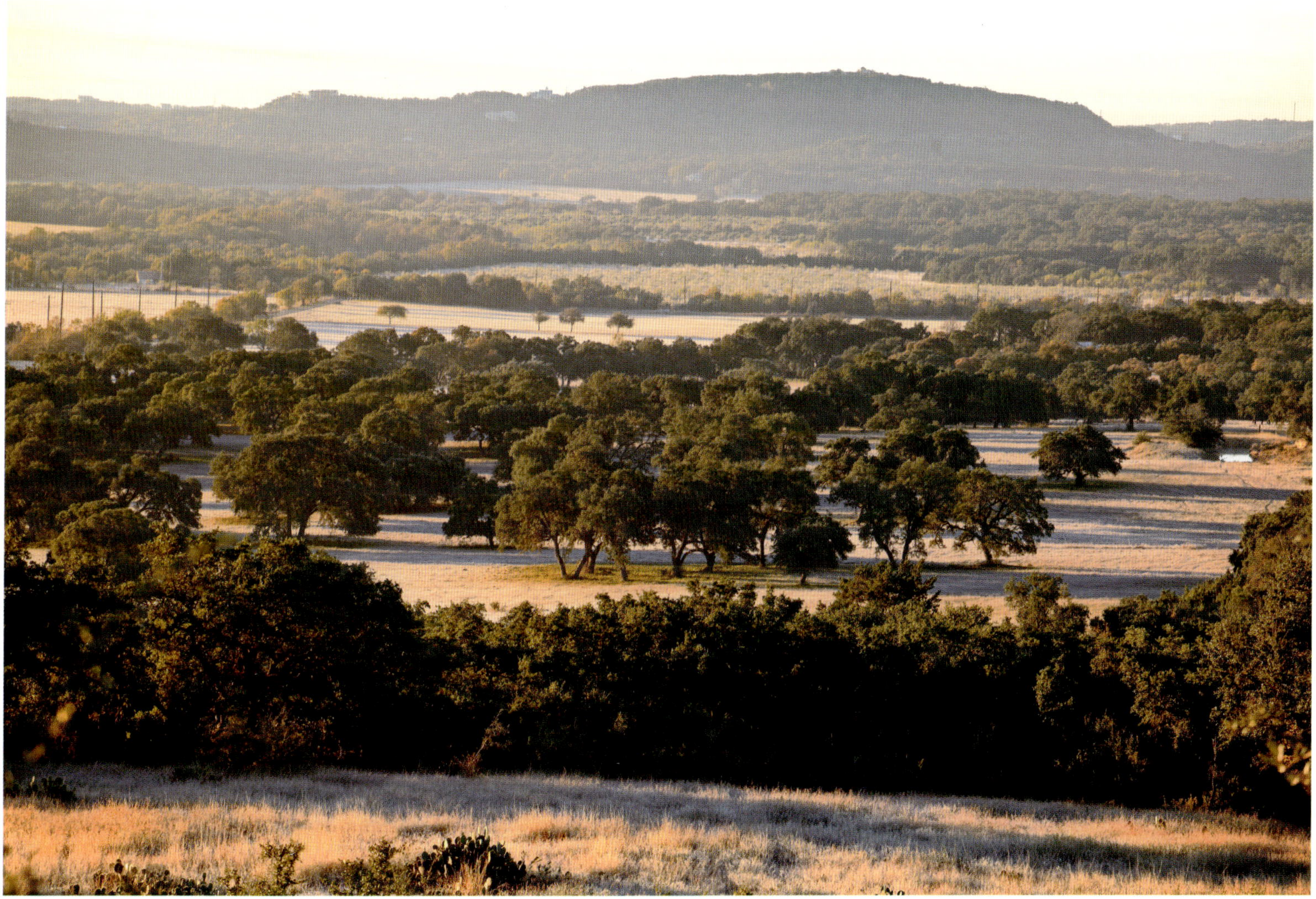

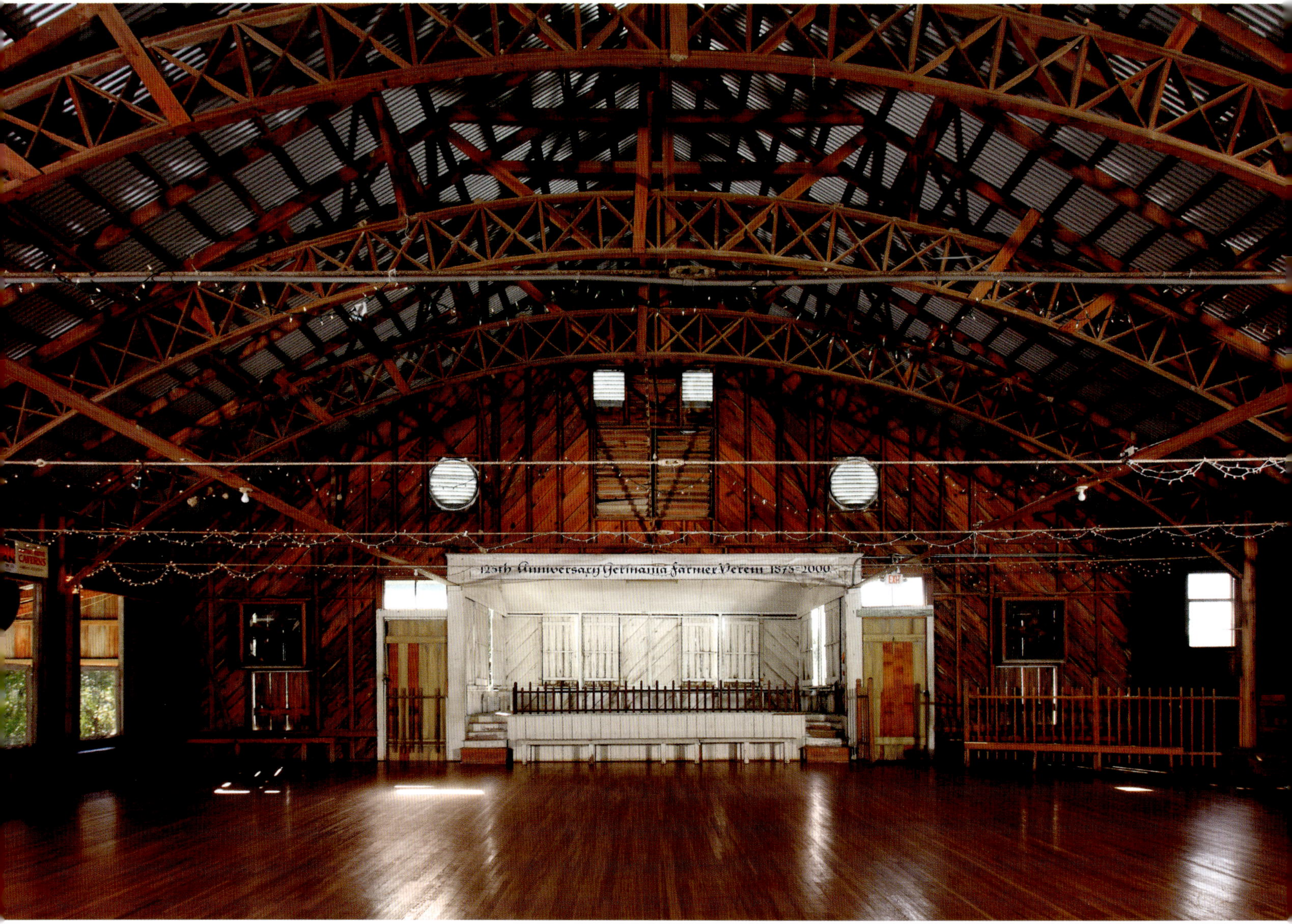

▲▶ Built in 1875 by a group of German settlers known as the Germania Farmers Verein, Anhalt Hall features stately arched trusses, wood-slat walls, and a 6,000-square-foot dance floor inside a gabled tin barn. Today it remains one of the most well-preserved and historic dance halls in the state.

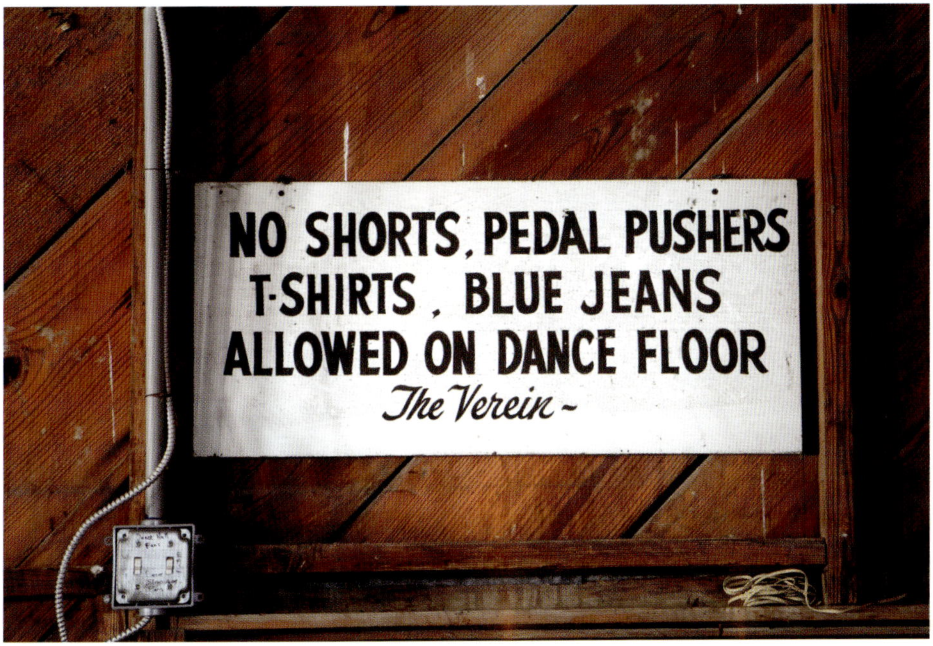
NO SHORTS, PEDAL PUSHERS
T-SHIRTS, BLUE JEANS
ALLOWED ON DANCE FLOOR
The Verein ~

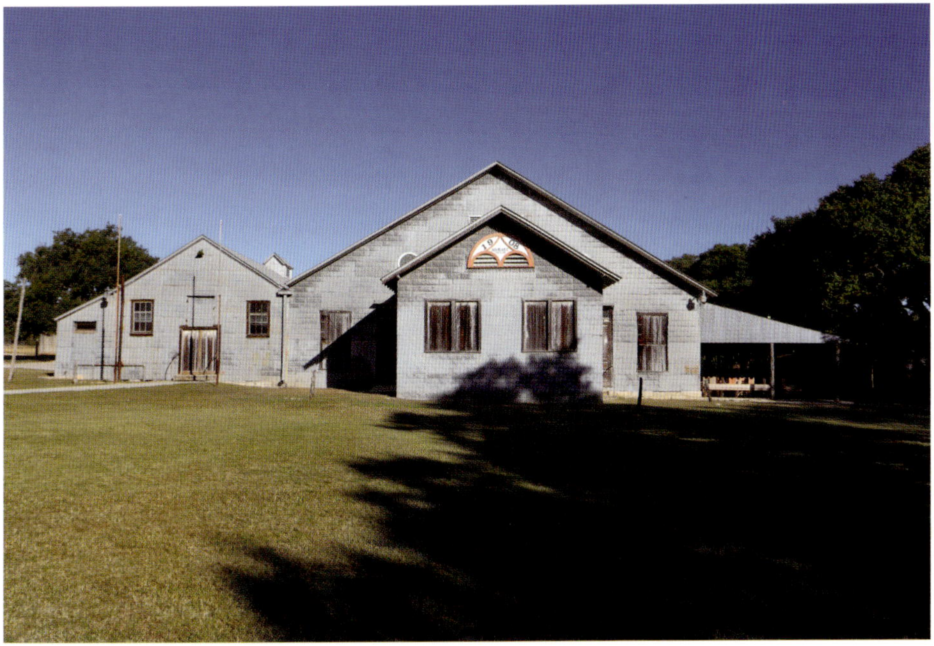
19 08

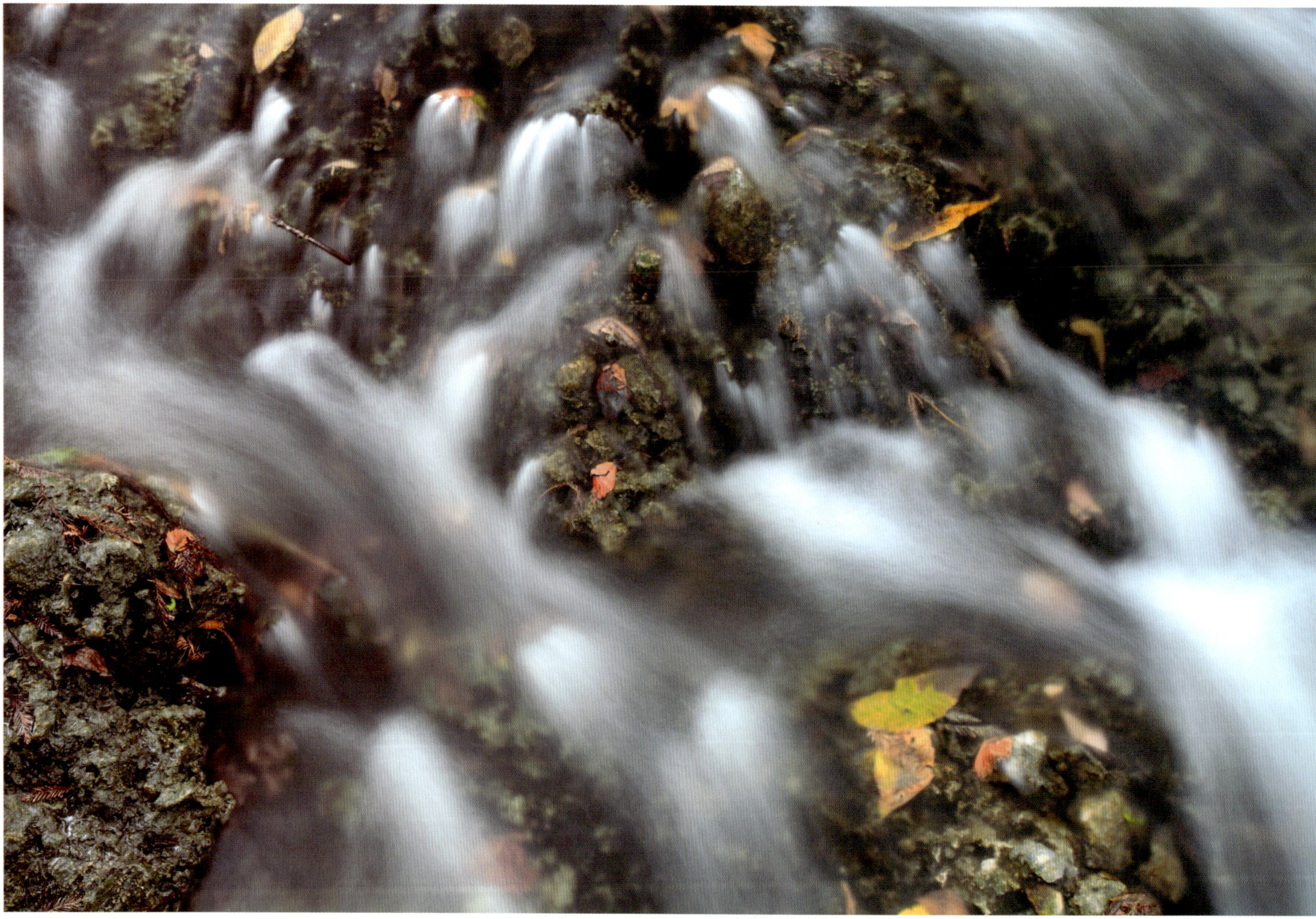

▲ The Texas Hill Country is also known as Flash Flood Alley, a well-chosen nickname given that shallow soil depth and steep topography can collude with rain storms to create walls of water rushing through otherwise placid streams and rivers.

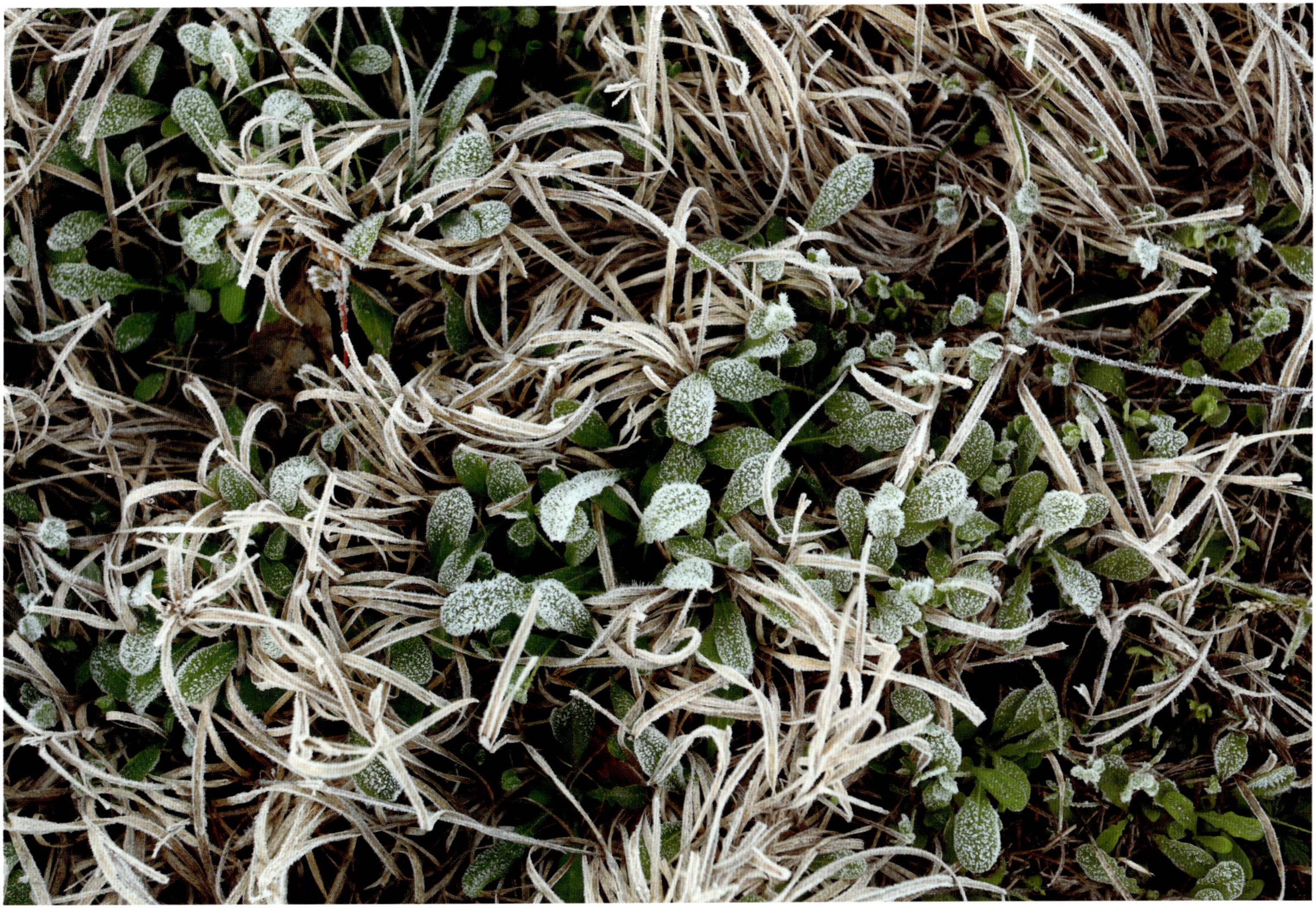

▲ Although Central Texas is known for its mild winters, the Hill Country will dip into freezing temperatures, glazing hillside flora with a soft layer of frost.

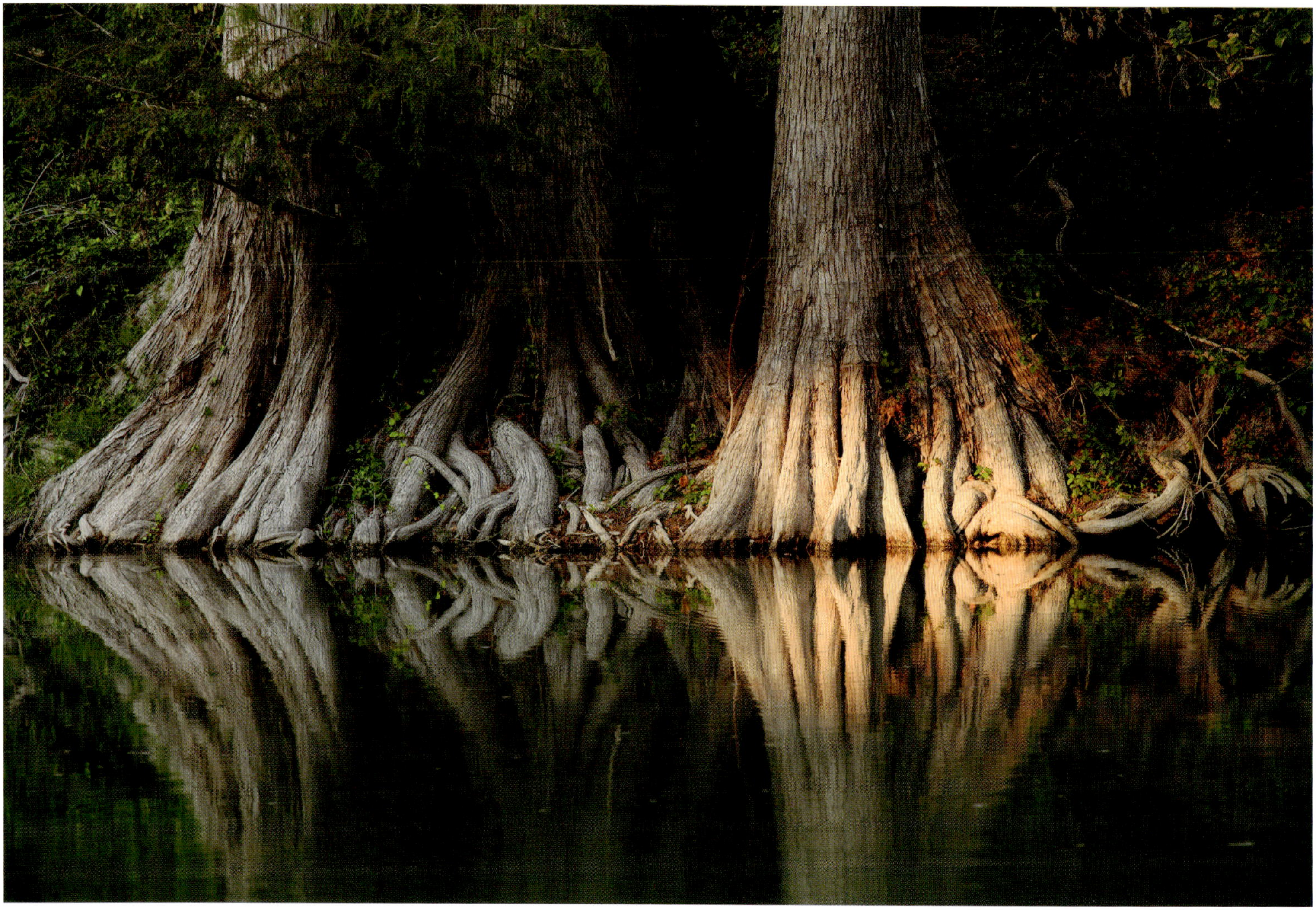

▲ A patch of afternoon sunlight casts light on the base of a large bald cypress tree reflecting off a still part of the Guadalupe River.

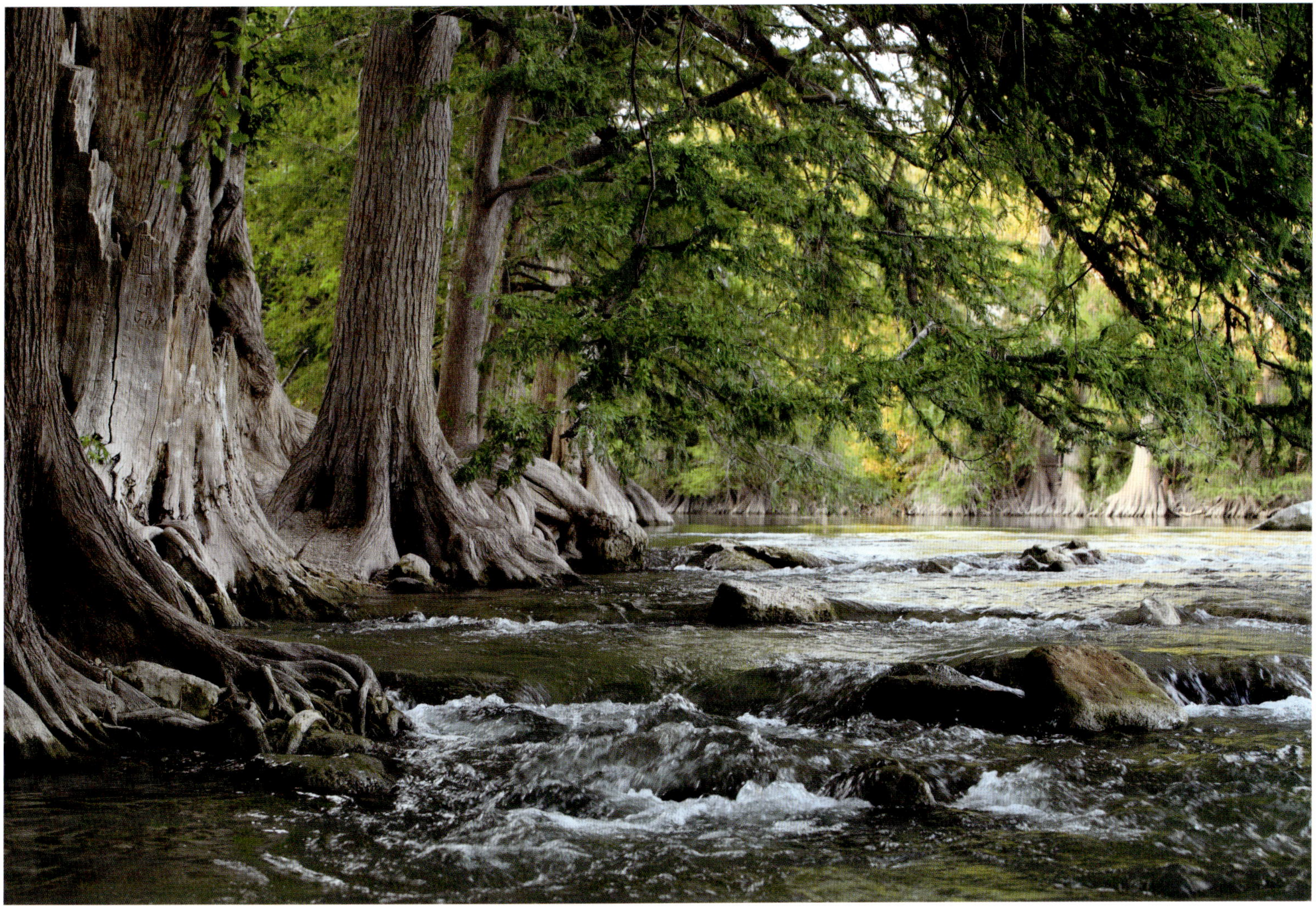

▲ From its headwaters west of Hunt, the Guadalupe River meanders across the Hill Country alongside towering limestone bluffs and rocky banks lined with old growth bald cypress trees.

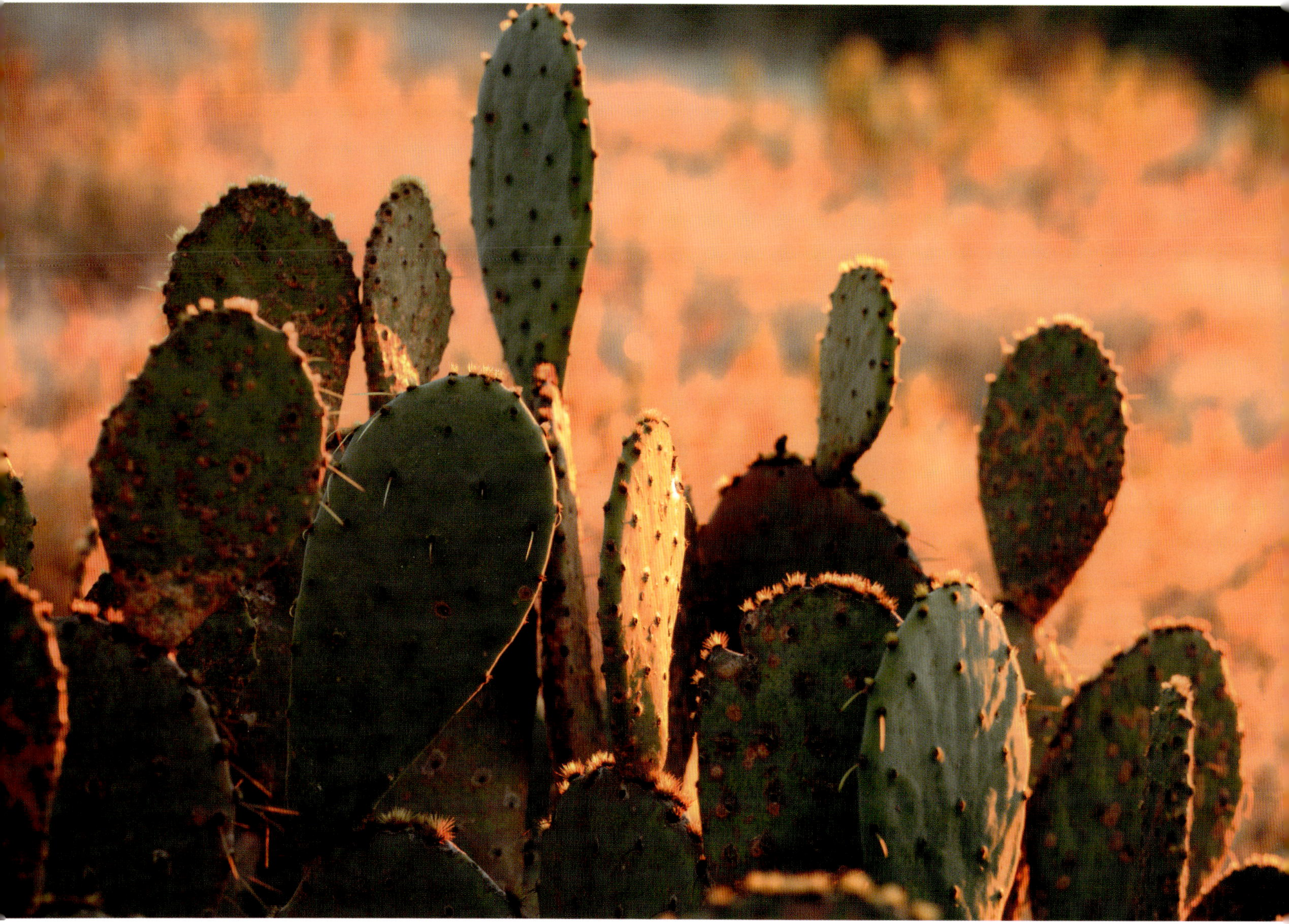

▲ A common site across Central Texas, the prickly pear is a spiny thick-skinned cactus that bears bowl-shaped flowers and fruit during different times of the year.

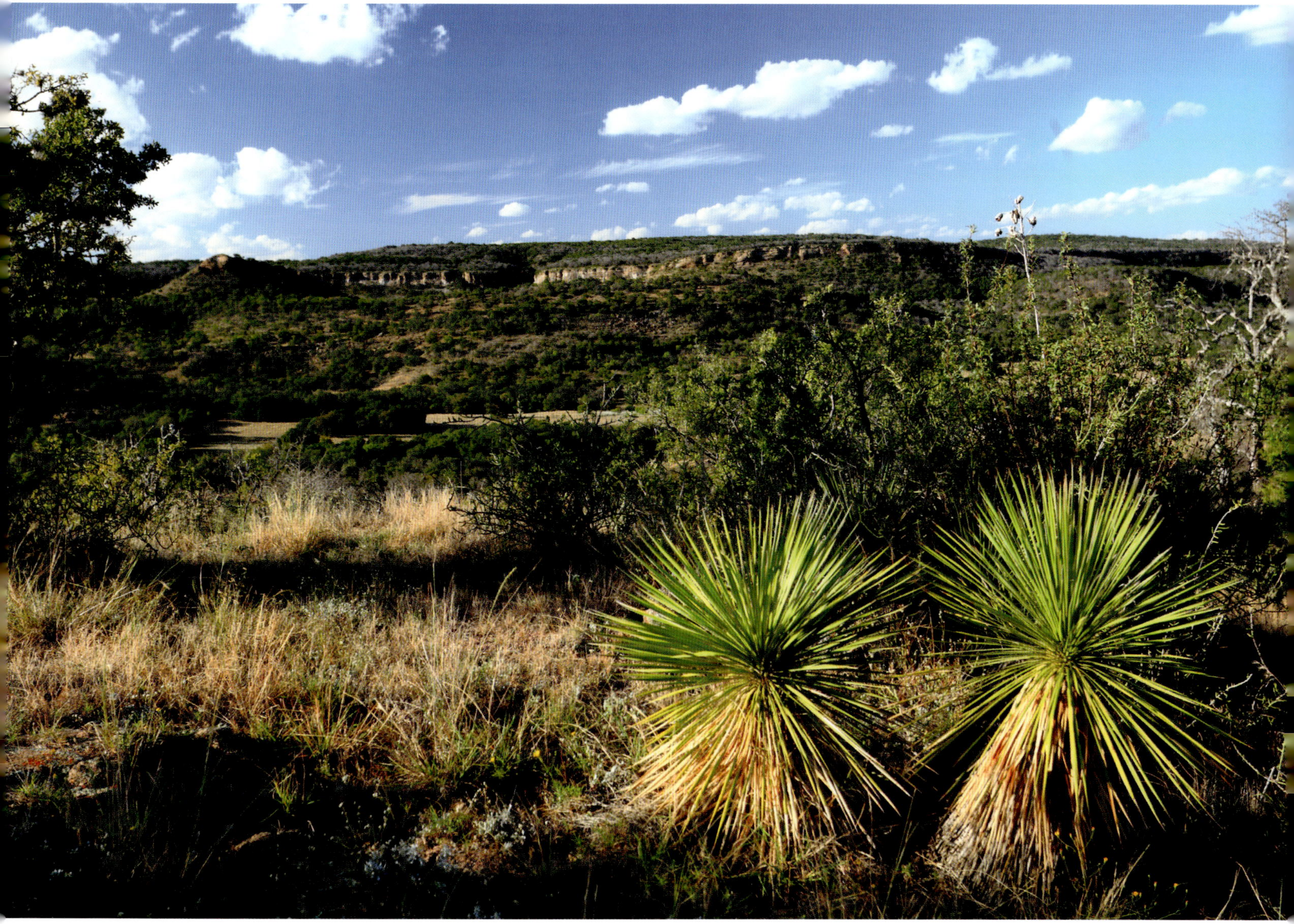

▲ The Willow City Loop is one of the most well-known and scenic byways in the Hill Country. In the spring, carpets of wildflowers abound amid deep canyons, creek bottoms, and panoramic views along a narrow thirteen-mile two-lane ranch road sixteen miles northwest of Fredericksburg.

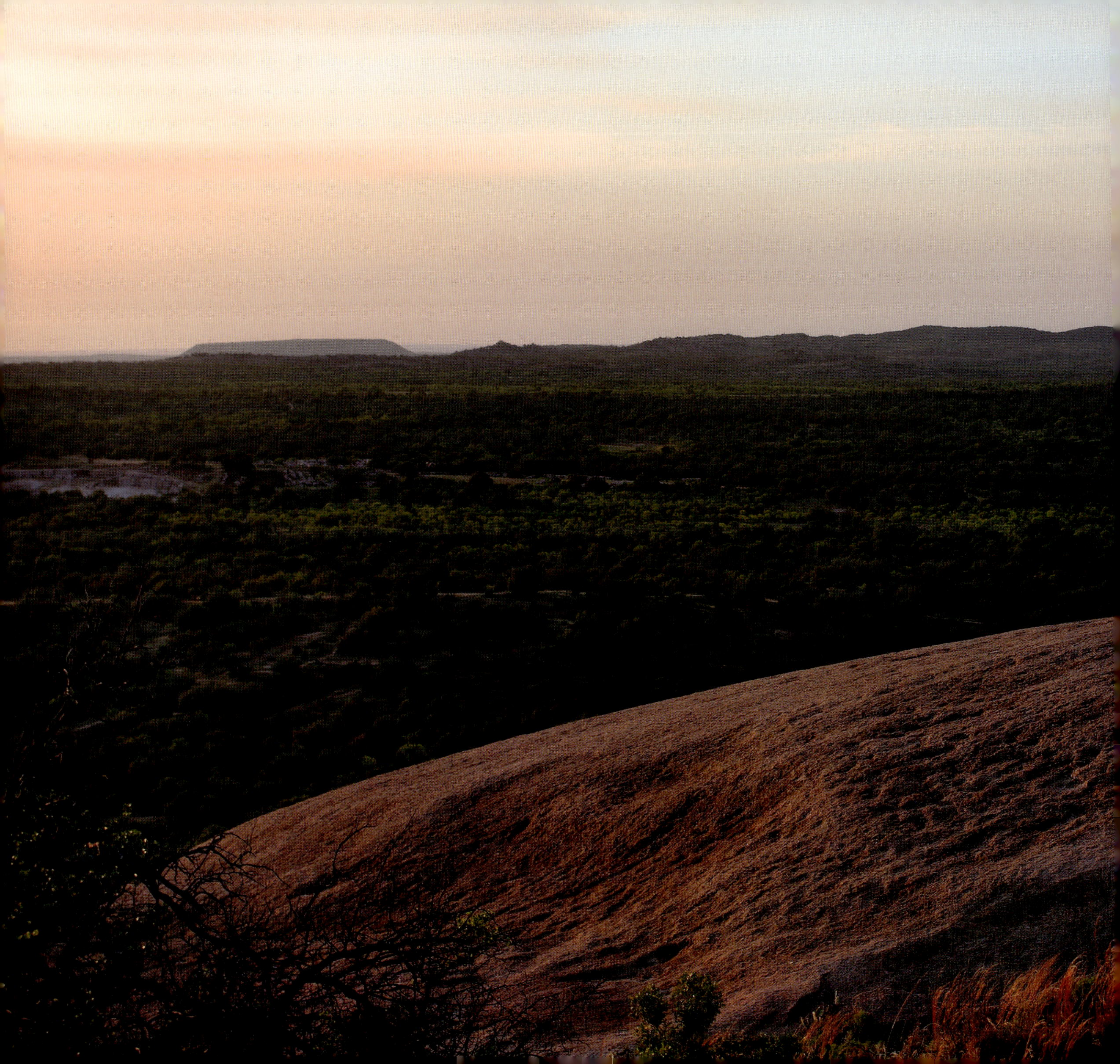

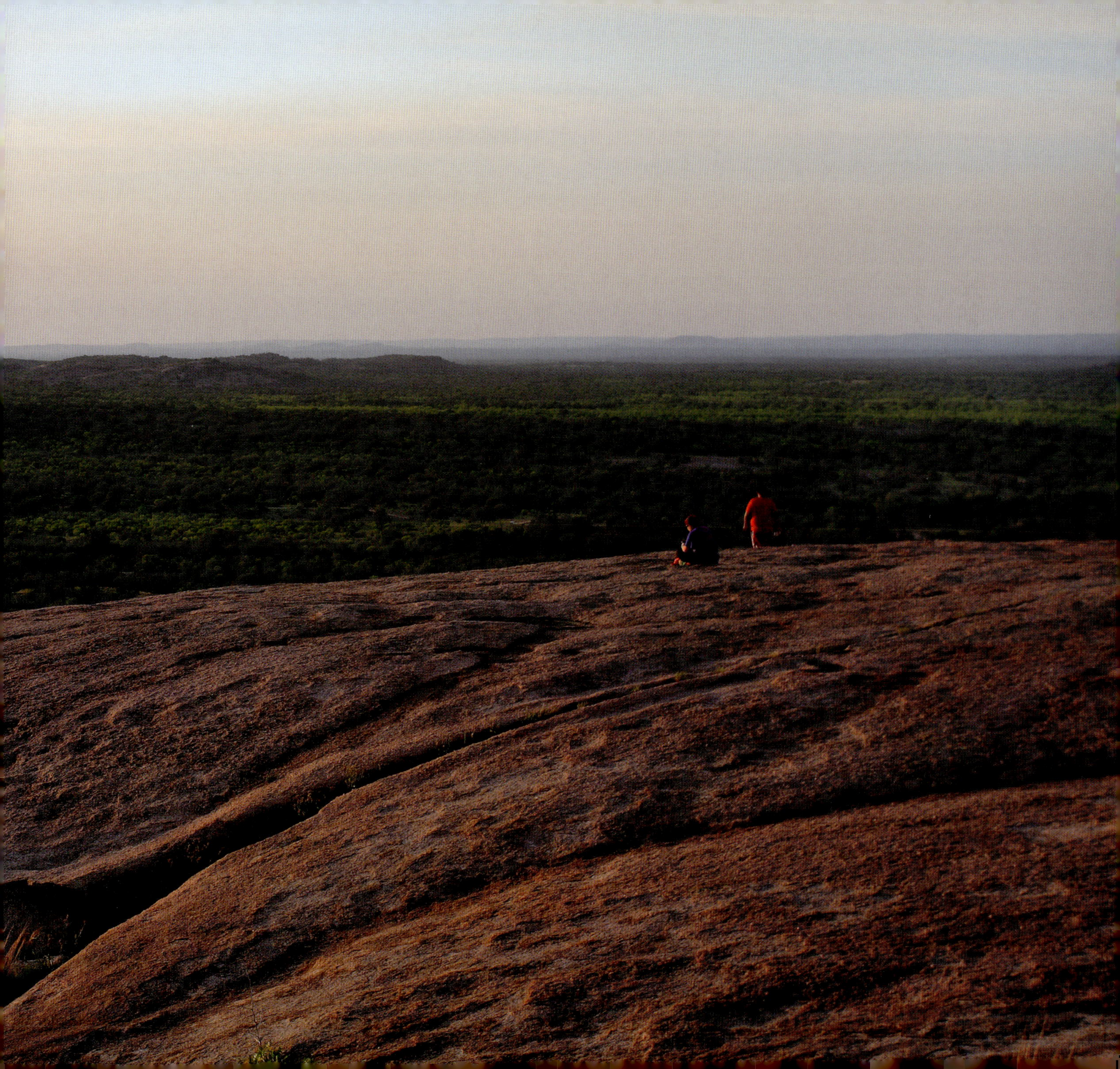

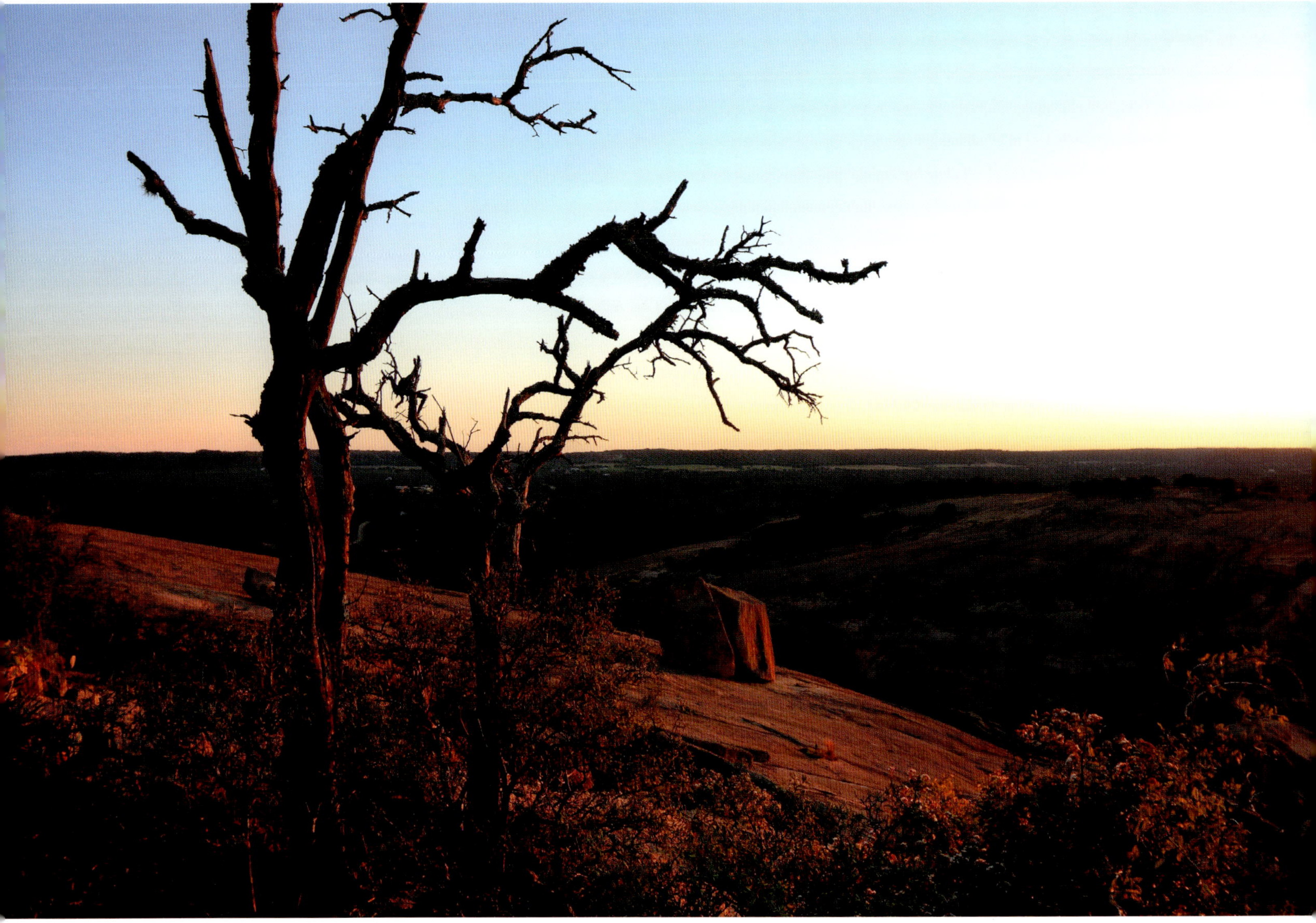

◀◀▲▶ One of the most visited parks in Texas, Enchanted Rock State Natural Area encompasses several monolithic pink granite domes that rise high above the surrounding countryside—the highest at 425 feet. The formations are more than a billion years old and are the result of ancient volcanic activity and later geologic forces that pushed the older rock to the surface.

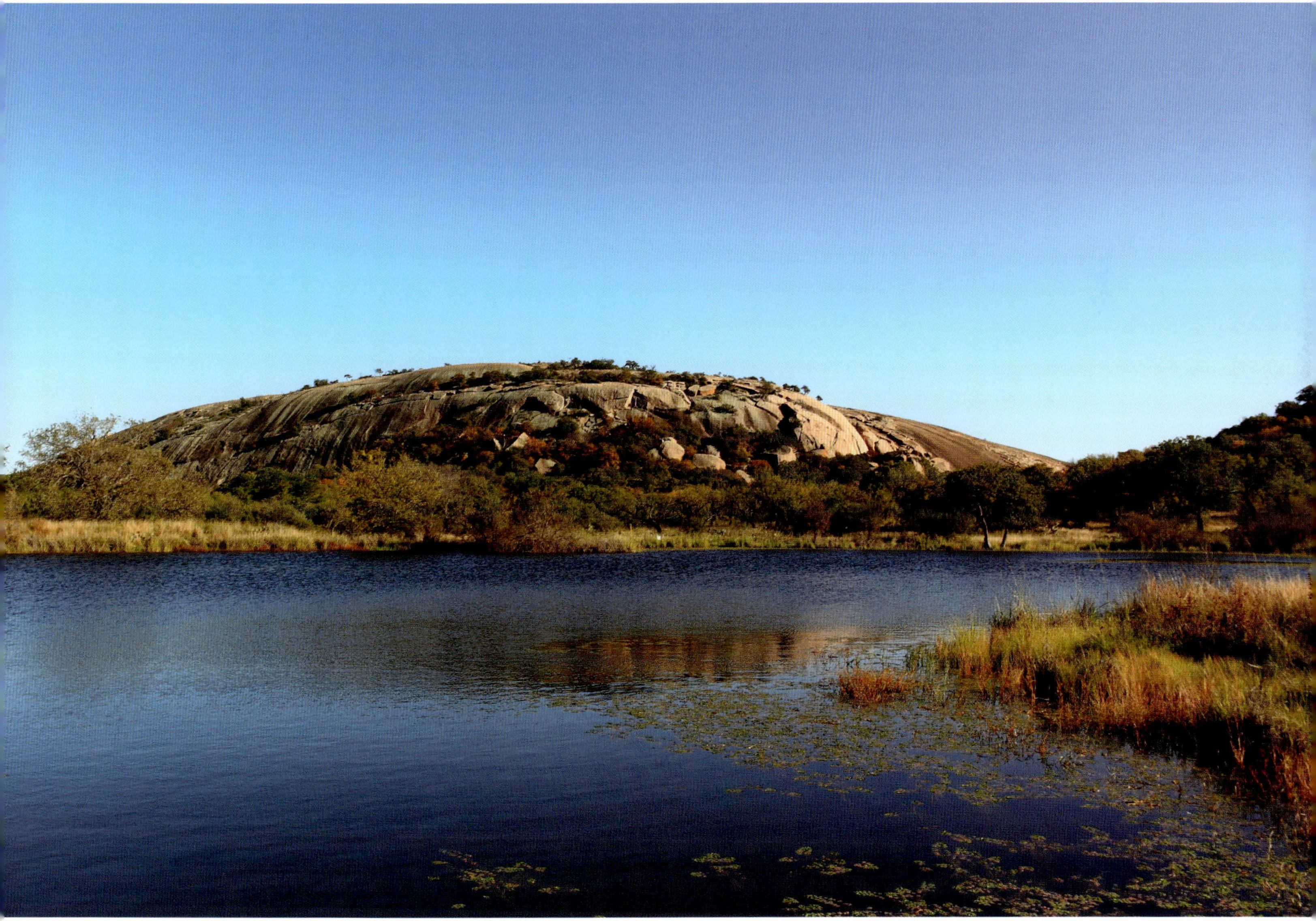

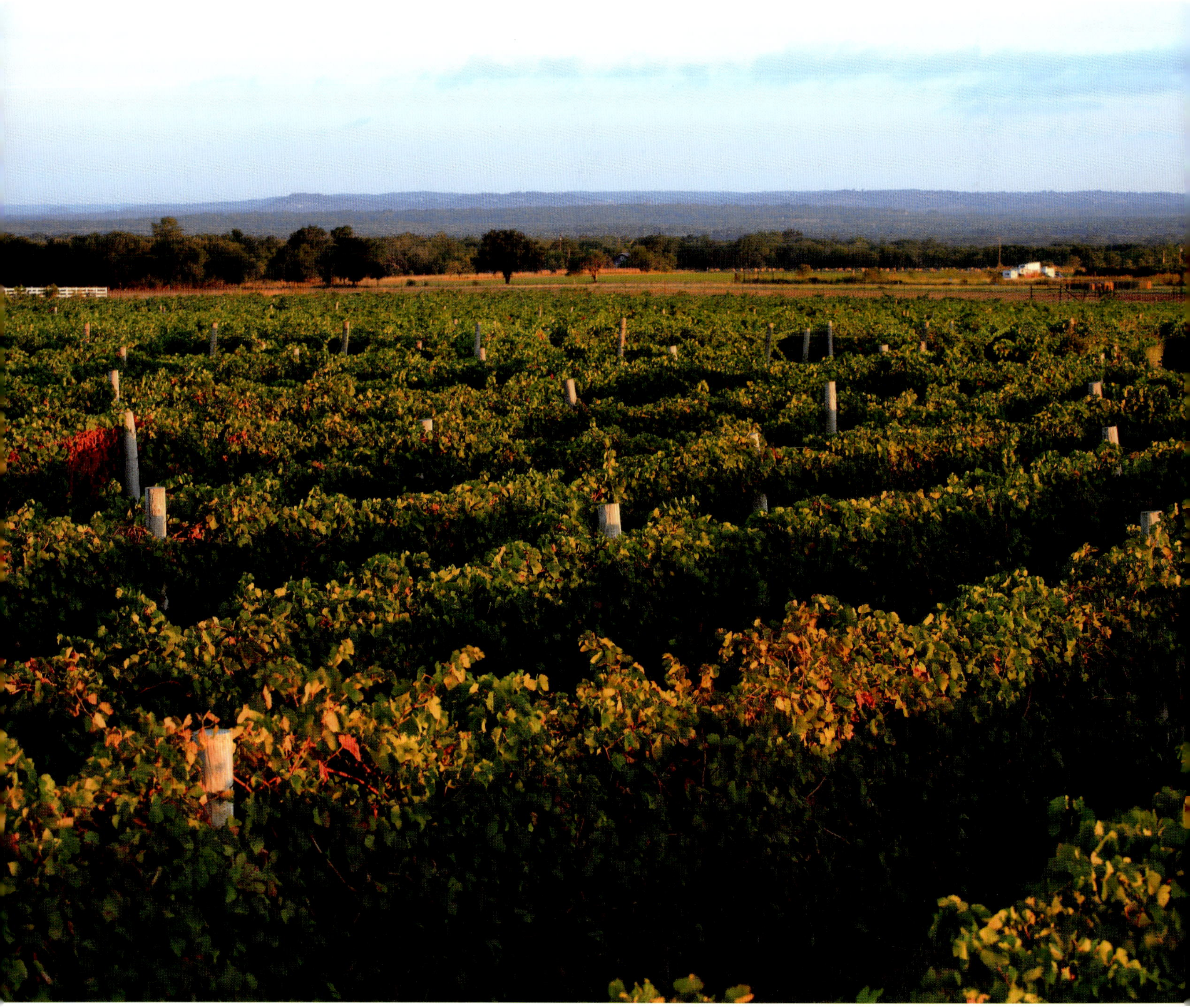

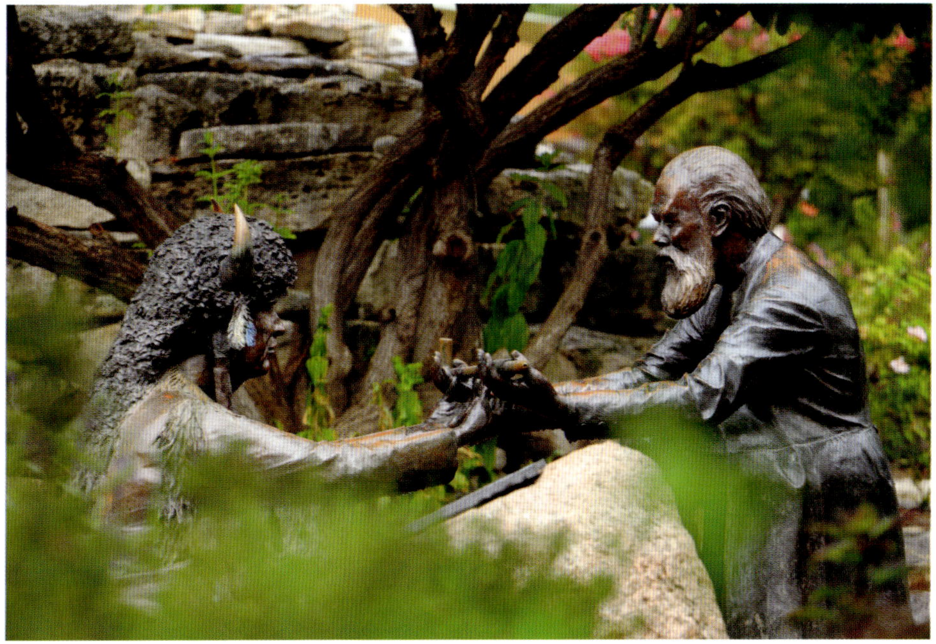

▶ A bronze sculpture in the Marktplatz called "Lasting Friendship," by Jay Hester, commemorates the 1847 agreement between John O. Meusebach (founder of Fredericksburg) and area Comanche tribes. The pact is thought to be the only unbroken peace treaty between US settlers and American Indians.

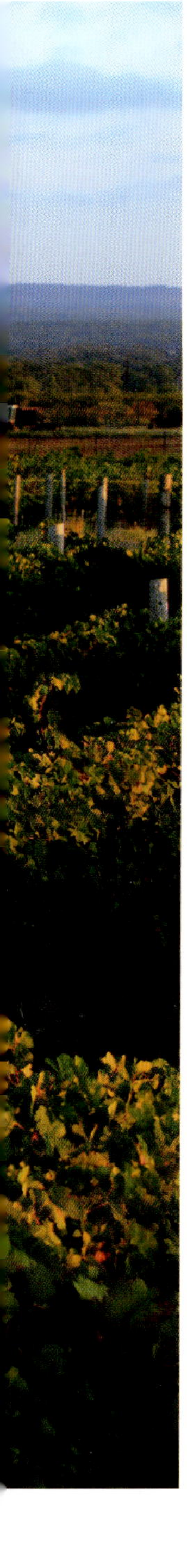

◀ The morning sun lights rows of petite sirah grapes at Becker Vineyards amid the rolling hills of Gillespie County. Pioneering vineyards like Becker have helped turn the Texas Hill Country into a world-renowned wine region with more than seventy wineries and dozens of award-winning wines.

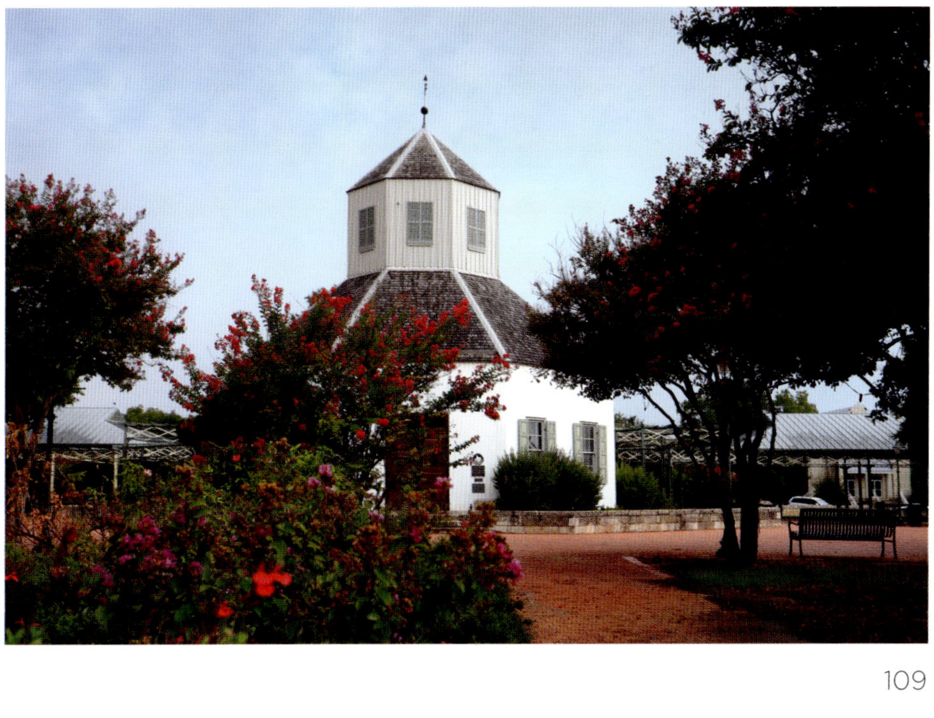

▶ Possibly the most well-known landmark in Fredericksburg, the Vereins Kirche is a 1935 replica of the original 1800s building that served as the first public building in Fredericksburg. Today it houses part of the Pioneer Museum.

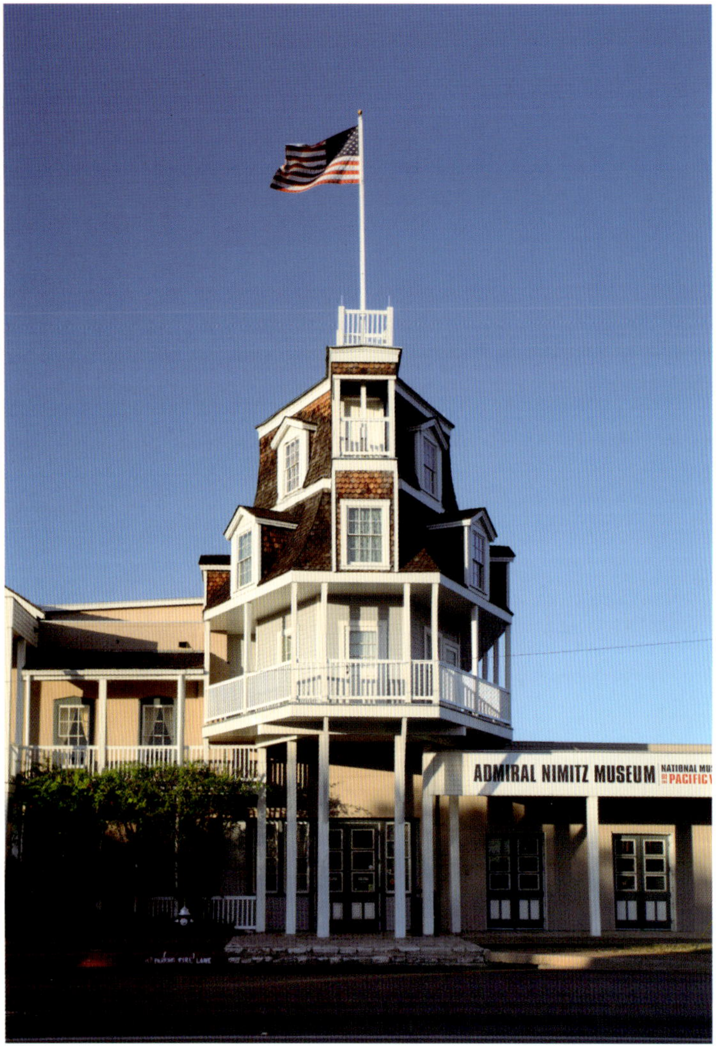

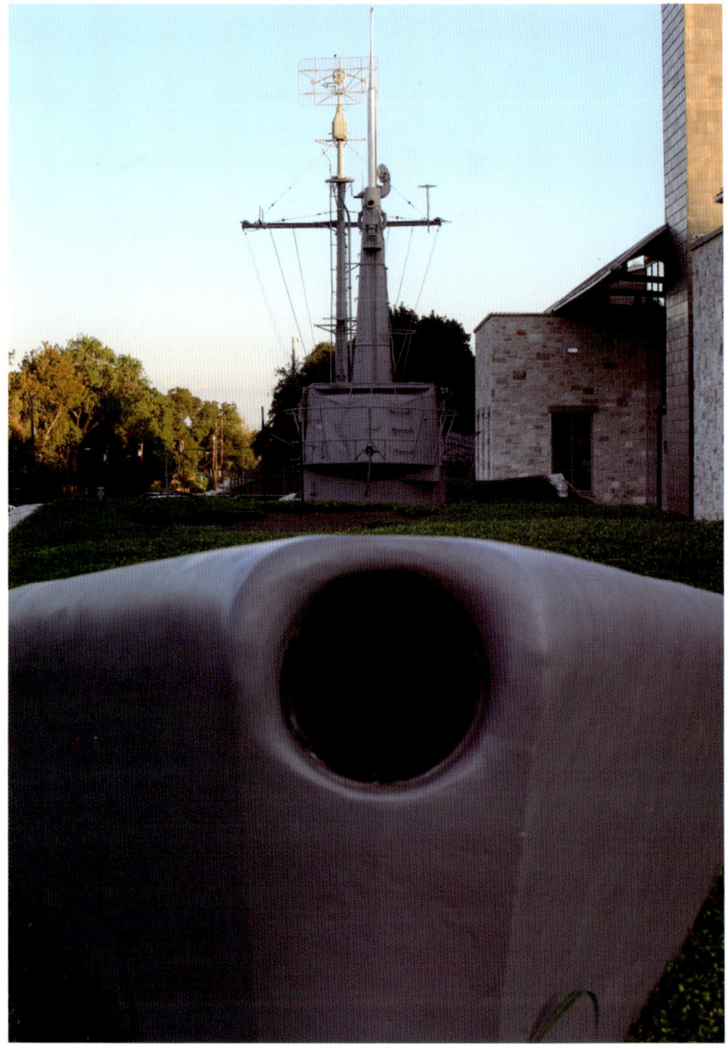

▲ Once known as the Nimitz Hotel, this grand building has been a prominent feature on Fredericksburg's main street since the mid-1800s. Originally built by pioneer and German merchant marine Charles H. Nimitz, the former hotel is now the headquarters of the National Museum of the Pacific War, memorializing Charles's grandson, Adm. Chester Nimitz.

▲ The National Museum of the Pacific War houses six acres of impressive exhibits preserving the history of the United States' WWII victory and educating the public about Pacific and Asiatic activity during WWII.

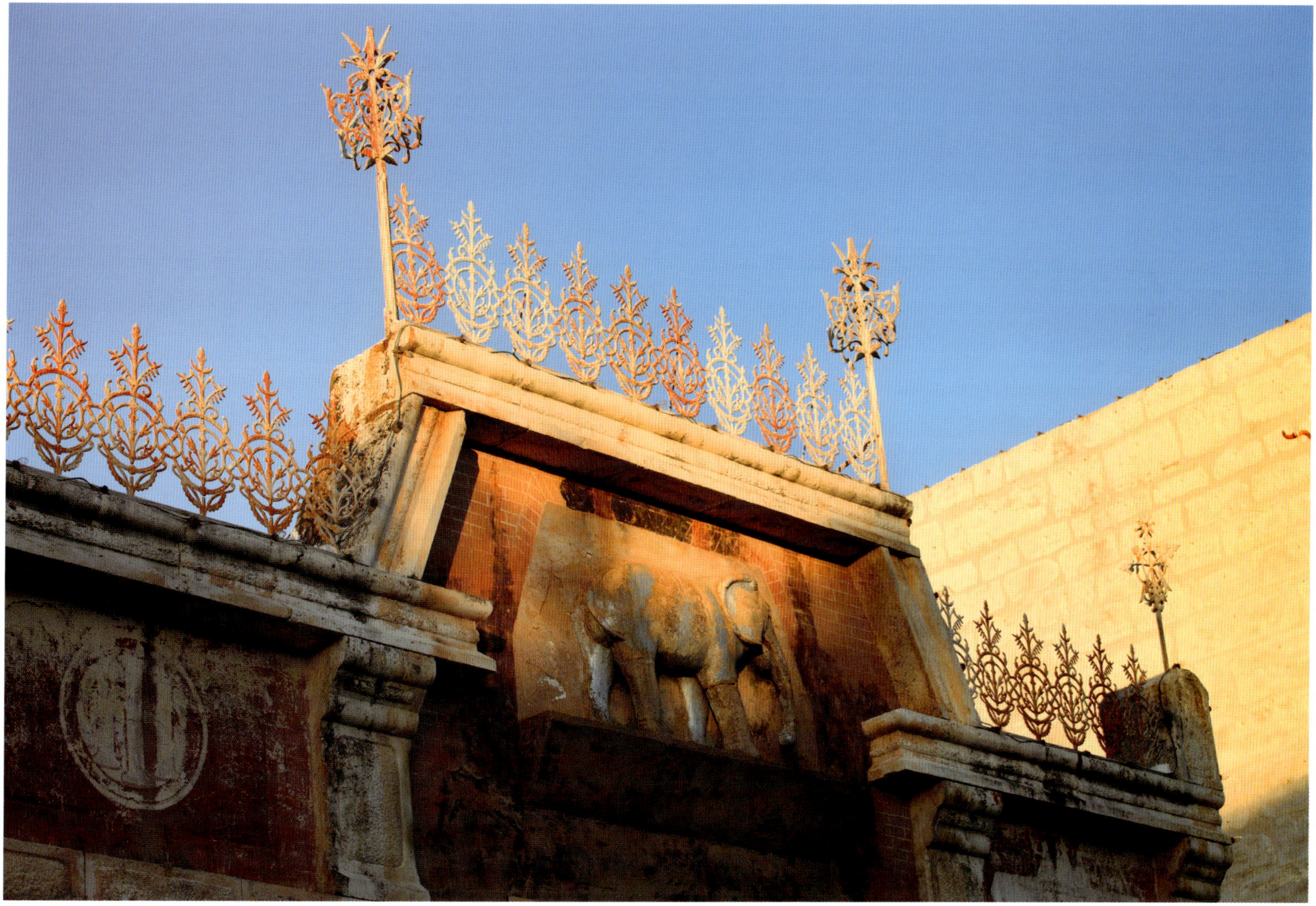

▲ The historic White Elephant Saloon building, notable for its ornate iron work and elephant relief sculpture, is a main street landmark in downtown Fredericksburg. It was built in 1888 by John W. Kleck and once housed a bar and gambling parlor.

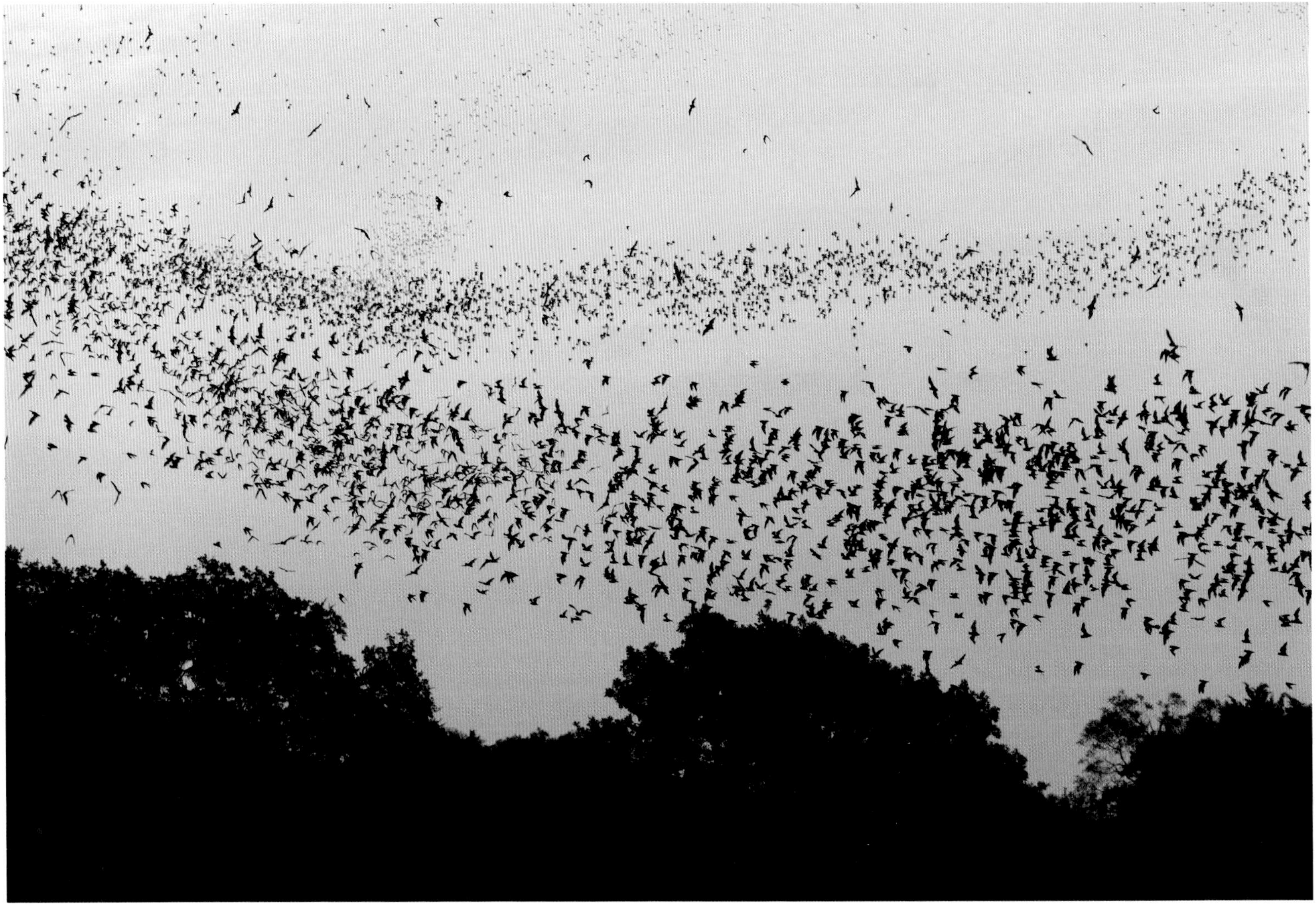

▲ Every evening from May through October millions of bats emerge from an abandoned railroad tunnel near Fredericksburg. The 920-foot tunnel was once part of the Fredericksburg and Northern Railway and operated until 1942. Today it is part of Texas' smallest state park and home to more than three million Mexican free-tailed bats and 3,000 cave myotis bats.

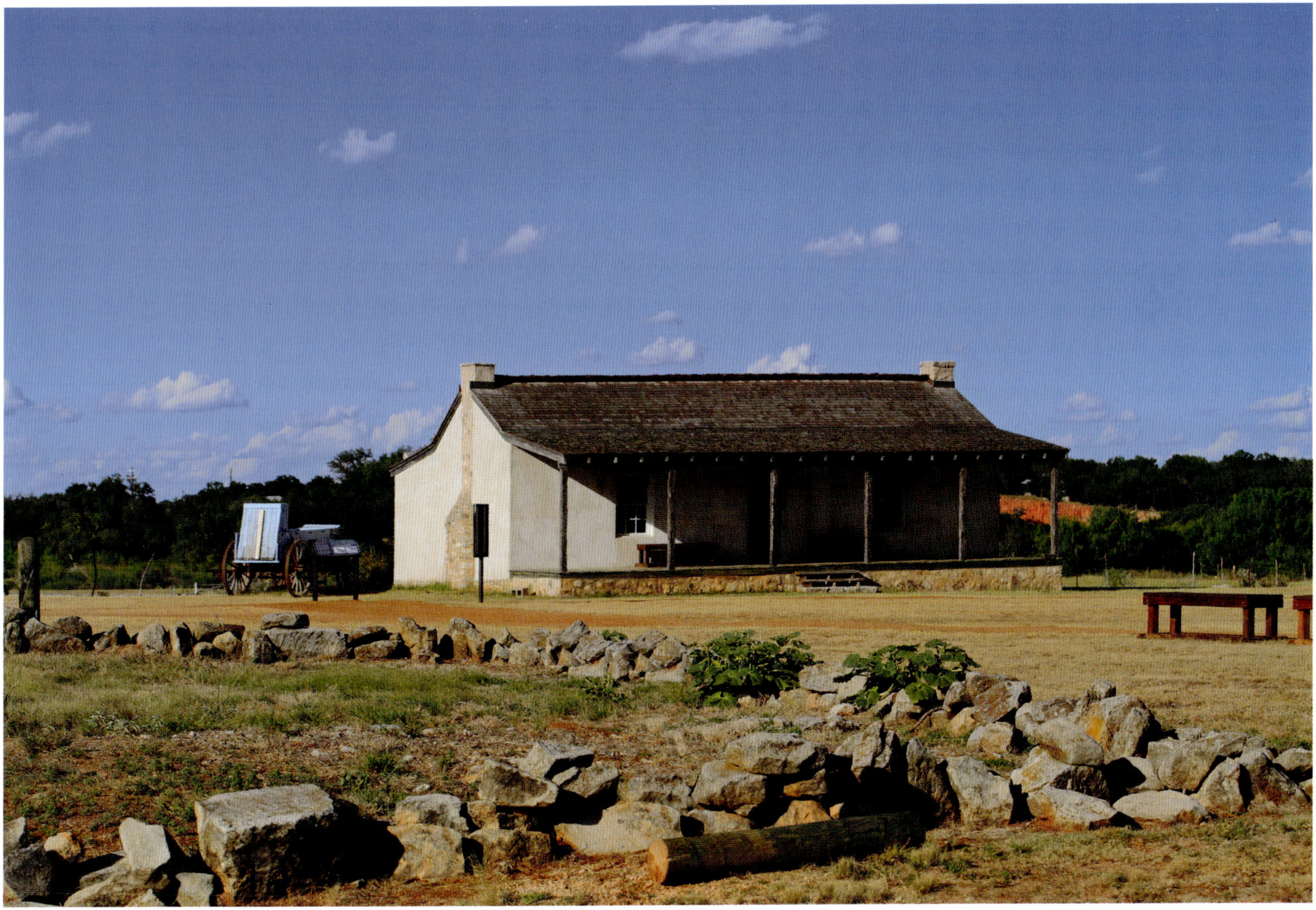

▲ Fort Martin Scott was established as the first US Army post protecting travelers and settlers on Texas' western frontier. Originally established as Camp Houston in December 1848, the name was changed to Fort Martin Scott the following year.

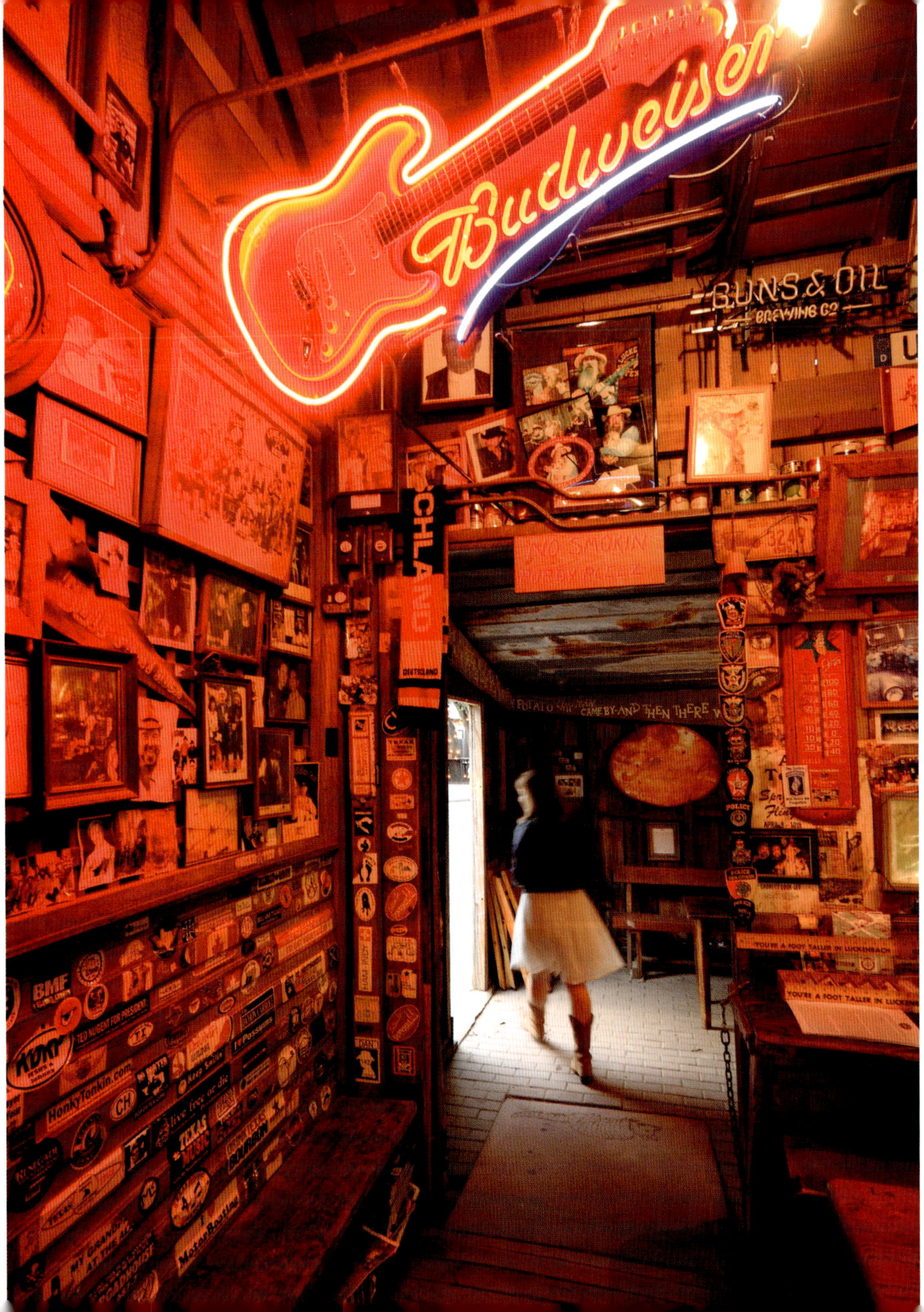
Budweiser
YOU'RE A FOOT TALLER IN LUCKENBACH

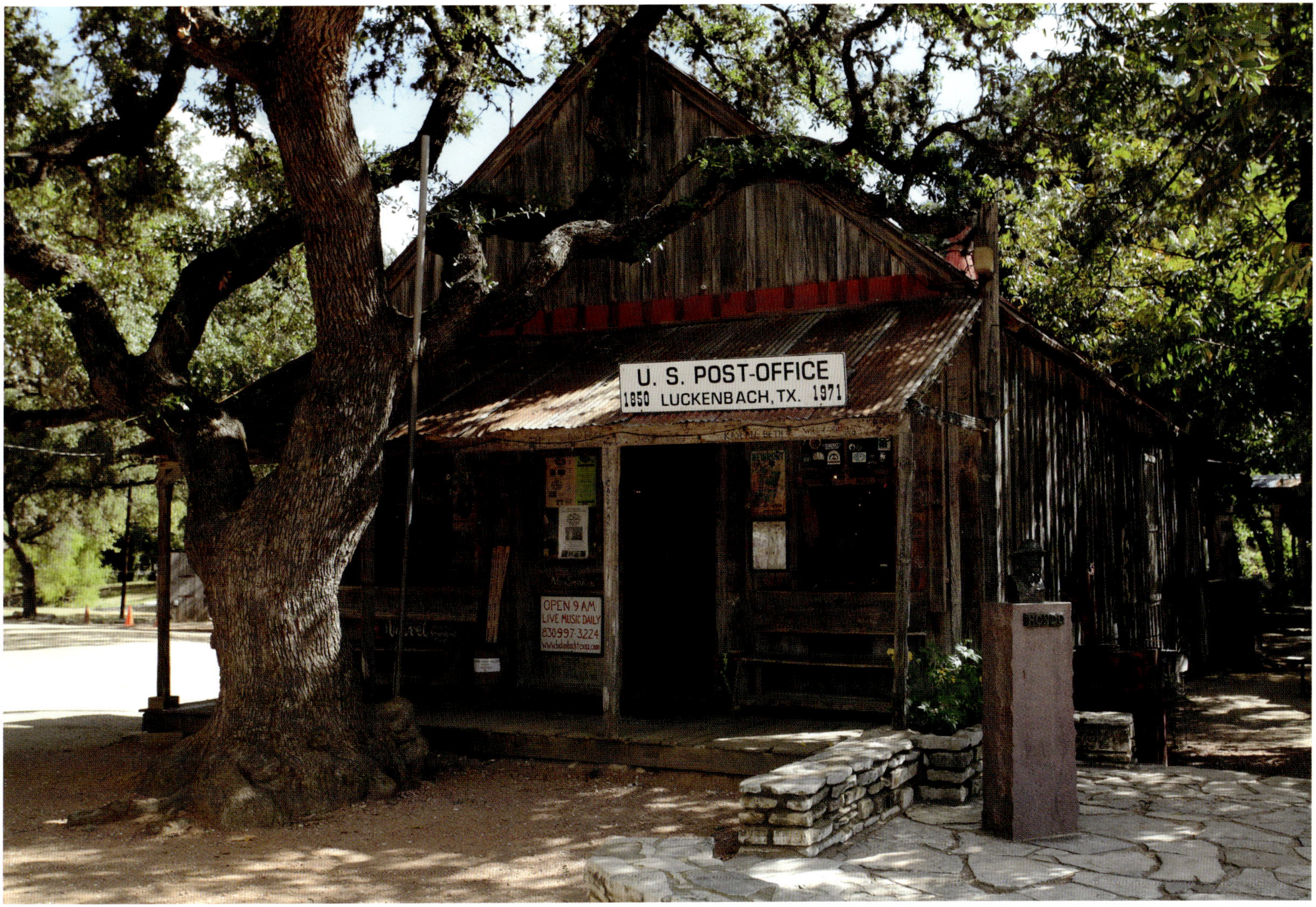

◀▲ Luckenbach was founded along Grape Creek in the mid-1800s. The town became famous 124 years later after Jerry Jeff Walker recorded a hit album in the Luckenbach dance hall, and in 1977, the Waylon Jennings song "Luckenbach, Texas" became a hit single. With its outdoor stage, saloon, and rustic dance hall, Luckenbach has become a tourist hotspot known for live music and events.

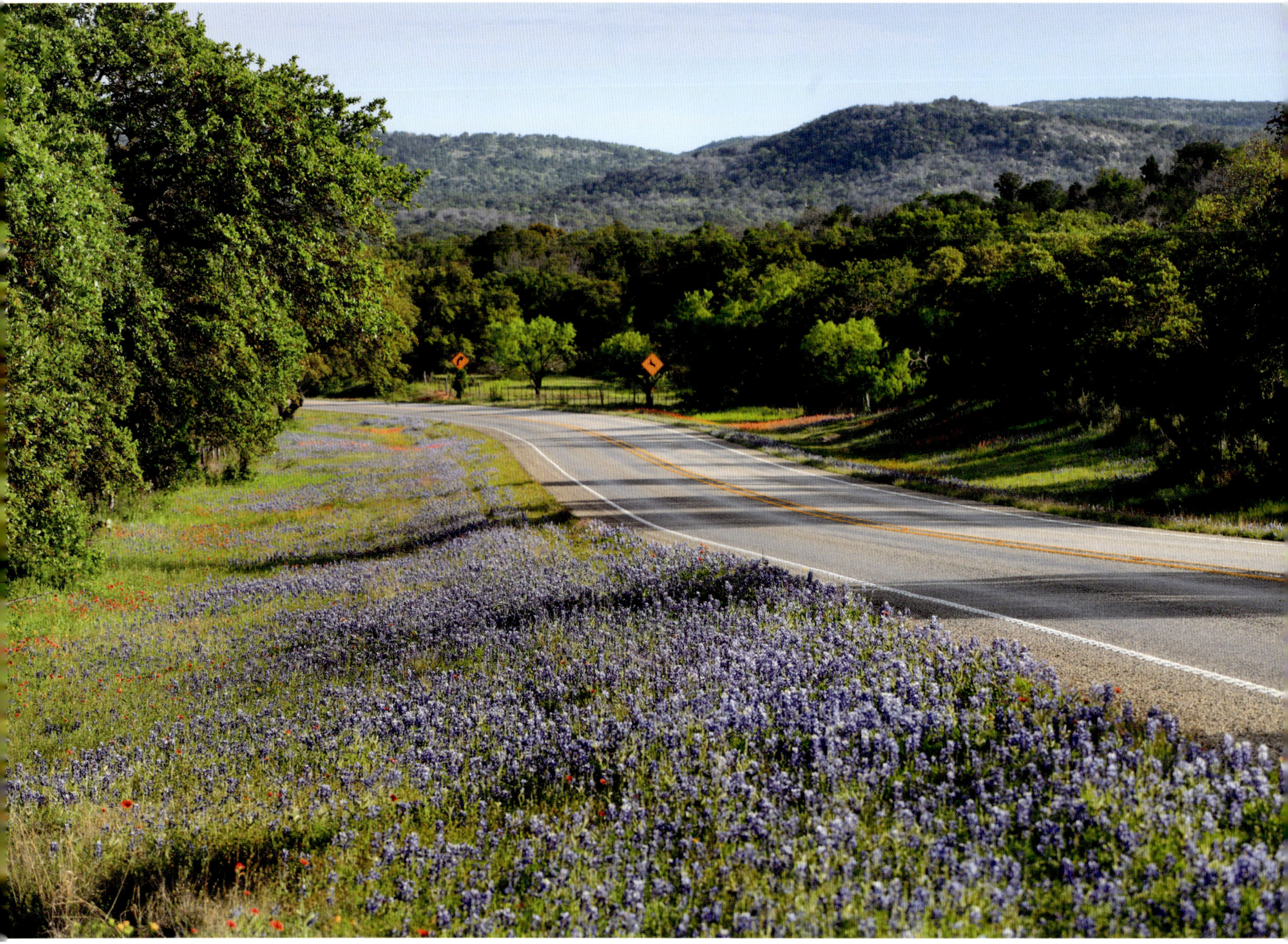

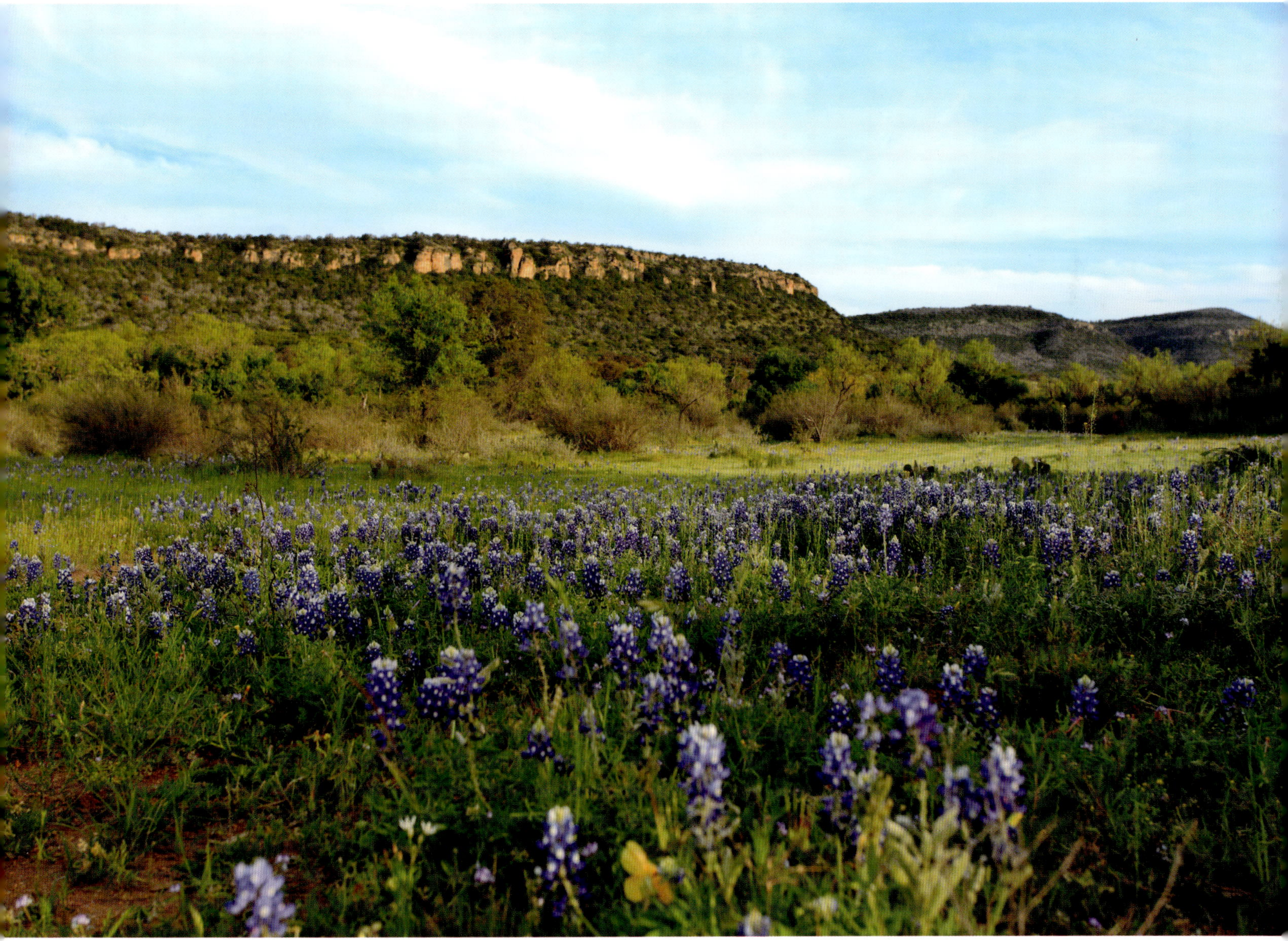

◀▲ Against an awe-inspiring backdrop of scenic vistas and rugged hills, the highways and byways of Gillespie County are known for their showy displays of spring wildflowers, including bluebonnets and Indian paintbrush.

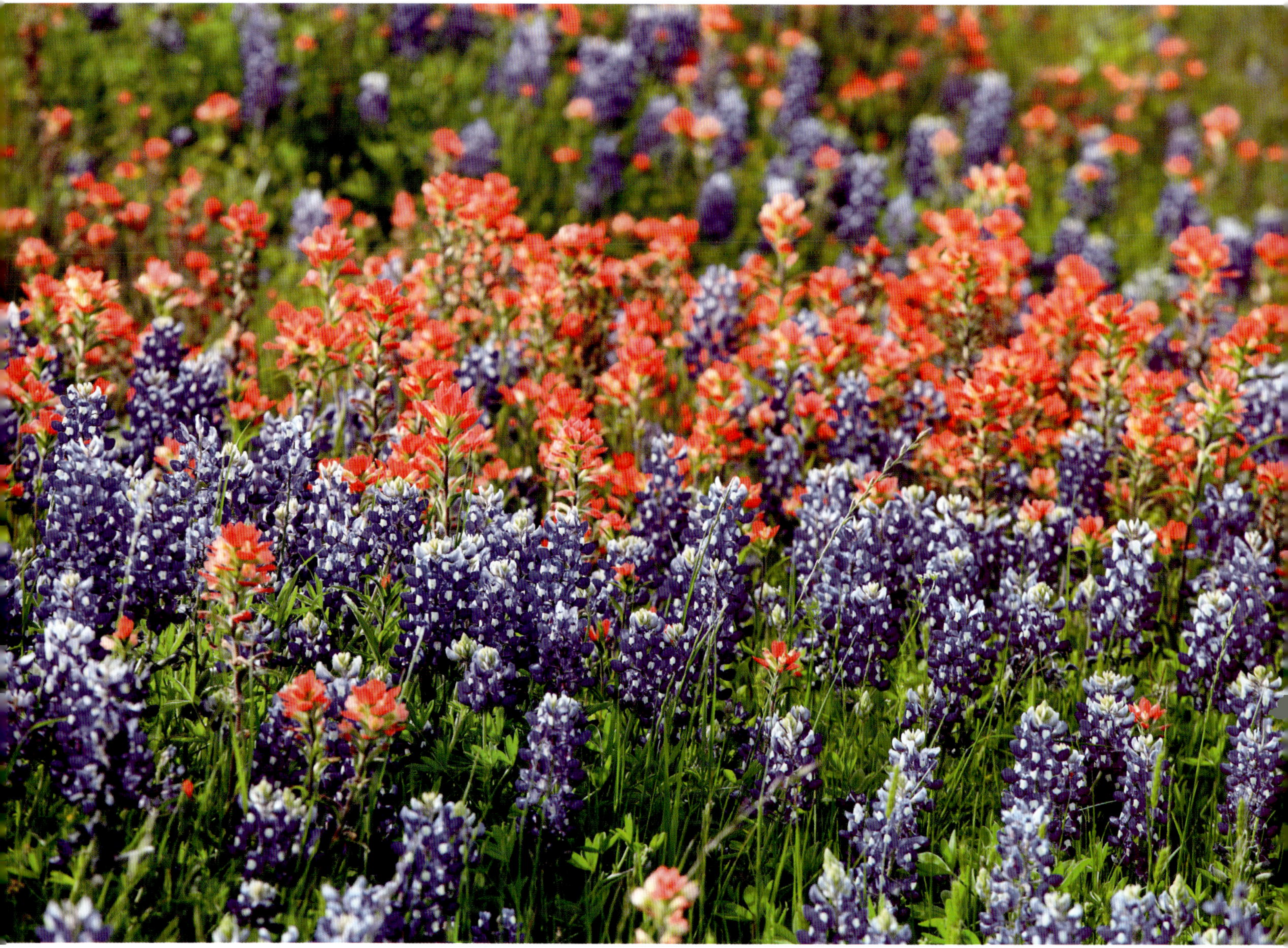

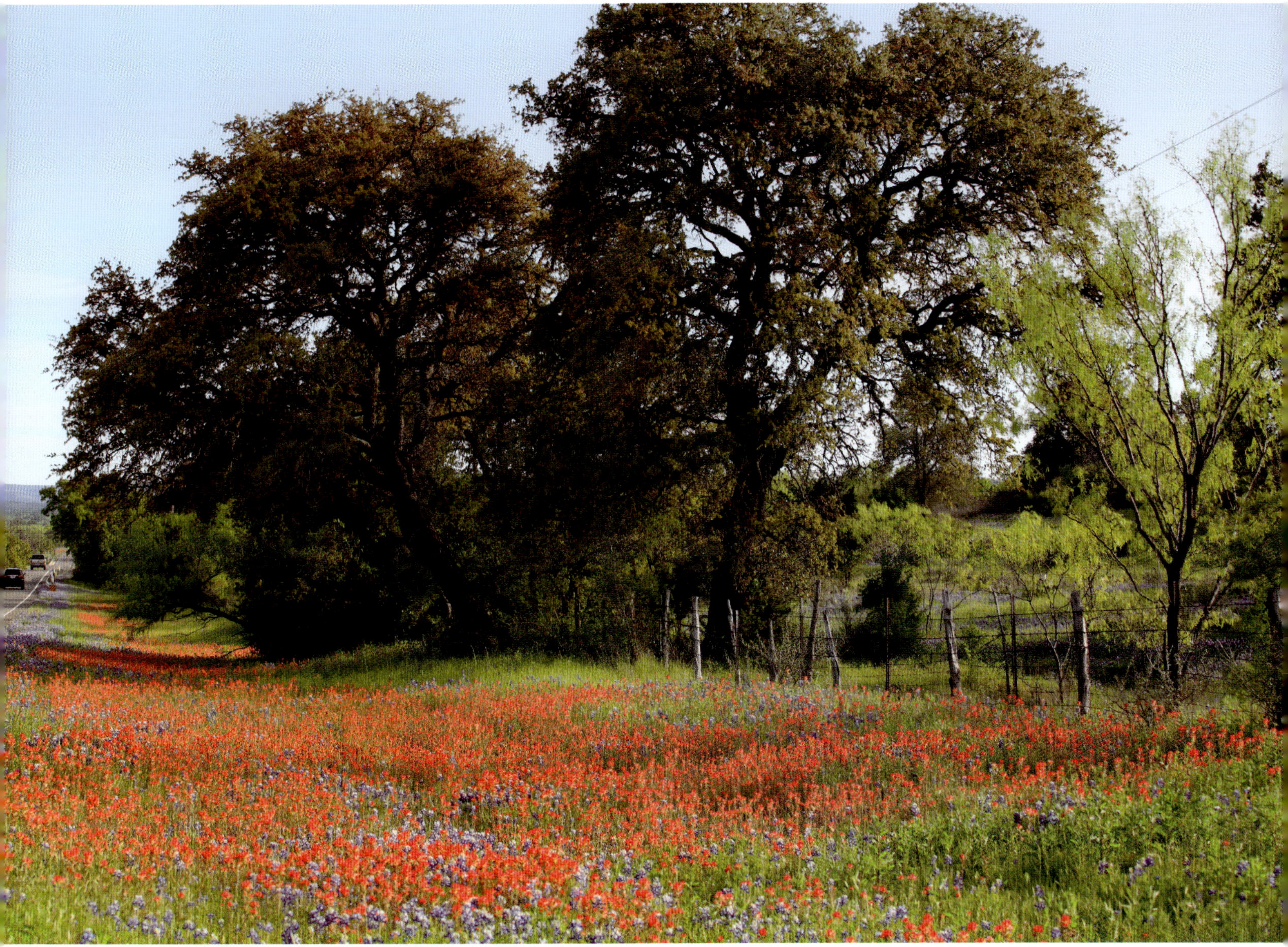

◀▲ Bluebonnets and Indian paintbrush blanket the ground just north of Fredericksburg, Texas.

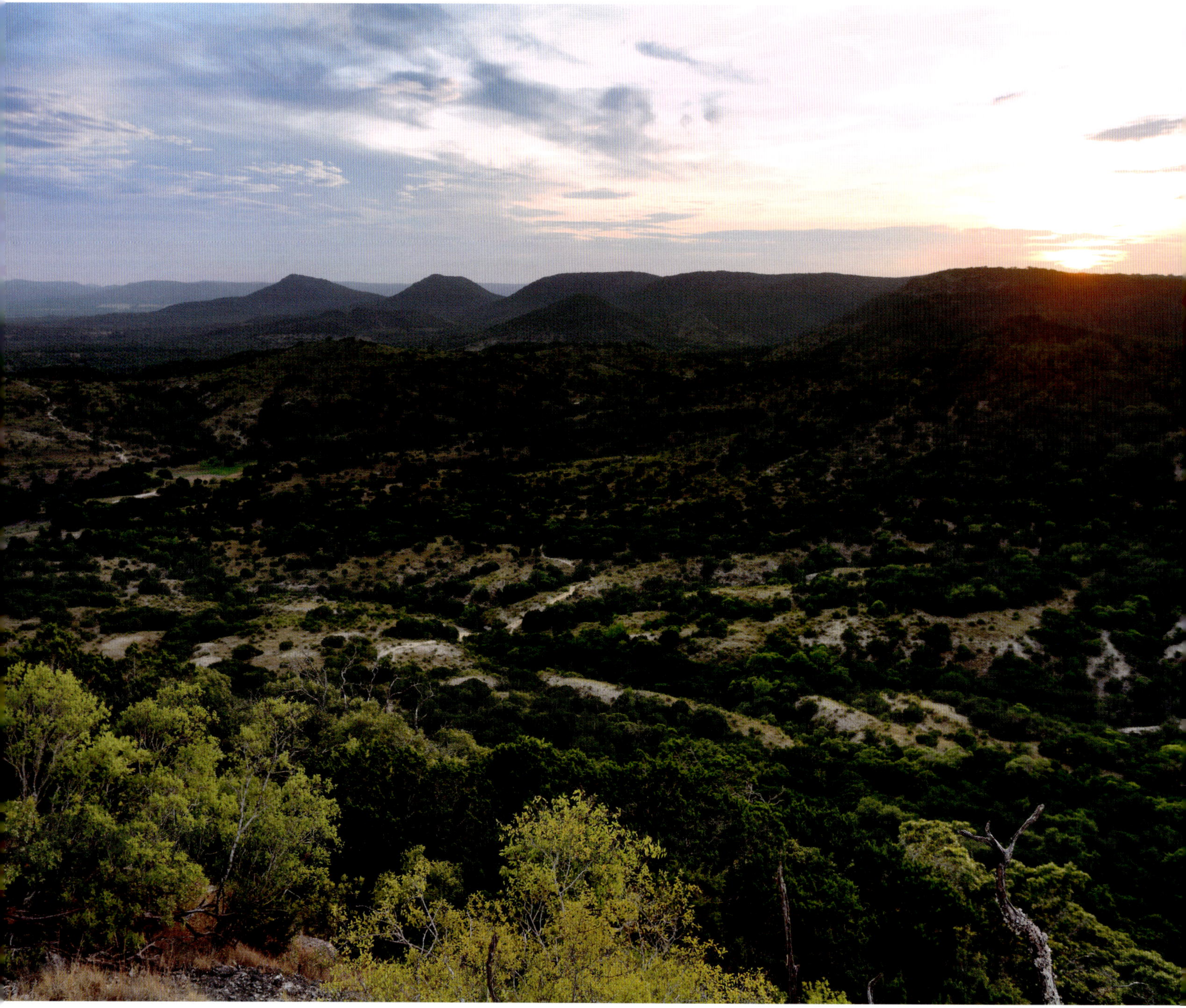

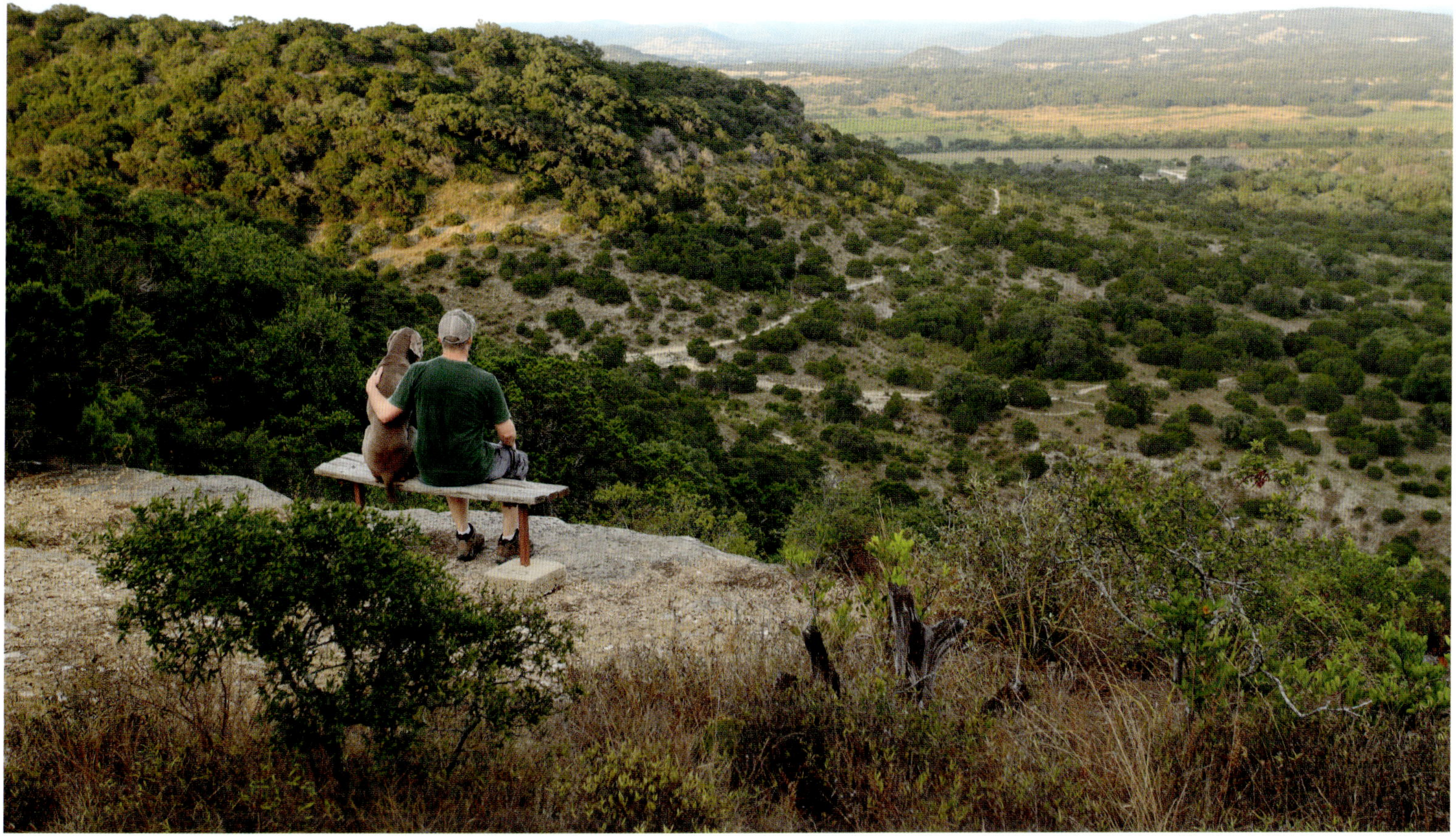

◀ The setting sun dips behind the rugged terrain of Hill Country State Natural Area as seen from the summit of West Peak, the park's highest point at over 2,000 feet.

▲ Mostly undeveloped, Hill Country State Natural Area sprawls across nearly 5,400 acres just forty-five miles northwest of San Antonio. Operating as the Merrick Bar-O Ranch until the early 1970s, the land was donated to the state of Texas under the provision that it "be kept far removed and untouched by modern civilization, where everything is preserved intact, yet put to a useful purpose."

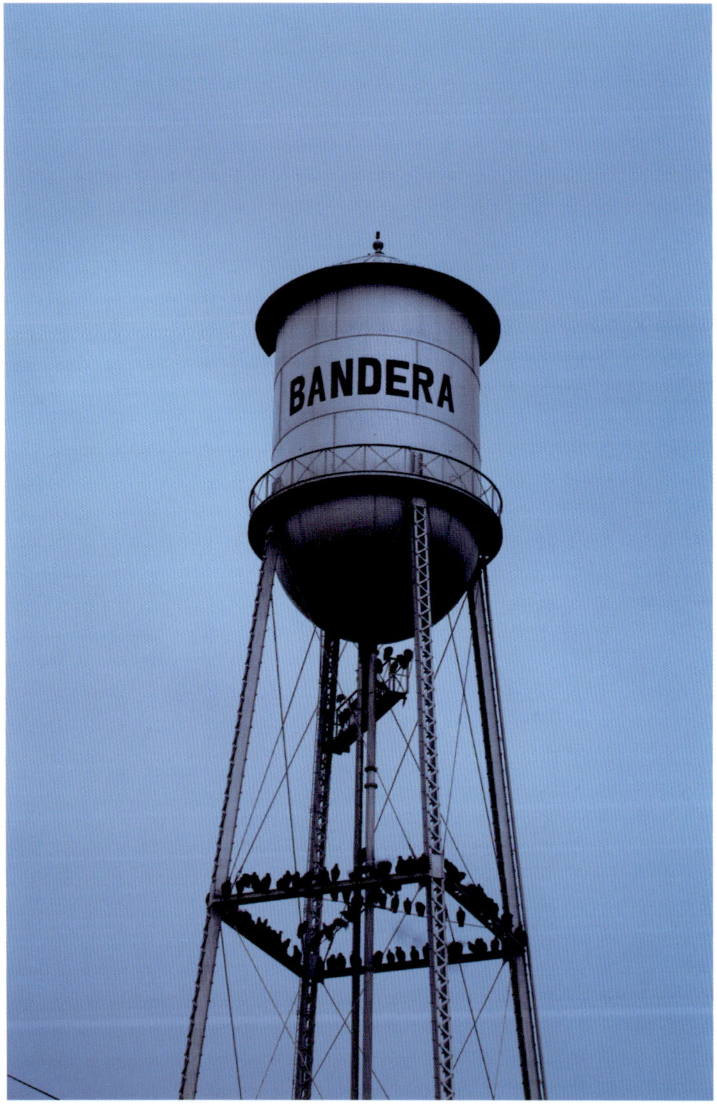

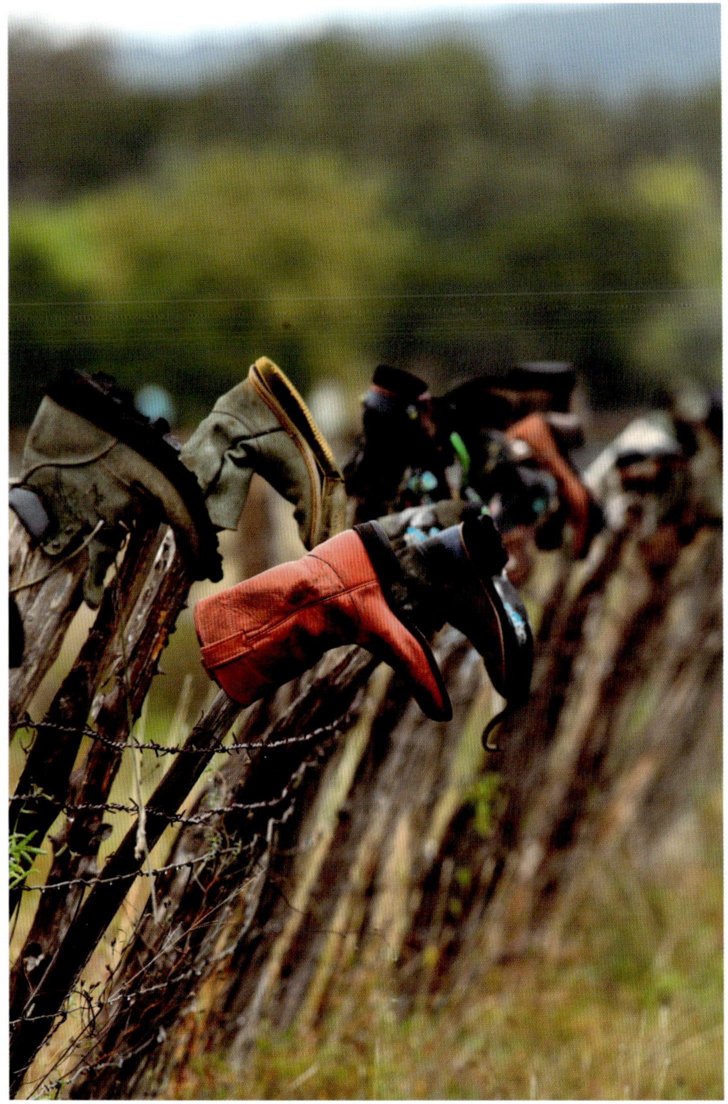

▲ Built in 1947, Bandera's 50,000 gallon "tin-man" style water tower gracefully stands over the town center as black vultures congregate on the tower's struts at dusk.

▲ On Highway 39, near Hunt, this cedar post fence is adorned with hundreds of boots of all sizes and styles. The boot fence was started in the 1970s by a Kerr County family.

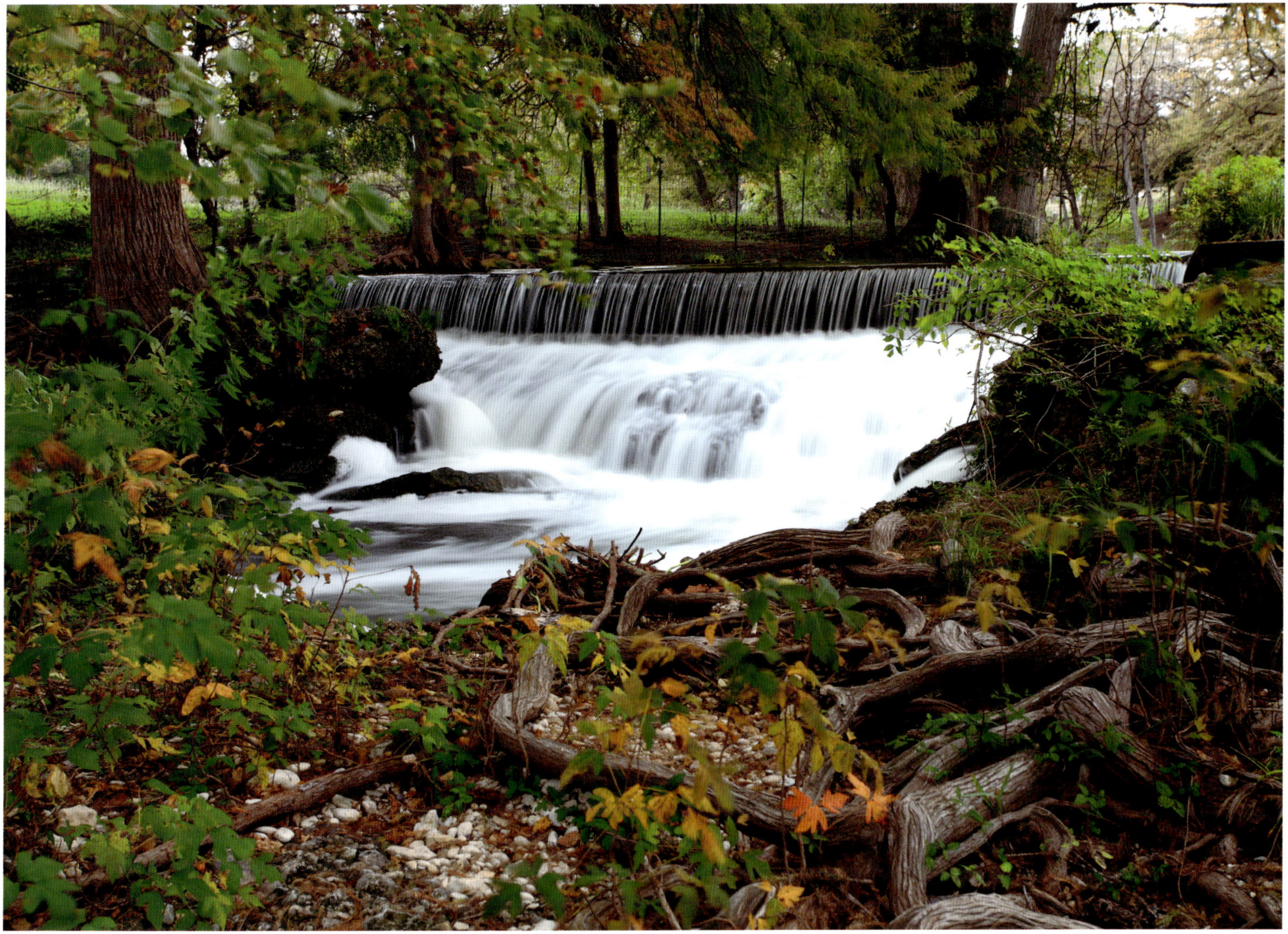

▲ Near the former site of an 1800s sawmill, the Schumacher family built a series of dams in the 1920s for flood control and a stream crossing. Today the cascading series of dams creates a scenic backdrop and a popular swimming hole on the Guadalupe River.

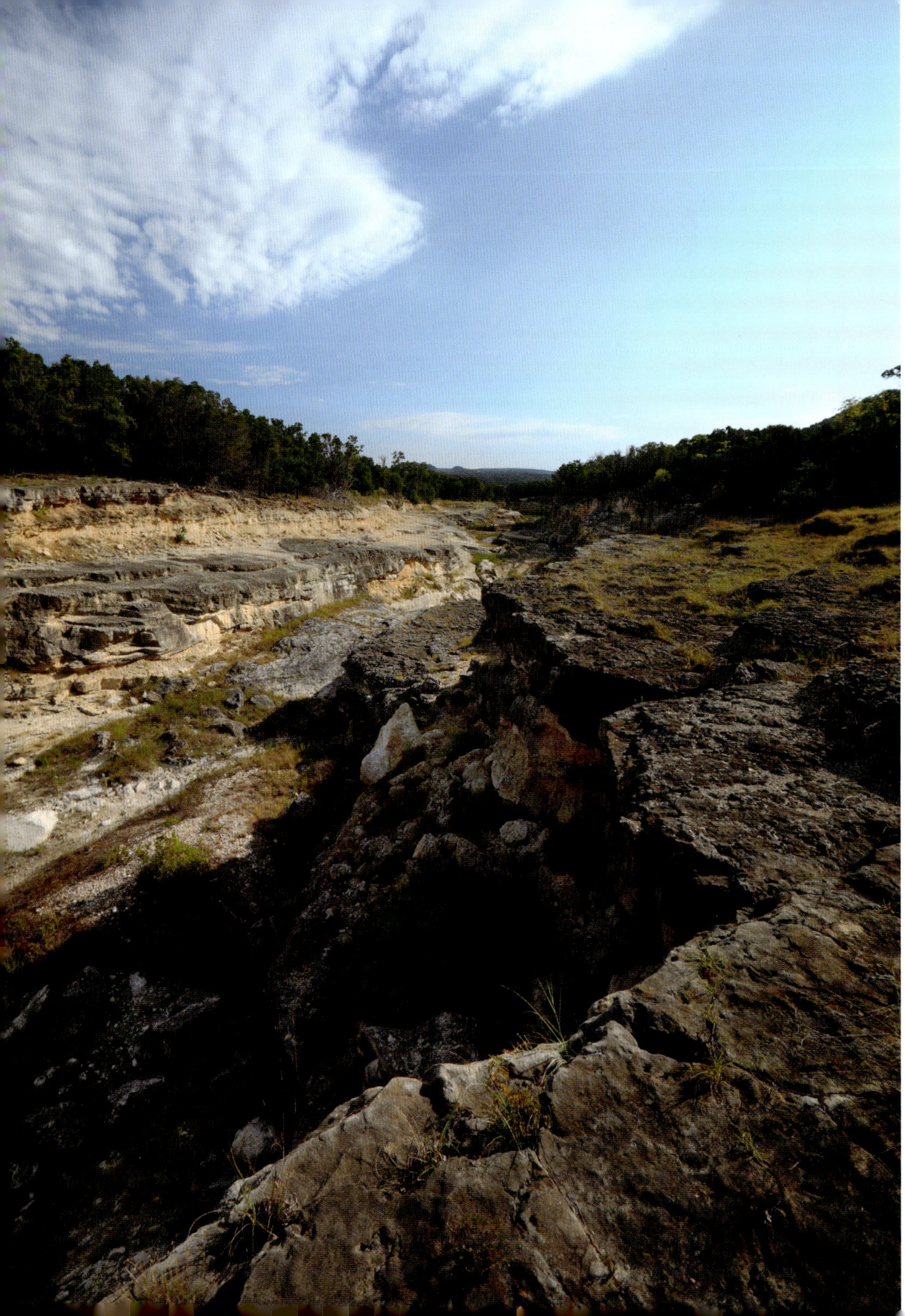

◀ In 2002, severe flooding sent one and a half times the amount of water stored in Canyon Lake over the spillway. This dramatic flood carved a gorge into the landscape southeast of the lake, revealing a treasure trove of geological formations, dinosaur tracks, and layers of marine fossil deposits. Filled with beautiful lagoons and waterfalls, Canyon Lake Gorge is open to the public by tour.

▶ New Braunfels was established in 1845 by a group of German noblemen who had formed an immigration company called Adelsverein. Prince Carl of Solms-Braunfels helped settle the first wave of colonists and the community soon prospered. Today those German roots and culture are still strong in New Braunfels.

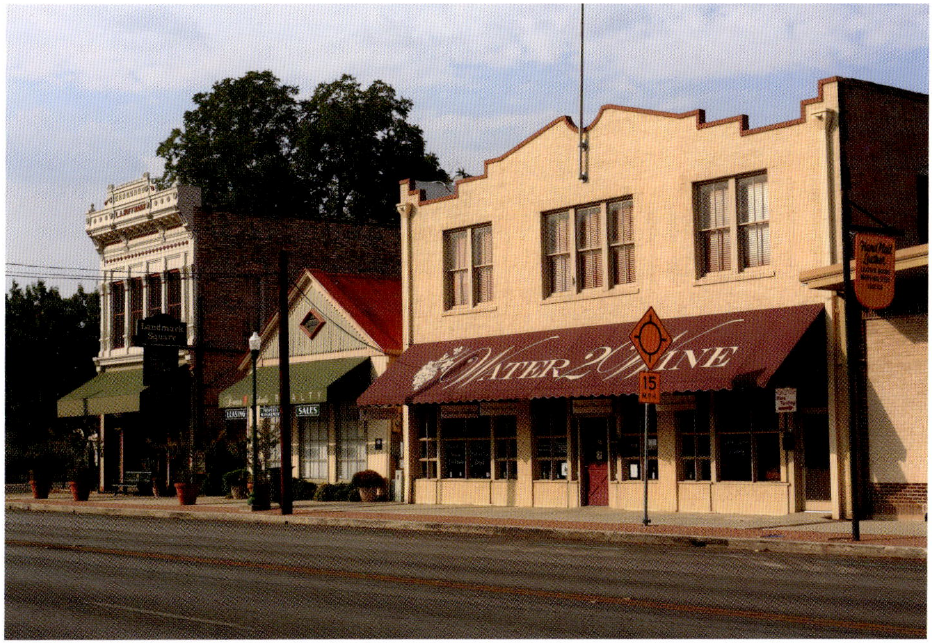

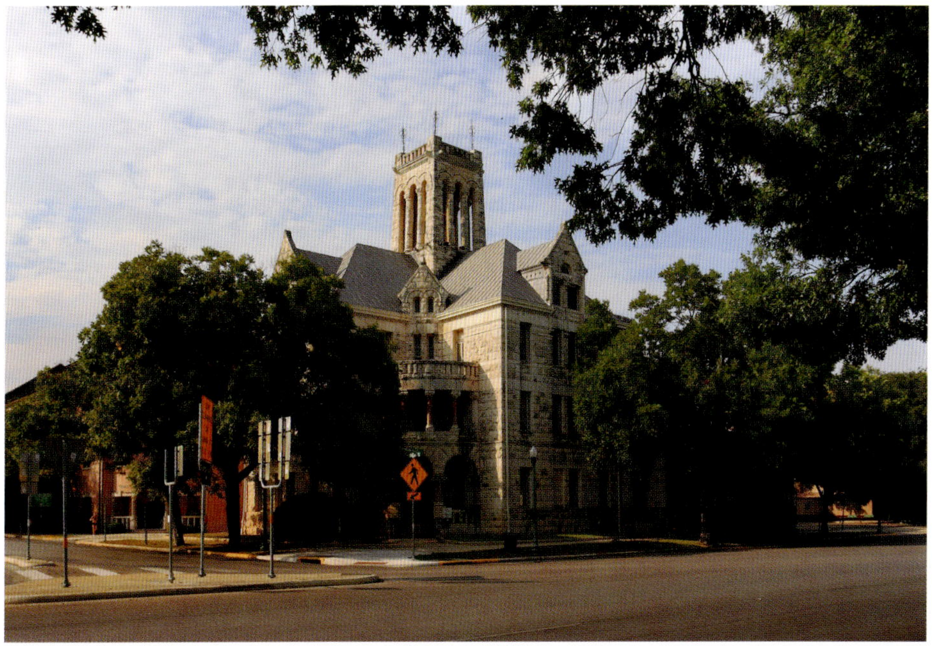

▶ Nationally renowned architect James Riely Gordon rose to prominence designing municipal buildings like the Comal County Courthouse in New Braunfels—a three-and-a-half story Romanesque Revival structure comprised of local limestone, red granite steps and columns, hipped metal roofs, and Gordon's trademark corner entrances.

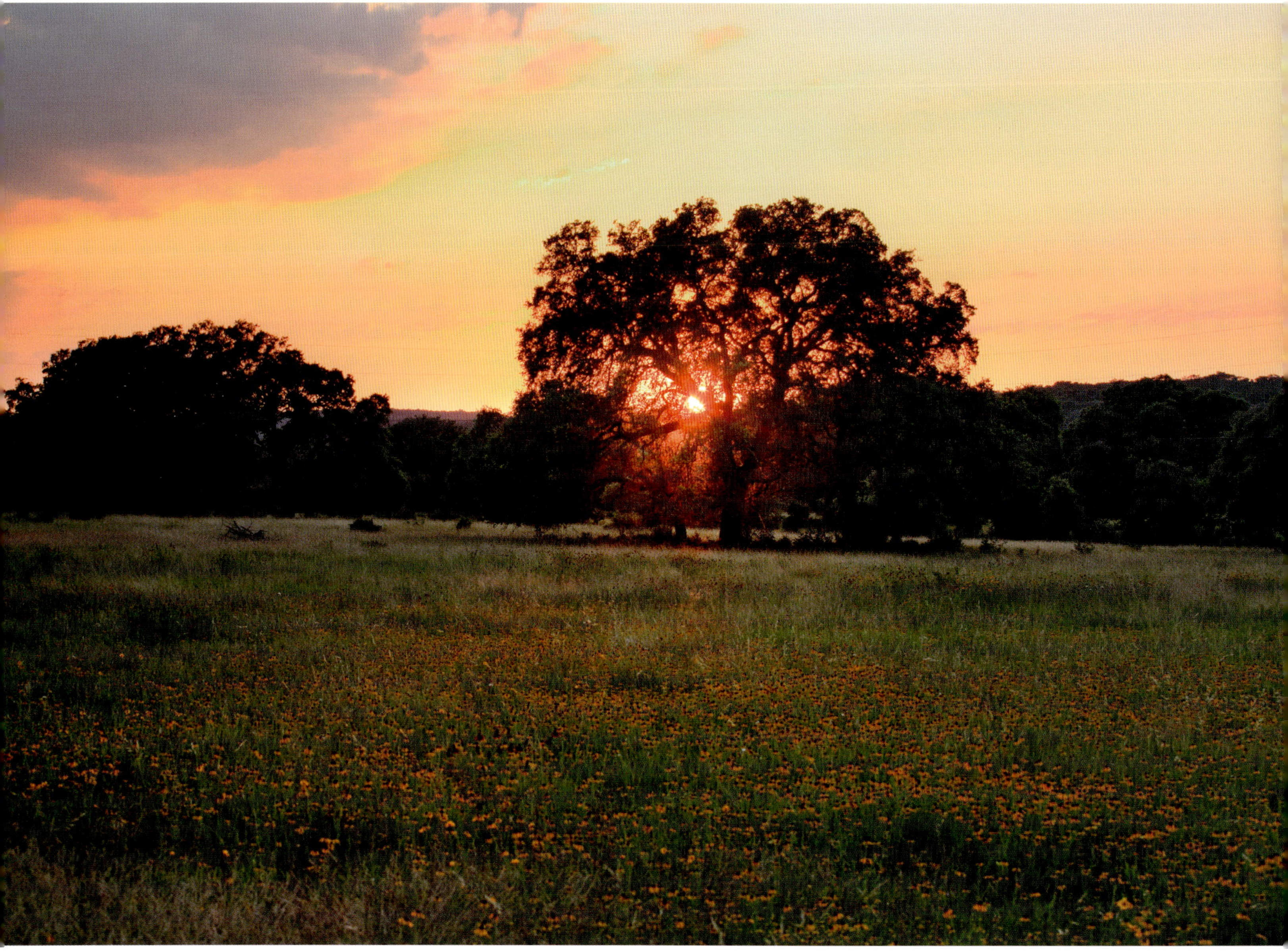

▲ The setting sun shimmers through live oaks over a field of Mexican Hat flowers in Comal County.

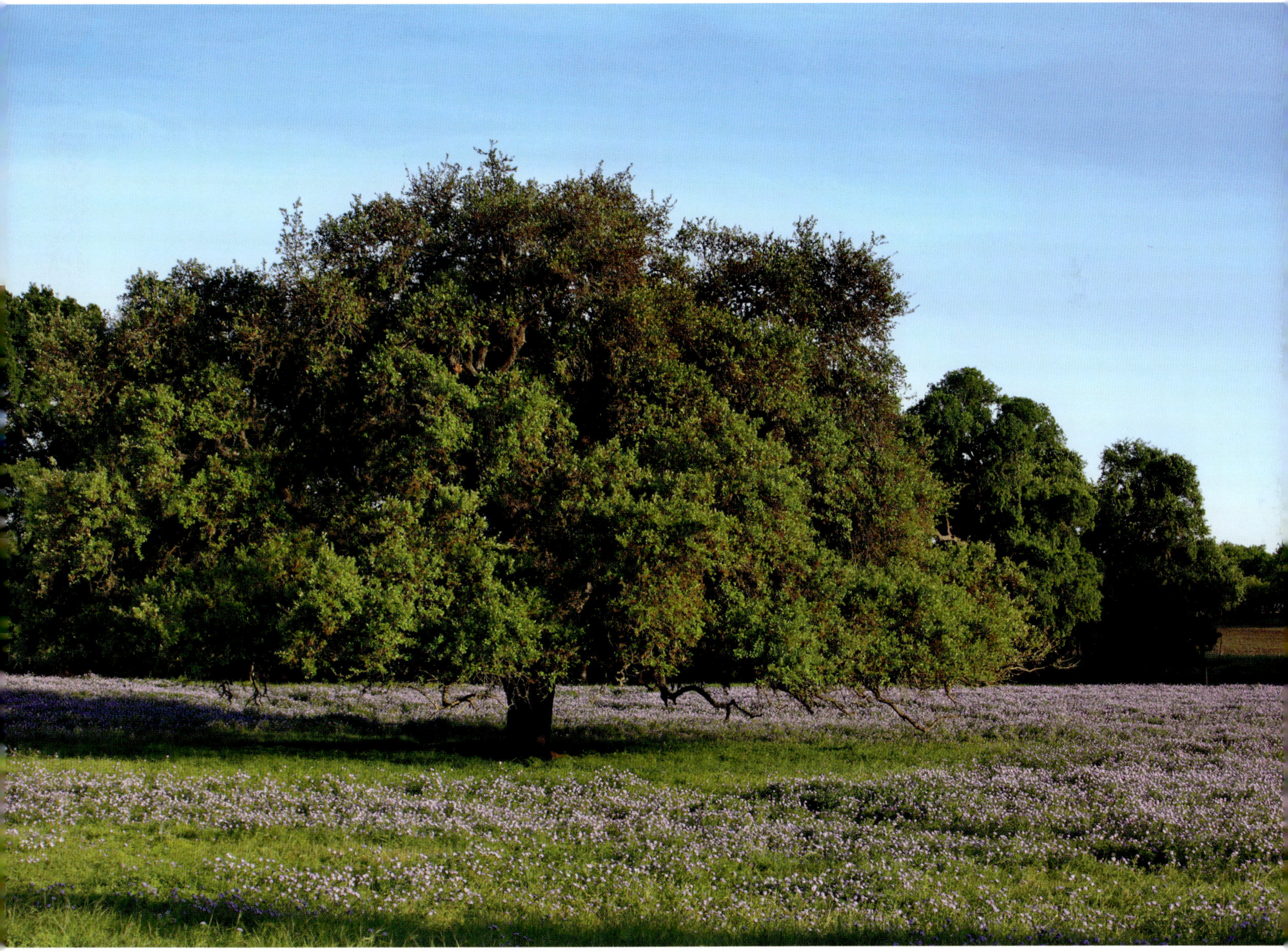

▲ A patchwork of flowering purple prairie verbena stretches out across a live oak savanna just west of New Braunfels.

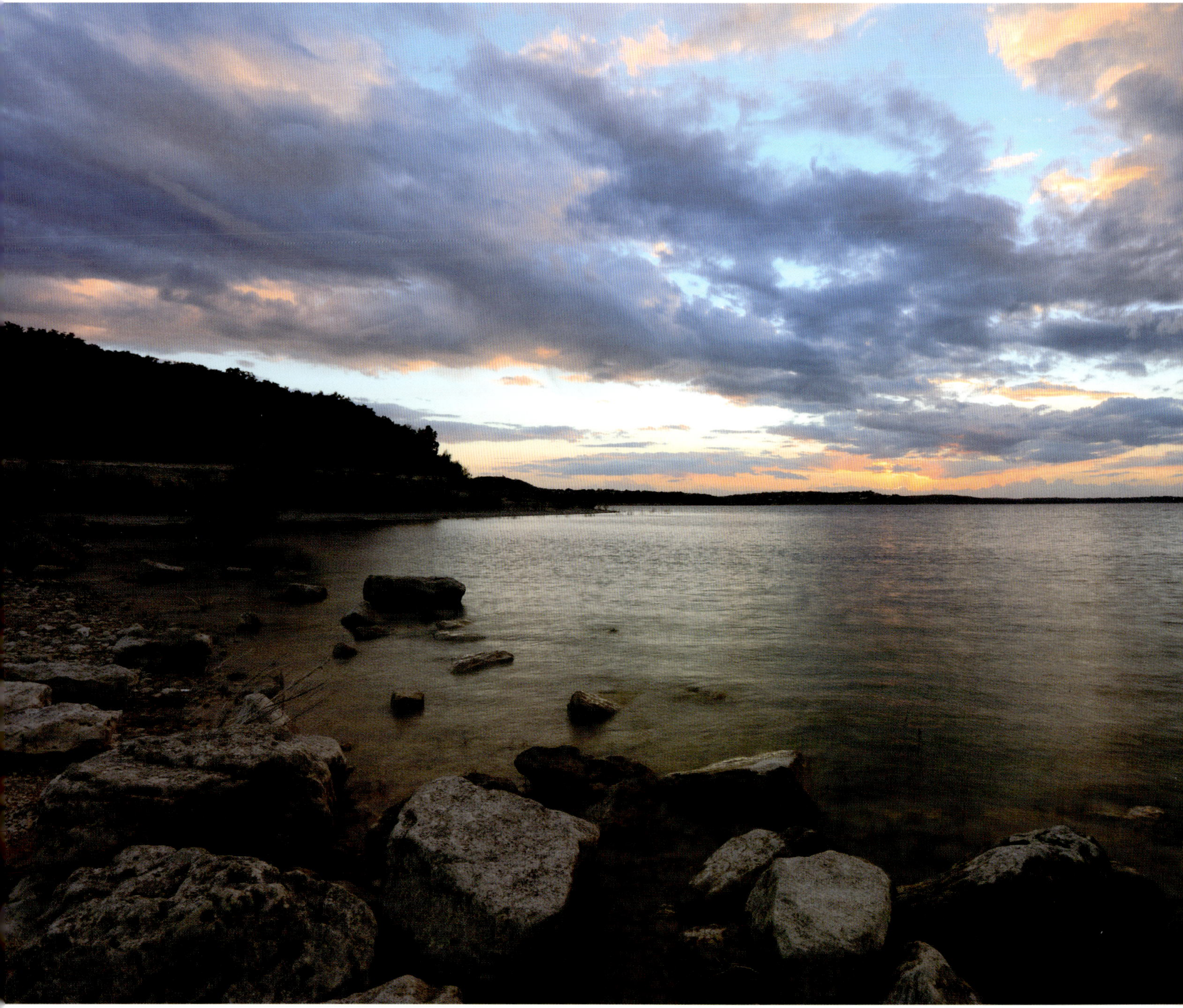

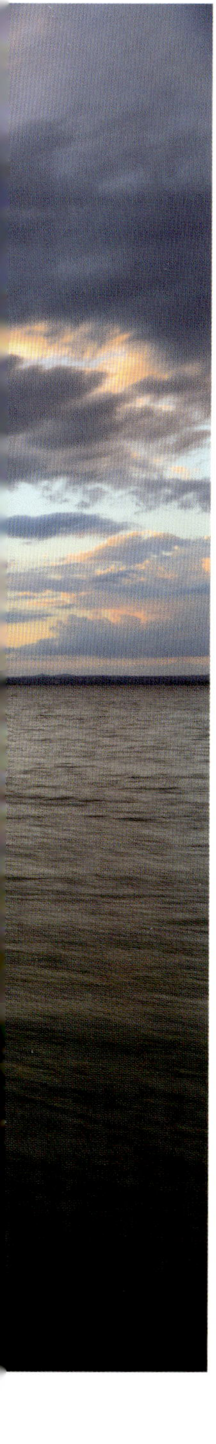

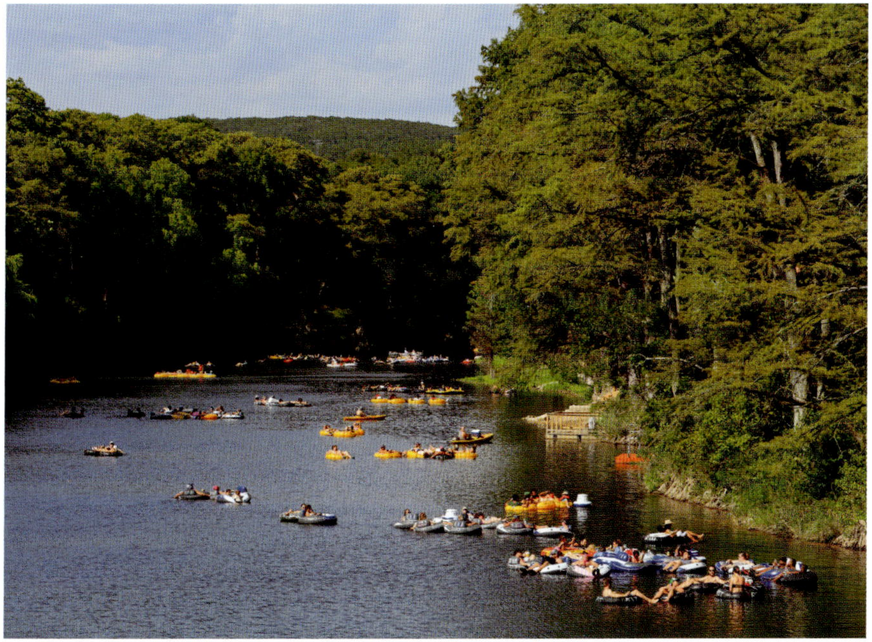

◀ Each summer throngs of people flock to the Texas Hill Country to go "tubing" on the region's scenic waterways. Cool, spring-fed rivers like the Comal, Frio, and Guadalupe become water-borne highways teeming with families and friends floating on inner tubes.

◀◀ Canyon Lake, a reservoir on the Guadalupe River, was built between 1958 and 1964. The lake's eighty miles of scenic shoreline and proximity to San Antonio and New Braunfels make it one of Texas' most popular recreational destinations.

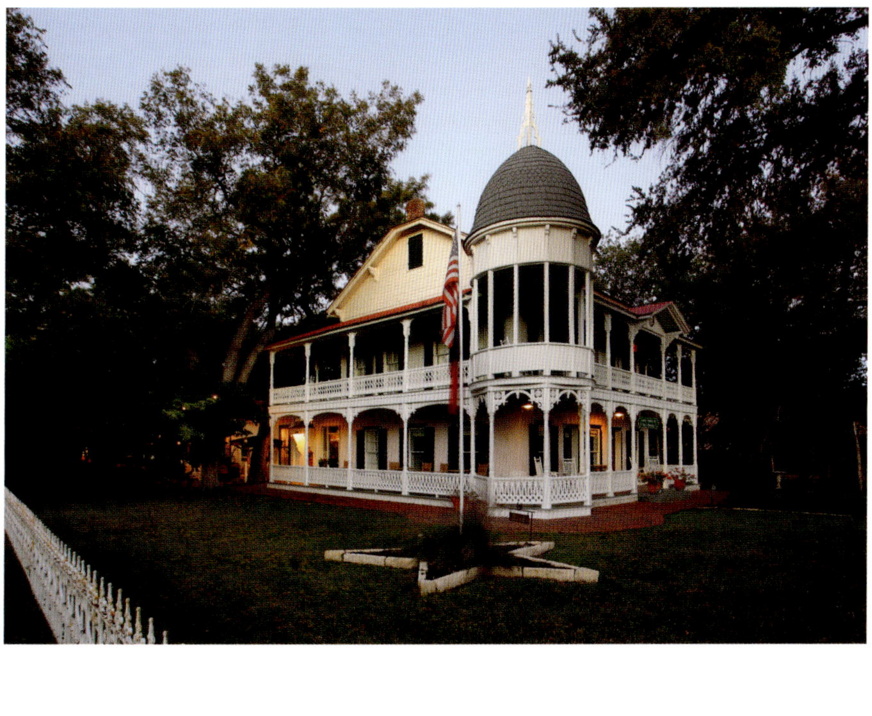

◀ This historic 1872 Victorian mansion and surrounding property was originally the home and cotton plantation of Henry D. Gruene. Henry, his brother, and father purchased land on the Guadalupe River and eventually developed it into a community aptly named Gruene, Texas.

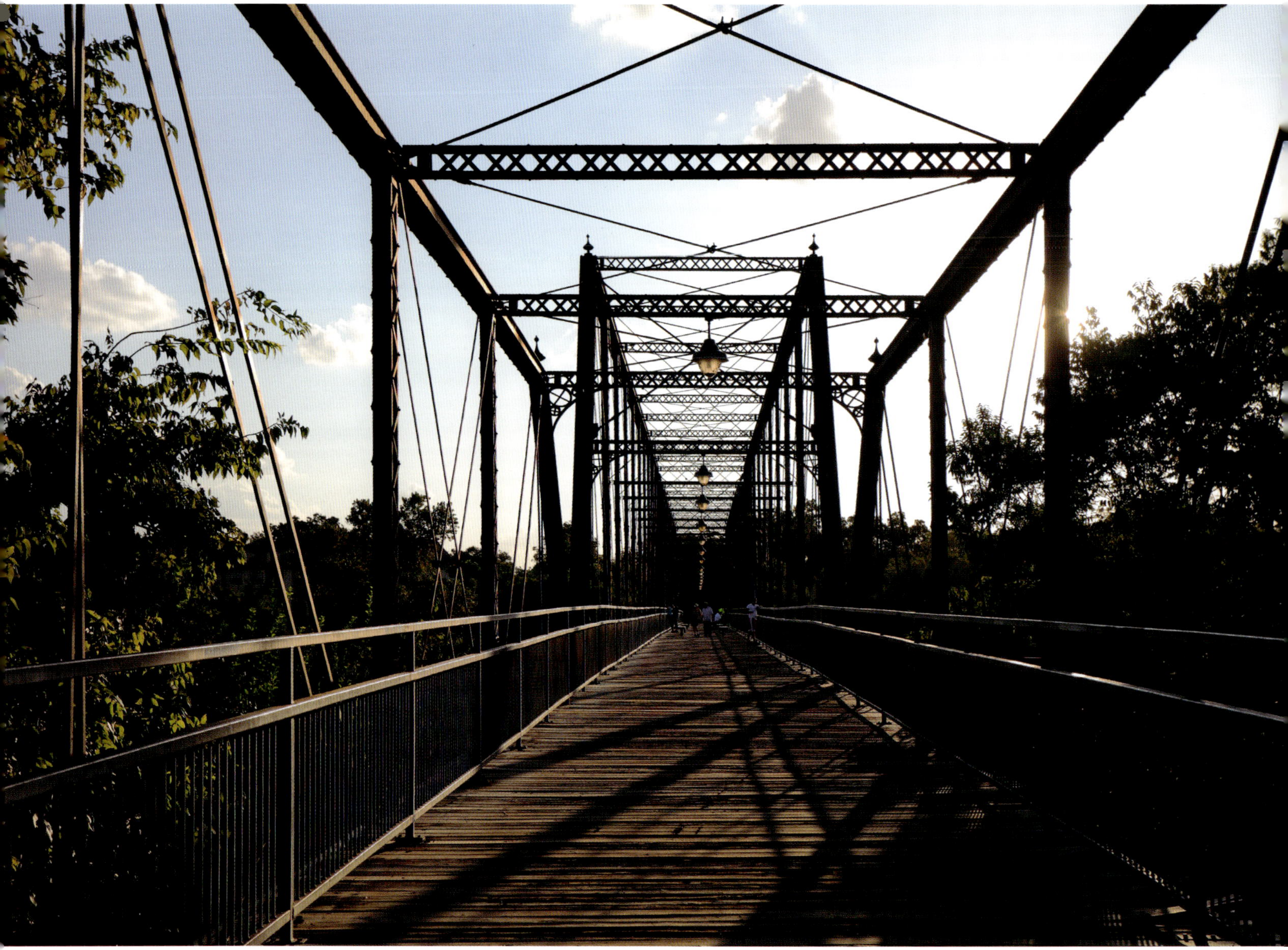

▲▶ Built in 1887 as a toll-free crossing, the historic Faust Street Bridge, with its double wrought iron trusses, spans 640 feet across the Guadalupe River in Comal County.

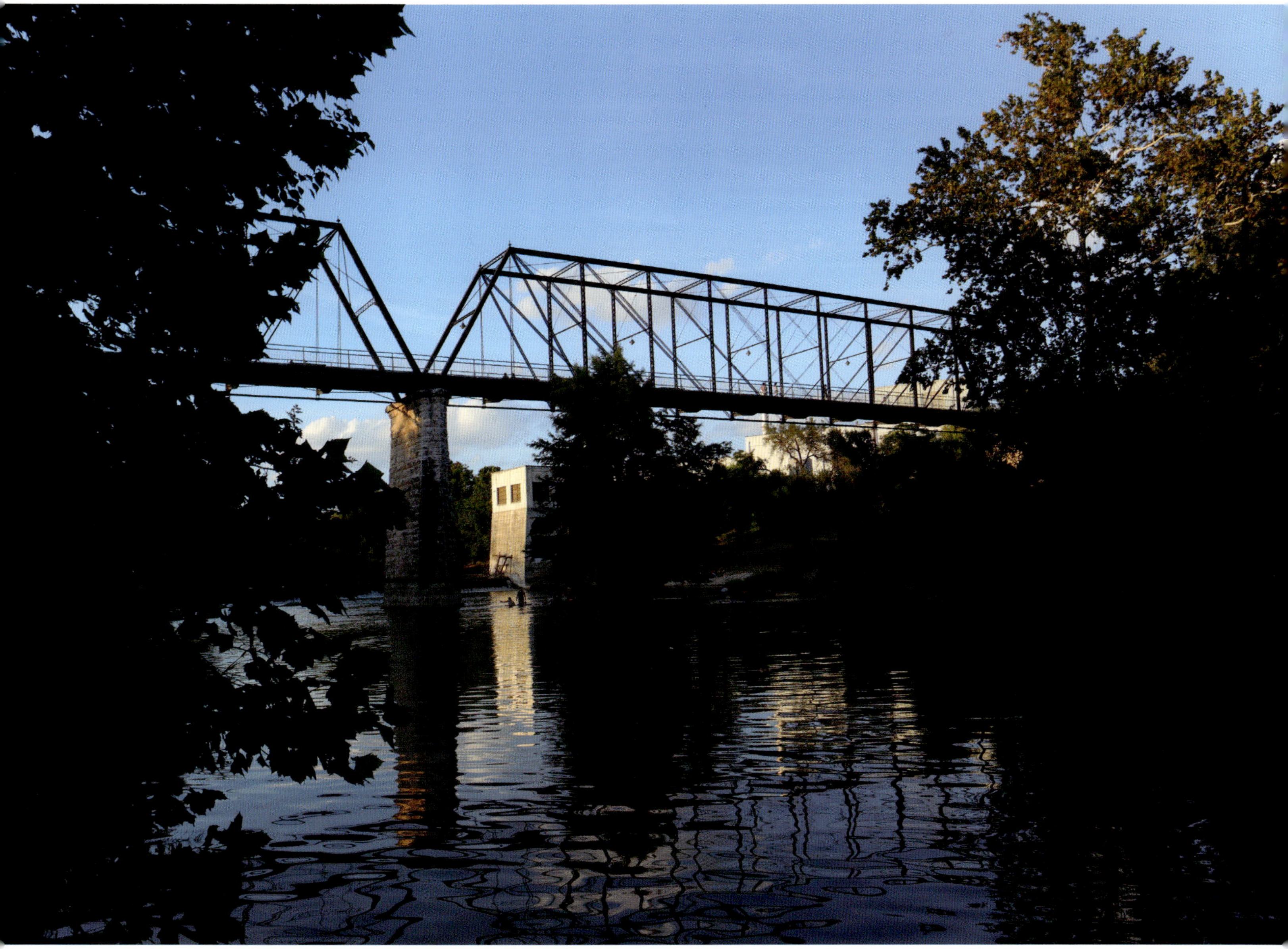

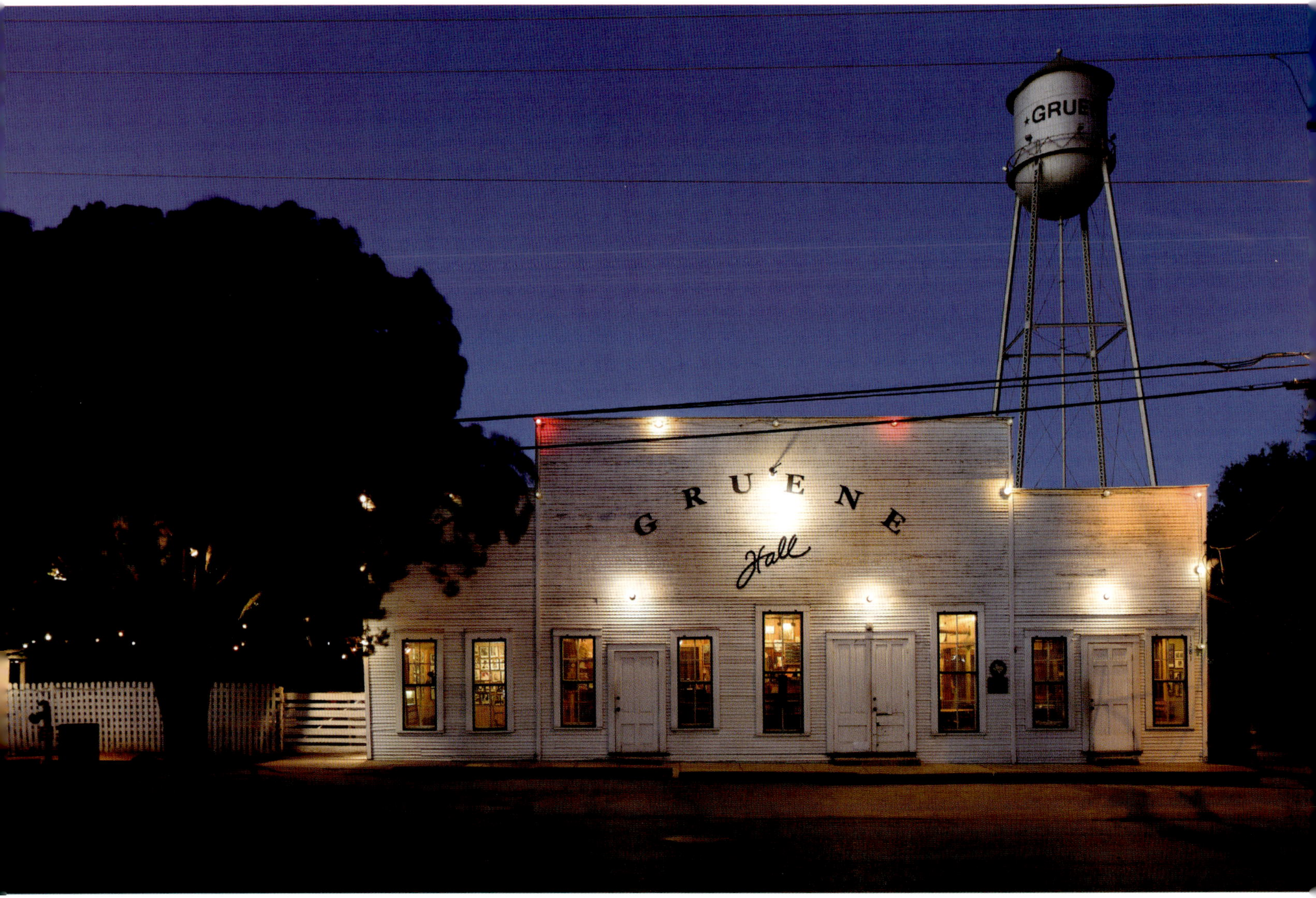

▲ Built in 1878, Gruene Hall is the oldest continually operated dance hall in Texas. The 6,000-square-foot open-air tin-roofed building has served as the social center of Gruene since the 1800s. Today it is famous for hosting musicians and recording artists such as Merle Haggard, Willie Nelson, George Strait, and Lyle Lovett.

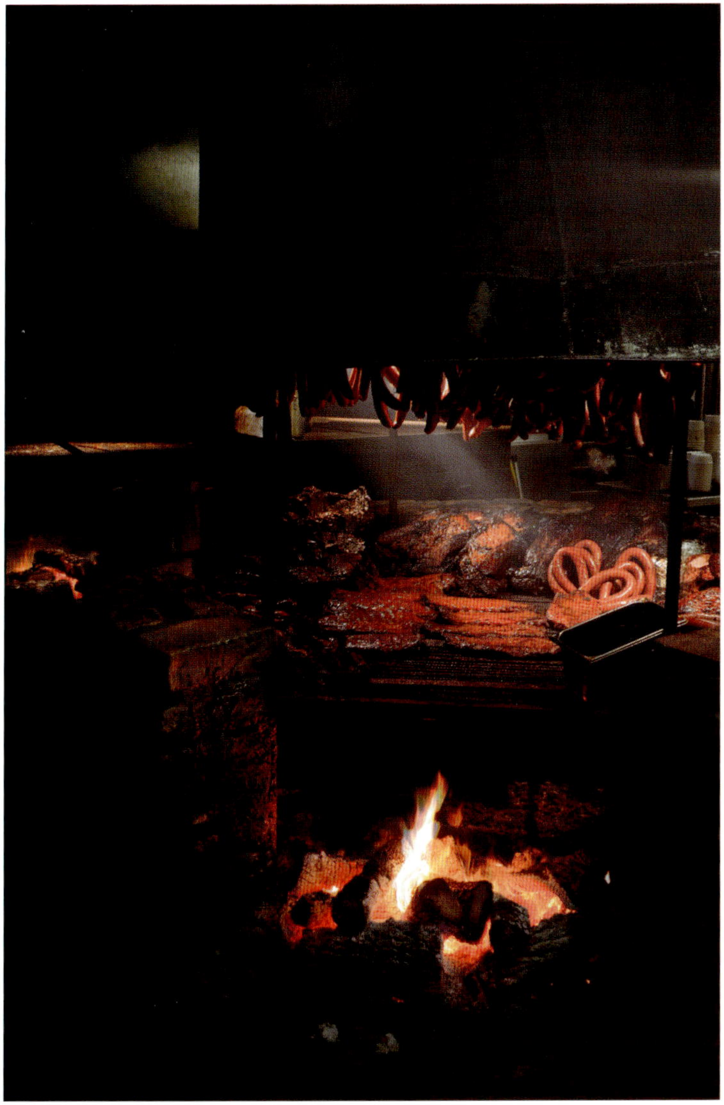

▲ In 1967, Thurman Roberts, a Driftwood local known for his tasty barbecue, and his two sons built a large barbecue pit to take a stab at cooking for paying customers. The restaurant and winery grew up over time around the pit and today it is a popular tourist attraction, serving thousands of customers each week.

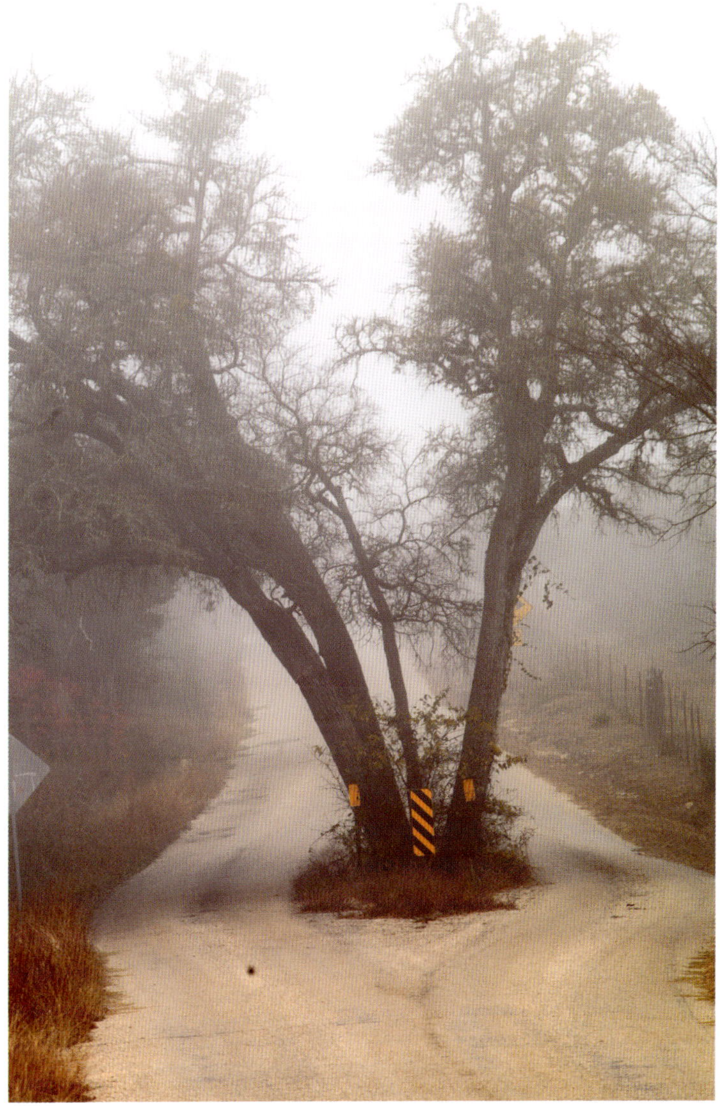

▲ In western Hays County, Mount Sharp Road splits around a cedar elm tree near Wimberley.

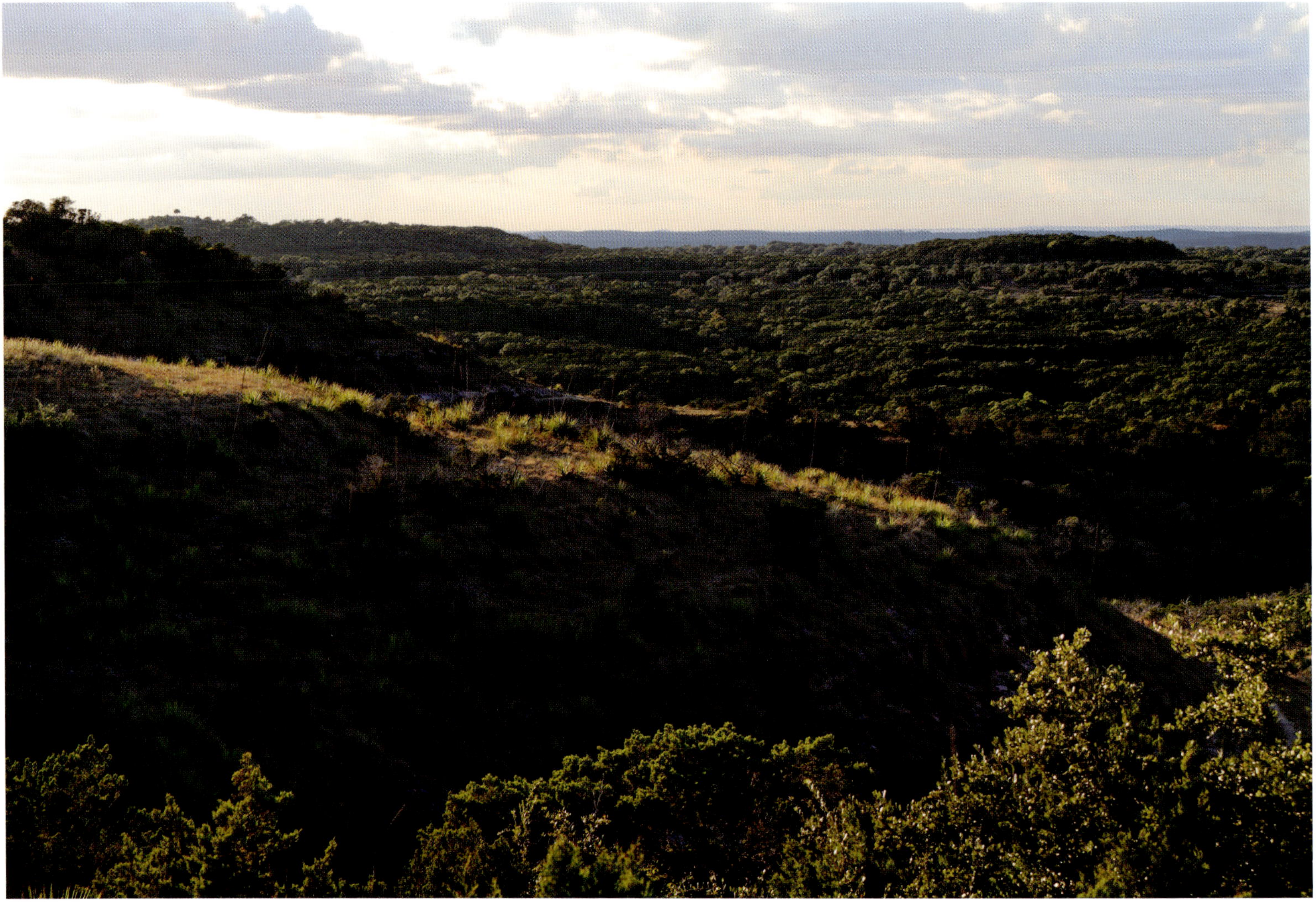

▲ One of the most scenic byways in Central Texas, Ranch-to-Market Road 32—known as the "Devil's Backbone"—winds along a spiny ridge surrounded by panoramic Hill Country views from Wimberley to Blanco.

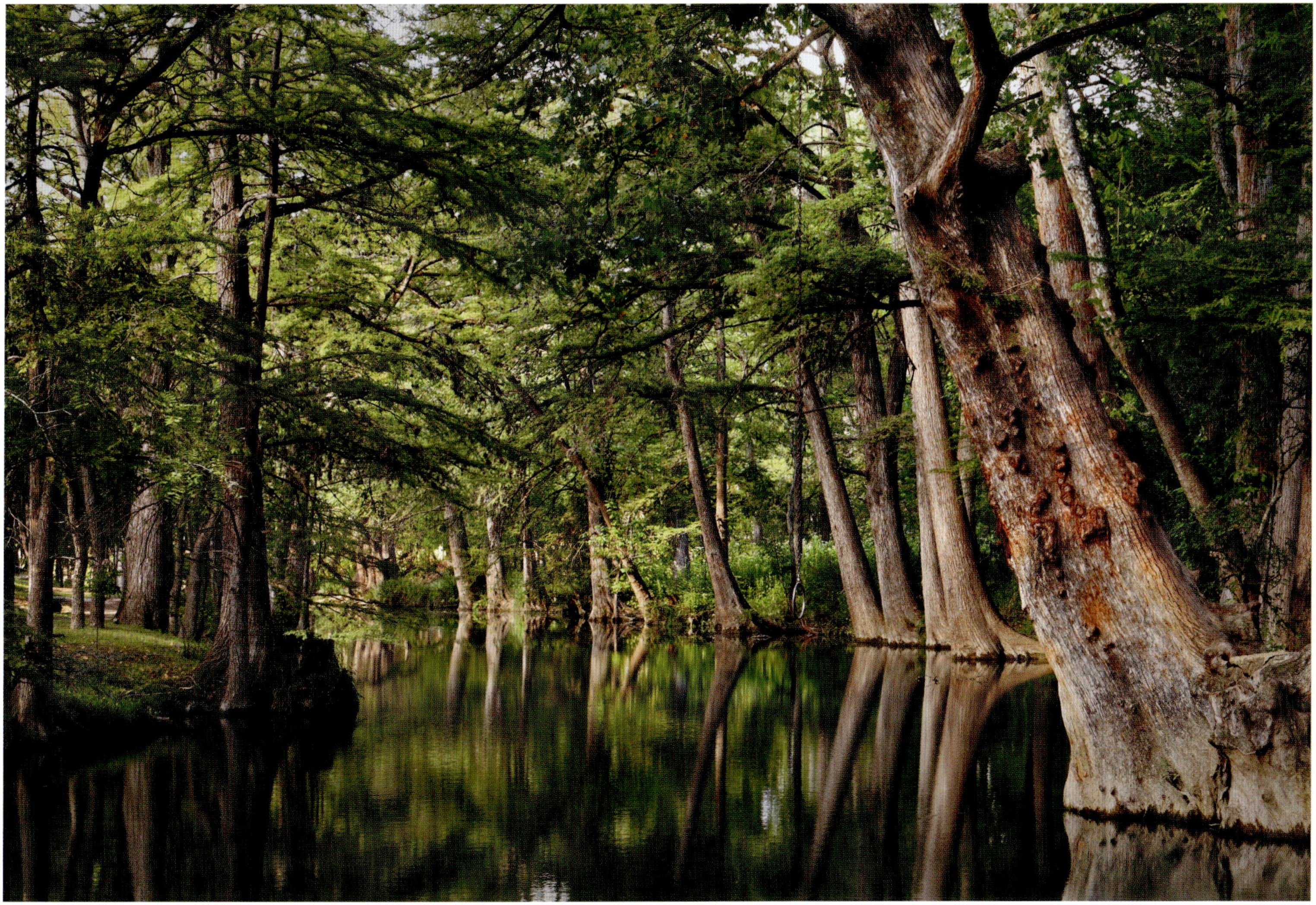

▲ One of the most popular natural swimming holes in Texas, Blue Hole encompasses a deep, wide section of Cypress Creek in Wimberley. Sparkling clear waters shaded by the bows of dozens of old-growth bald cypress trees make it a picture perfect spot to jump in or just wet your feet.

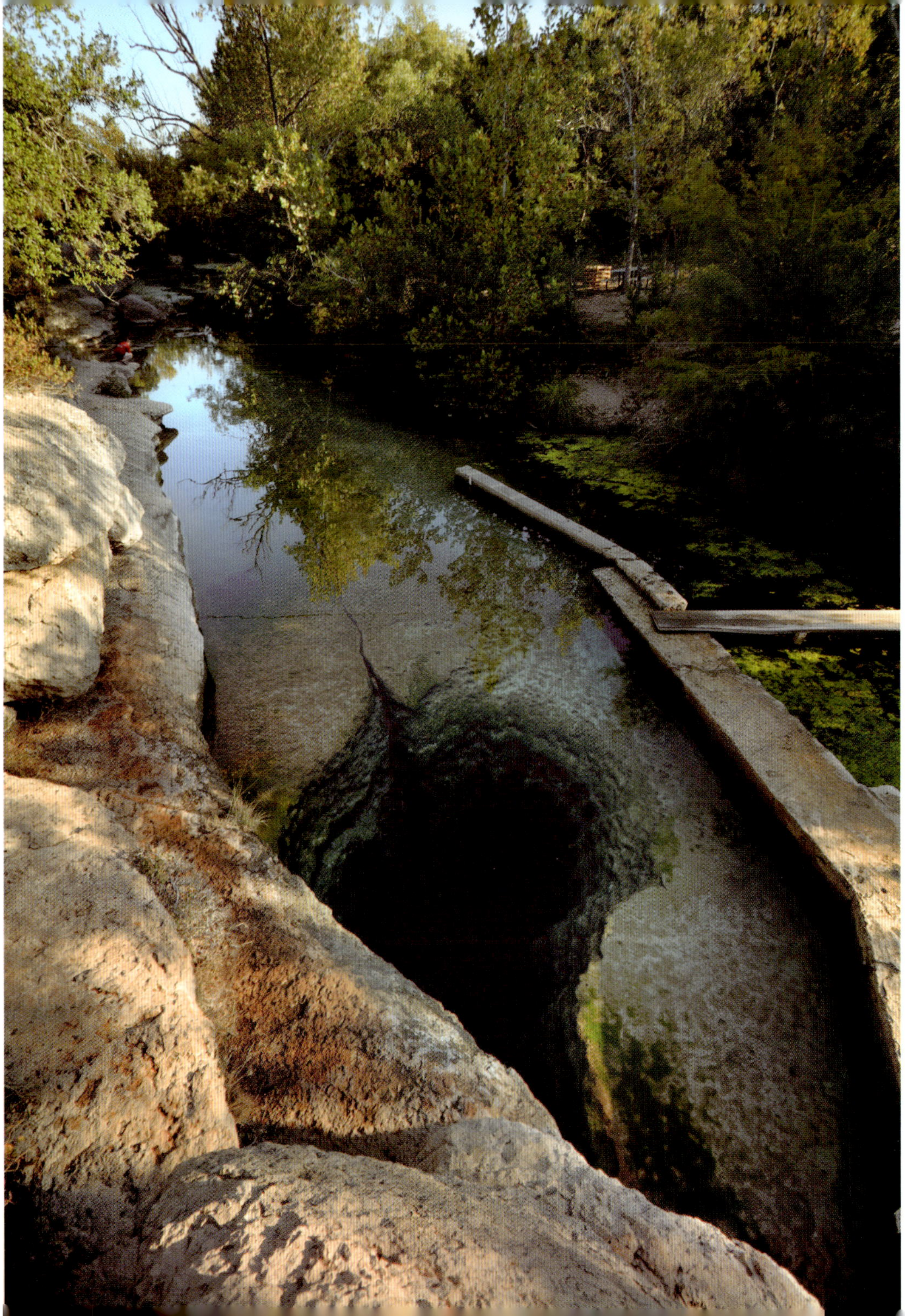

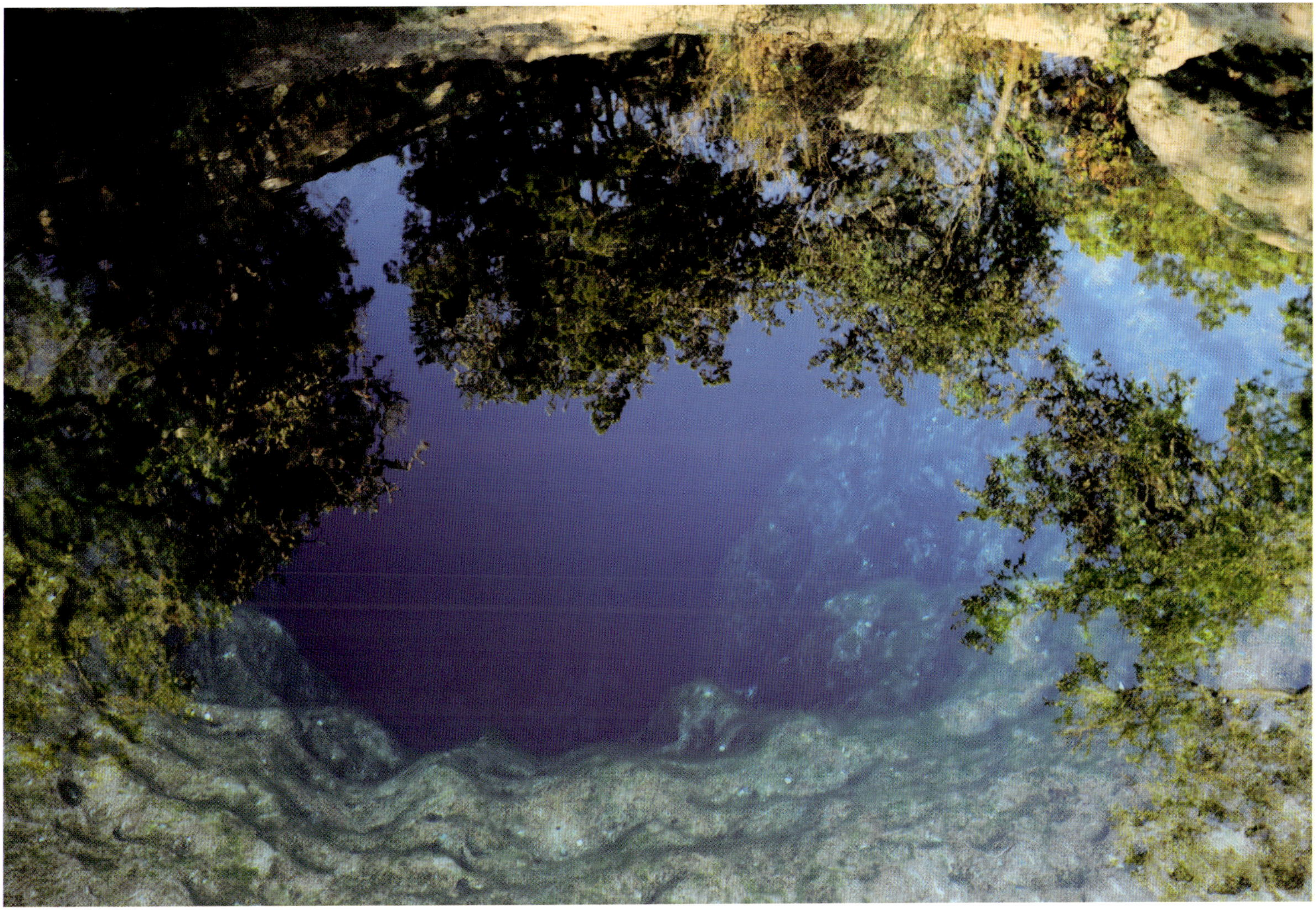

◀▲ Northwest of Wimberley, an artesian spring and popular swimming hole known as Jacob's Well bubbles up from the Trinity aquifer to form the headwaters of Cypress Creek. Summer thrill seekers dive from the adjacent limestone bluff into the twelve-foot-wide deep blue opening to the well. Beneath the surface is an extensive cave system that has only been partially explored.

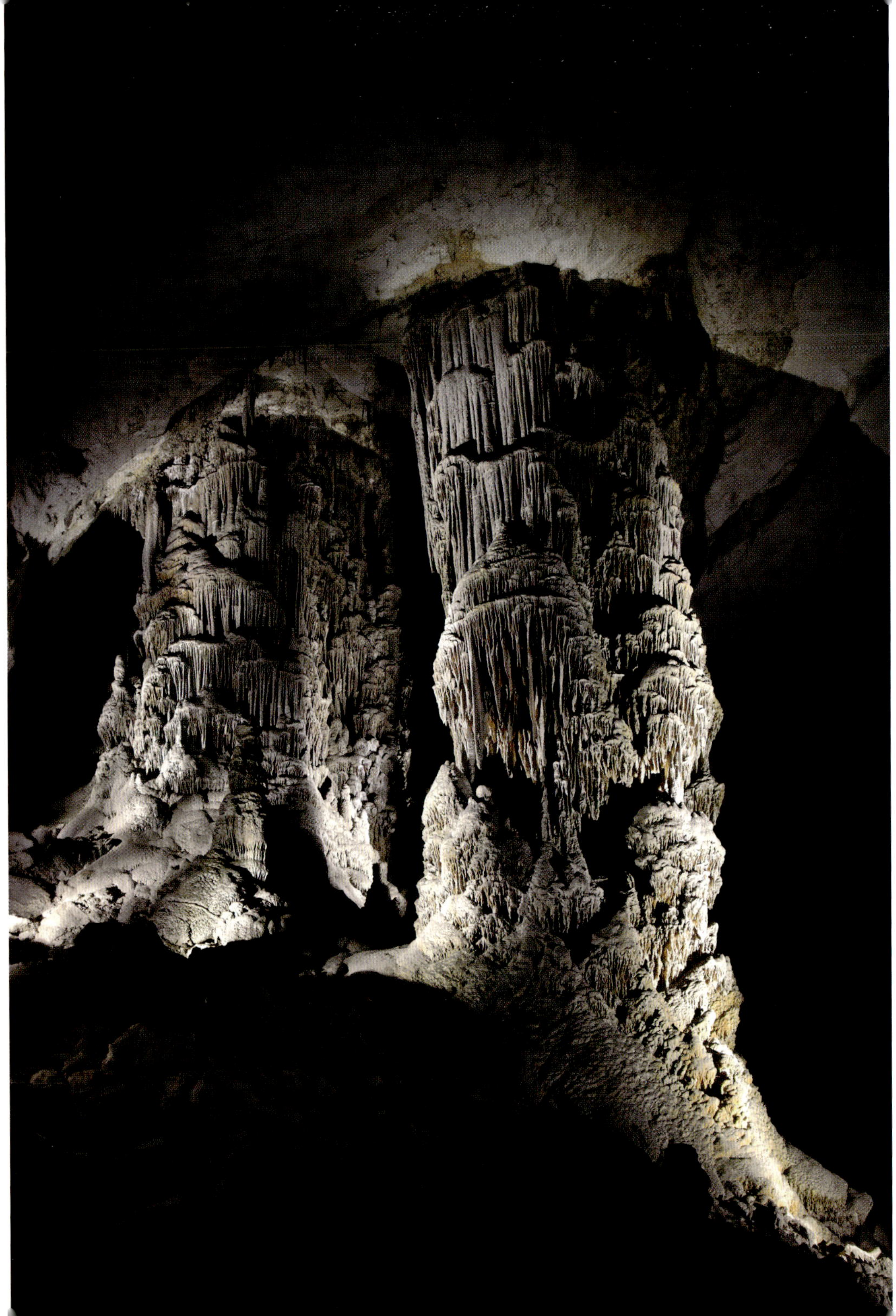

◀ North of Brackettville, in the southwest corner of the Hill Country, Kickapoo Caverns is famous for its impressive columns—the largest known cave formations in Texas. These massive columns rise as tall as an eight-story building and divide the upper and lower chambers of the cave.

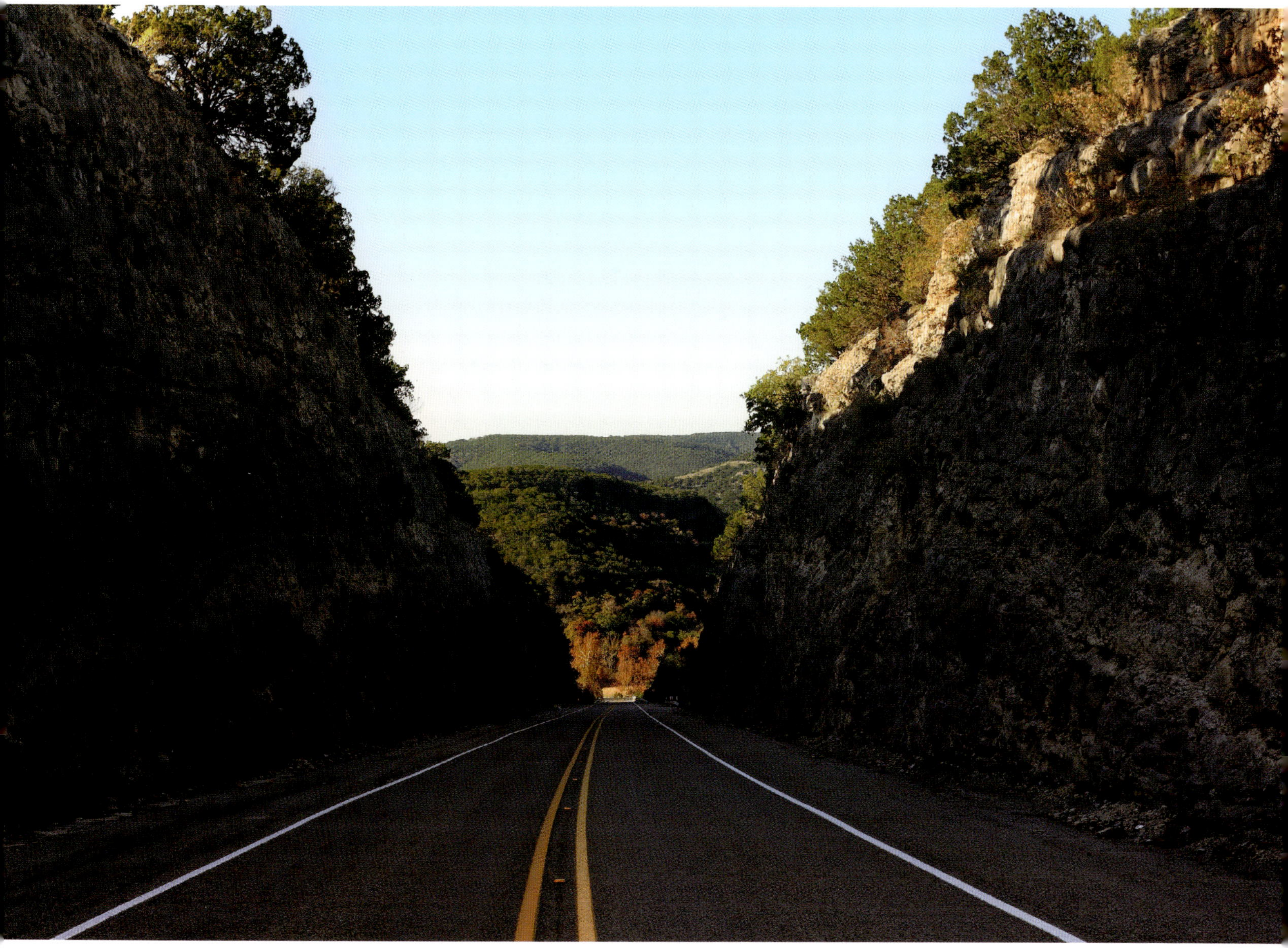

▲ One of the most scenic roads in Texas, Ranch-to-Market Road 337 winds fifty-six miles through scenic canyons, shady creek crossings, and breathtaking panoramas, with sharp turns around mountain sides and steep climbs up to elevations as high as 2,200 feet.

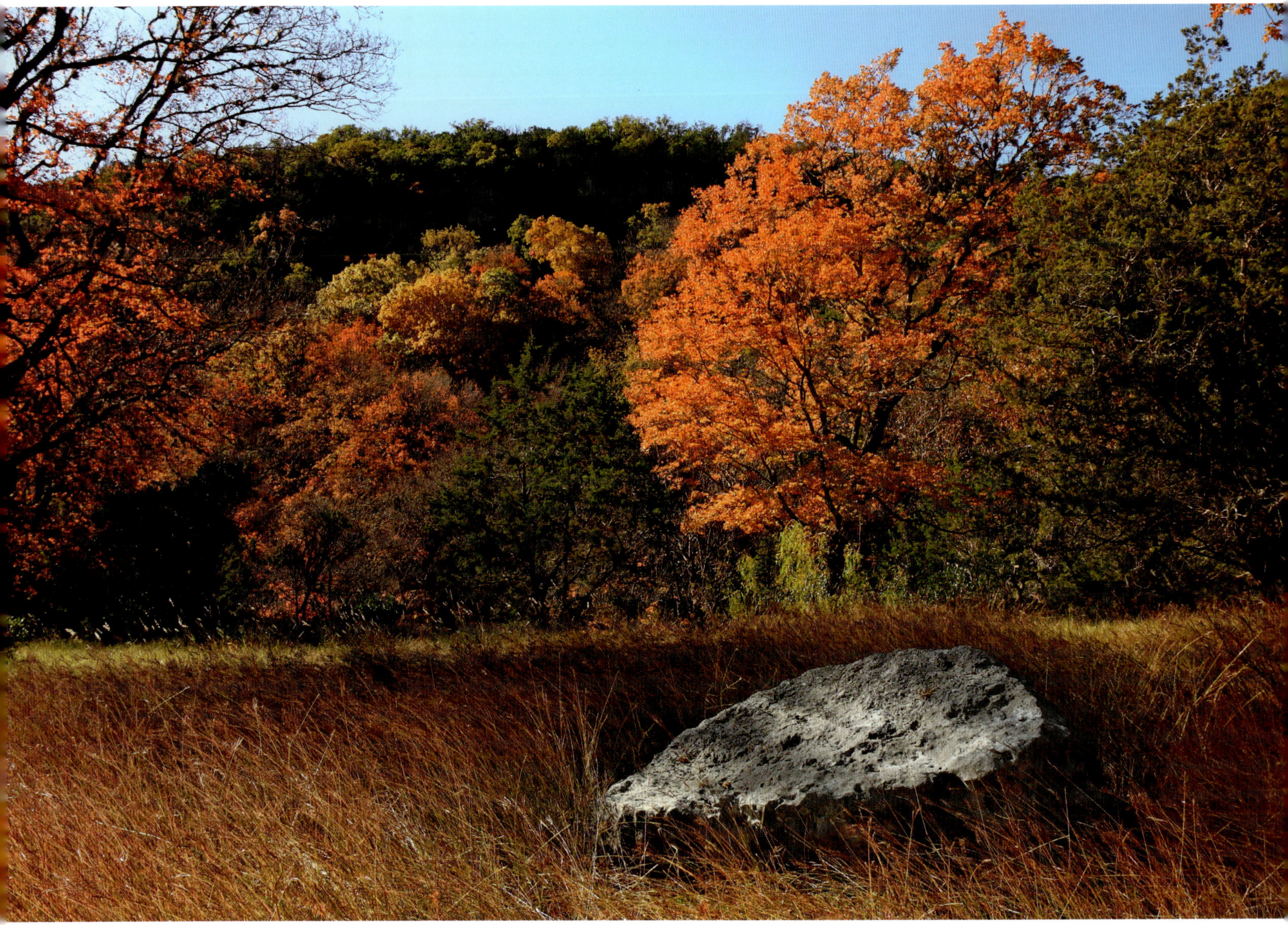

▲ Sheltered canyons, steep rugged terrain, wooded rocky slopes, intimate spring-fed pools and streams, and hilltop grasslands showcase the variety of natural features found within Lost Maples State Natural Area. Yet the gem of this 2,174-acre park is its isolated population of Uvalde big tooth maple trees which paint the valleys and hillsides in vibrant autumn color.

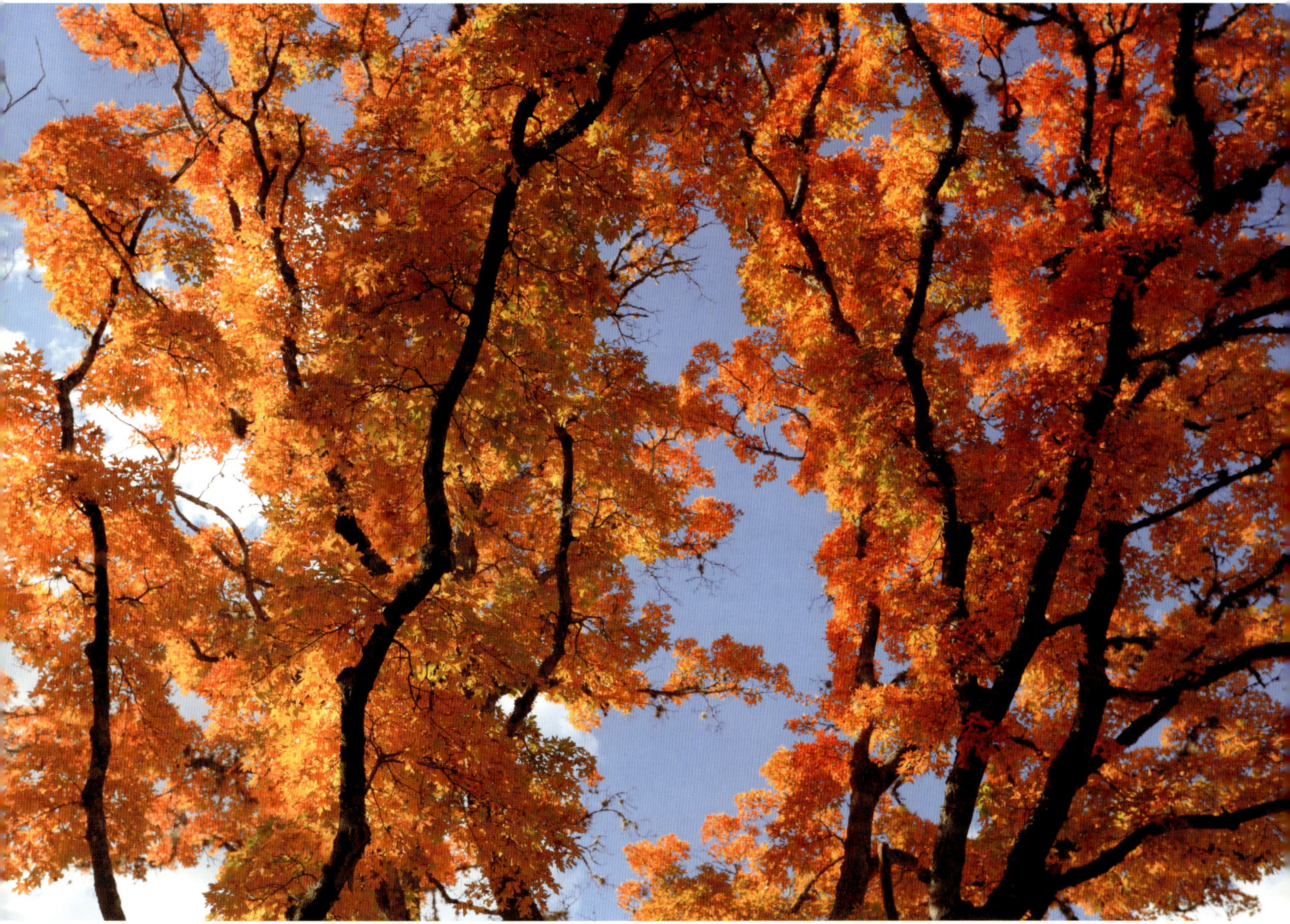

▲ Veins of dark maple branches and brilliant orange leaves contrast against a crisp blue sky in Lost Maples State Natural Area. The uncommon Uvalde big tooth maples are endemic to parts of Central Texas and the mountains of the Trans-Pecos region.

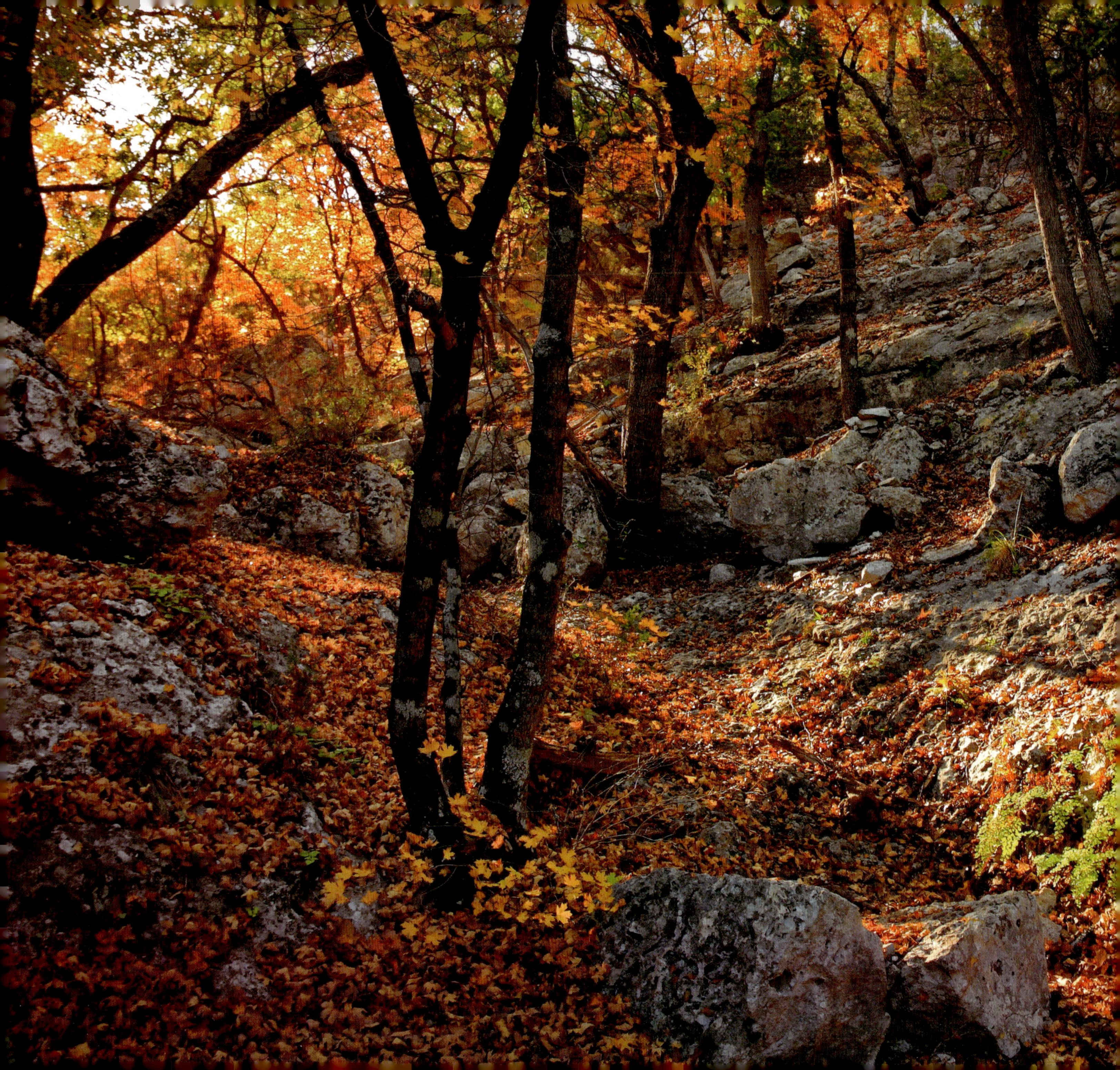

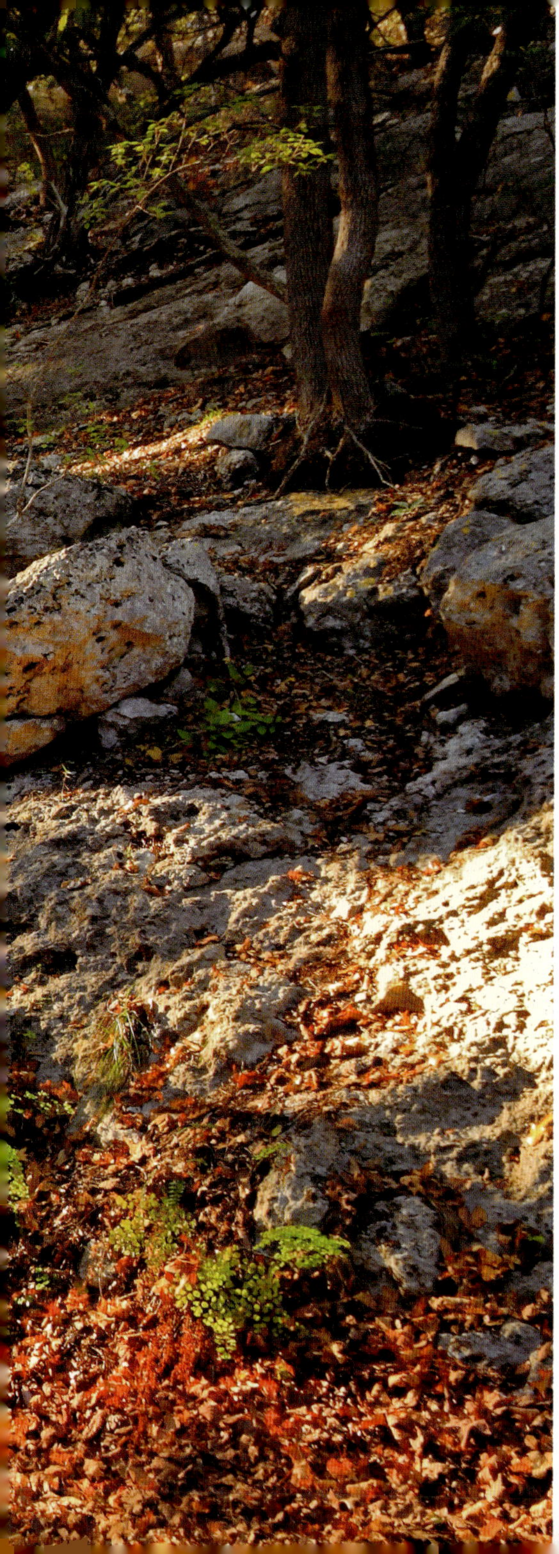

◀ Yellow and orange maple leaves glow as the afternoon sun streams into a stair-stepped ravine in Mystic Canyon in Lost Maples State Natural Area.

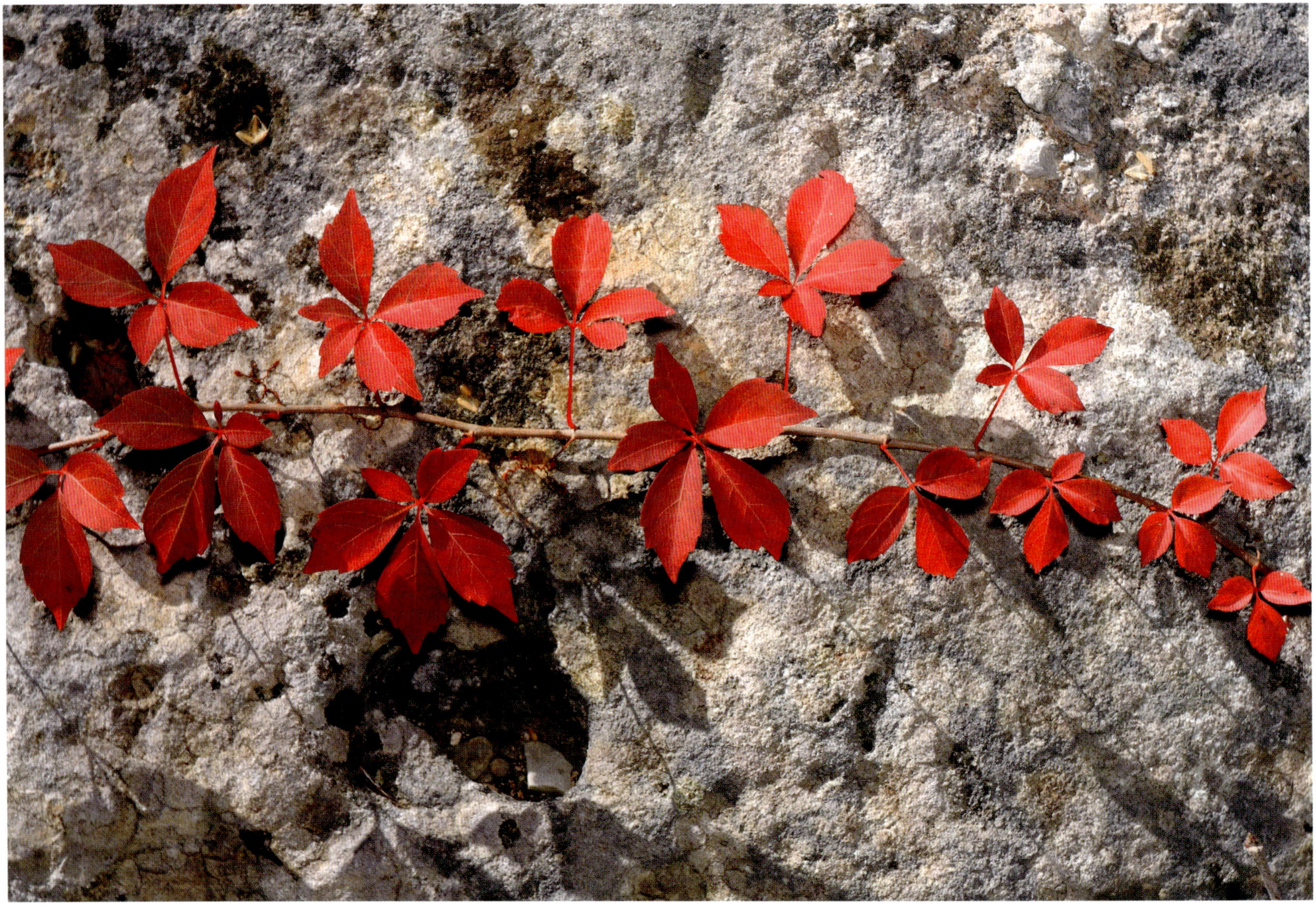

▲ One of dozens of climbing flora species in Texas, Virginia creeper stands out in autumn amid the limestone outcroppings and tree trunks with its vivid eye-catching red foliage.

▶ A pool on the shallow Sabinal River reflects a medley of colors cast by the sky and from the seasonal hues of the Uvalde big tooth maples found in Lost Maples State Natural Area.

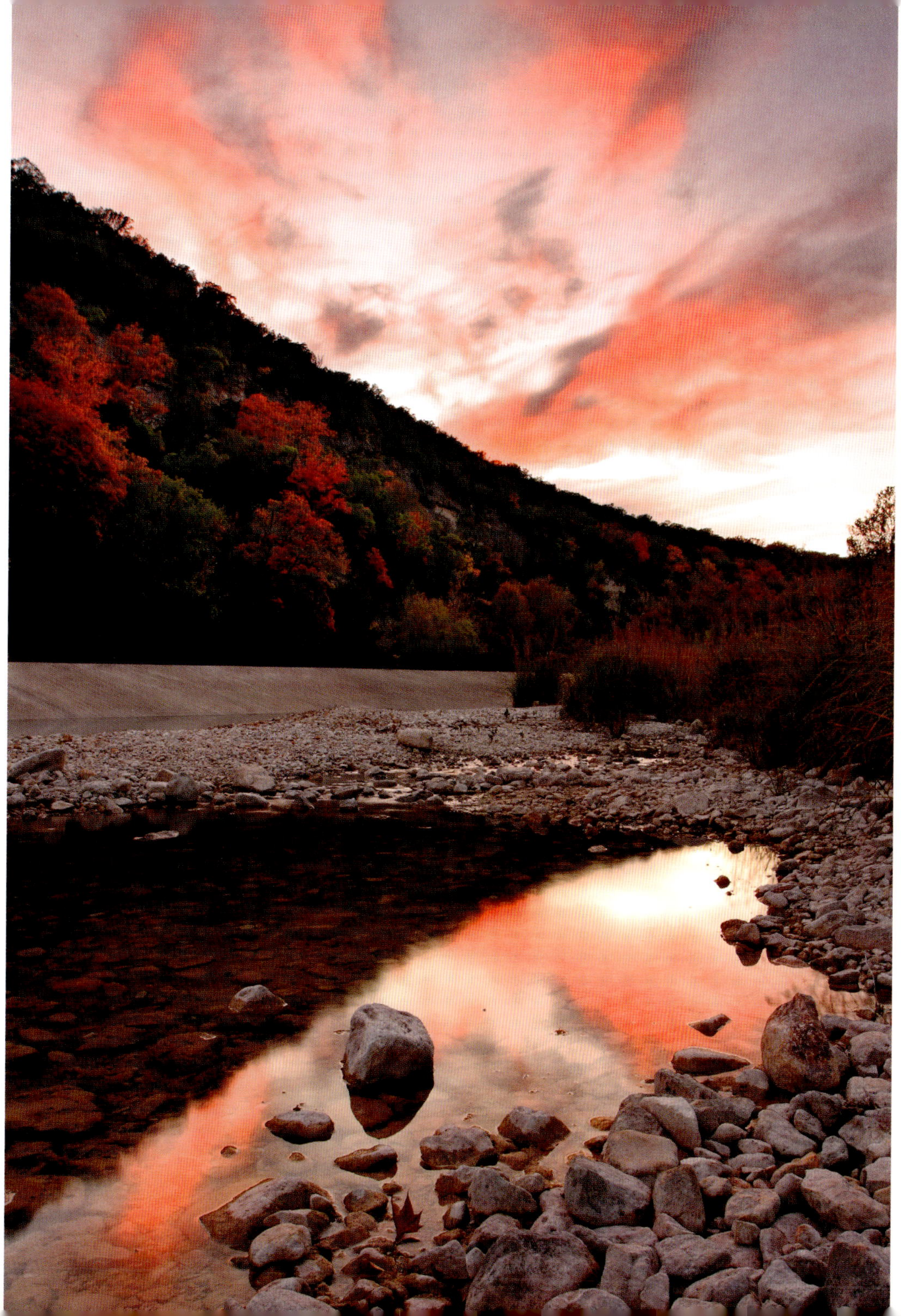

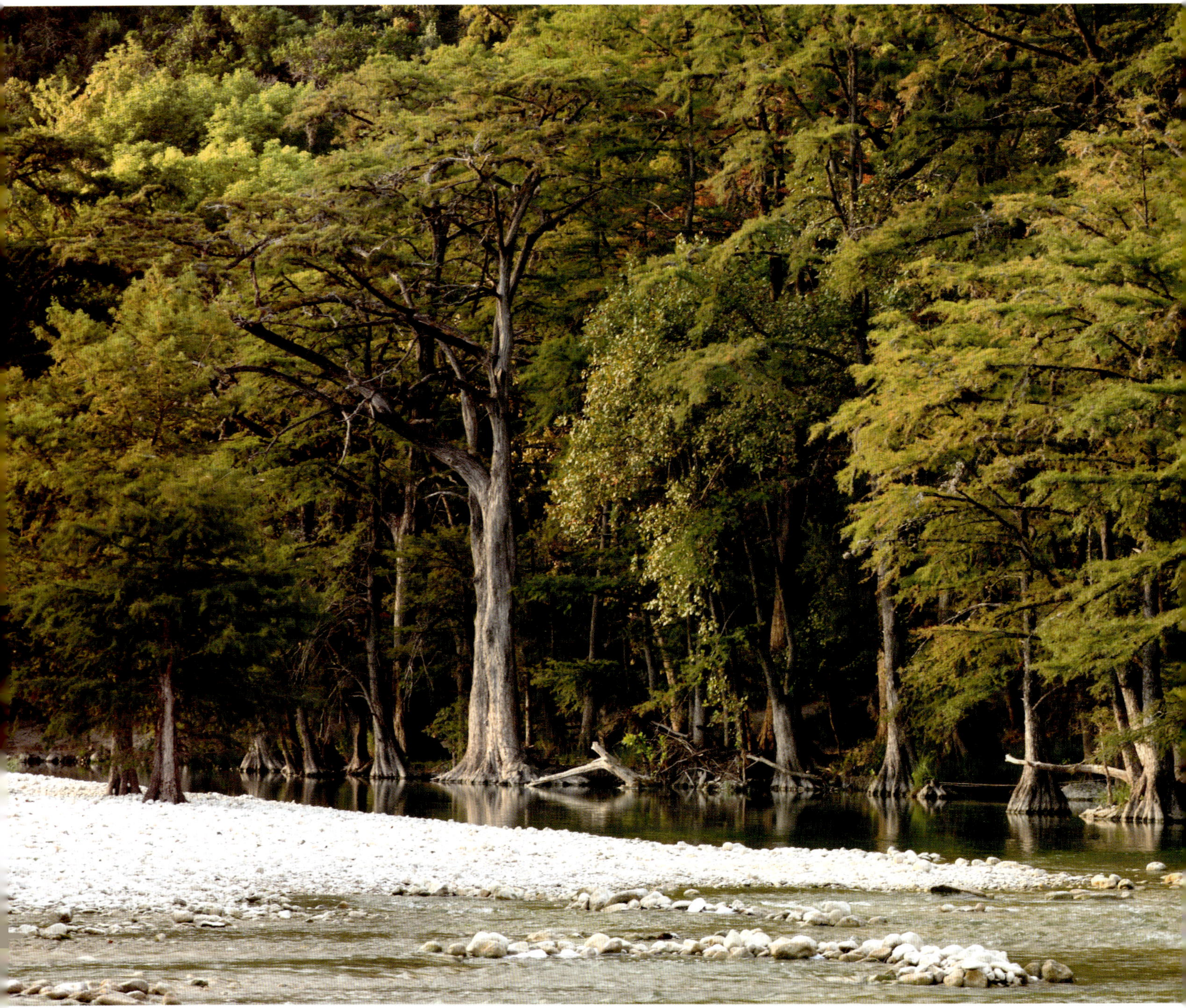

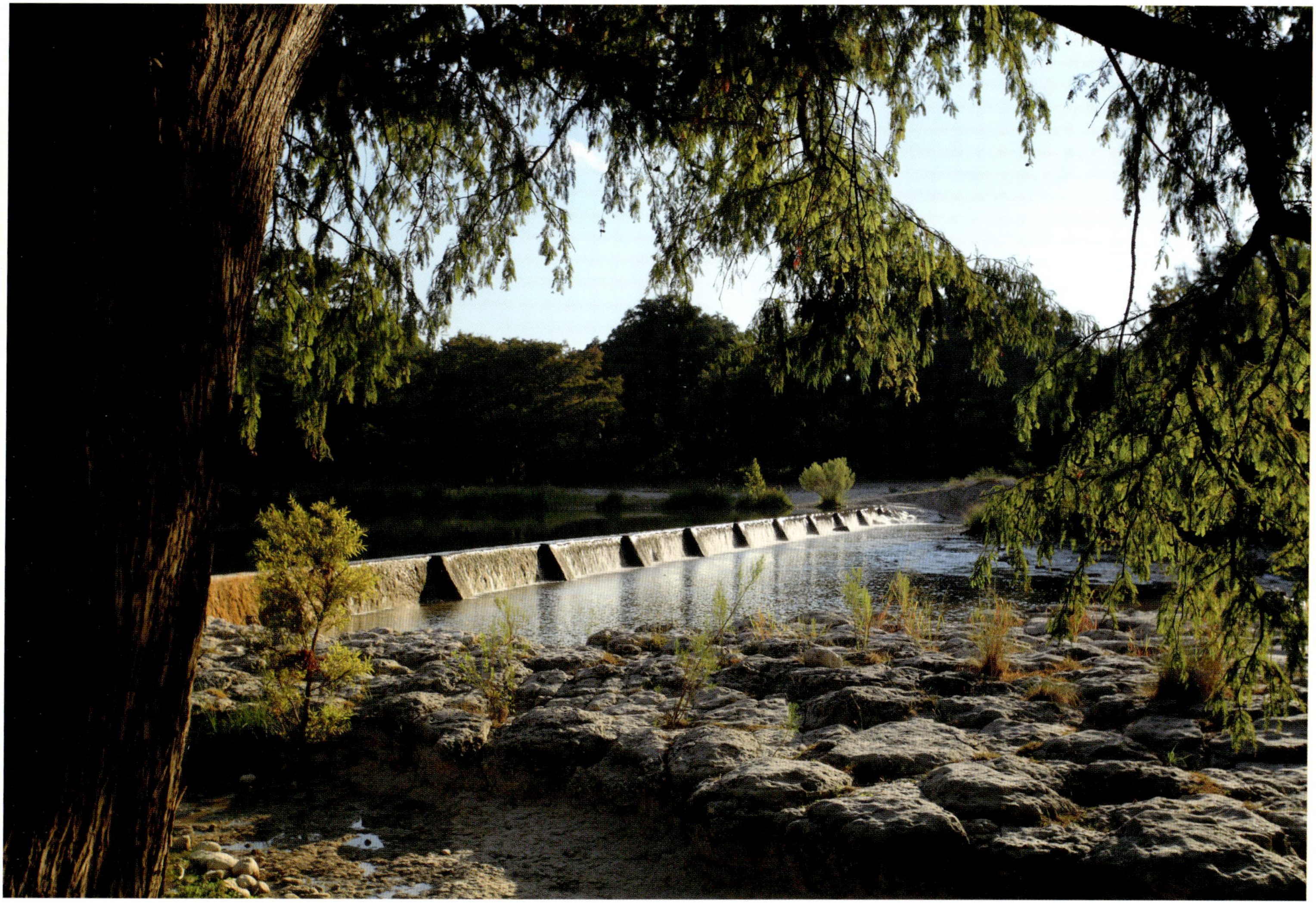

◀ Old and young bald cypress trees stand as sentinels along the banks of the Frio River in Garner State Park.

▲ Tranquil canyons, dramatic panoramas, and the cool waters of the Frio River provide a picturesque setting, making Garner State Park one of the most popular parks in Texas. The 1,774-acre park takes its name from former local resident, congressman, and Vice President John Nance Garner.

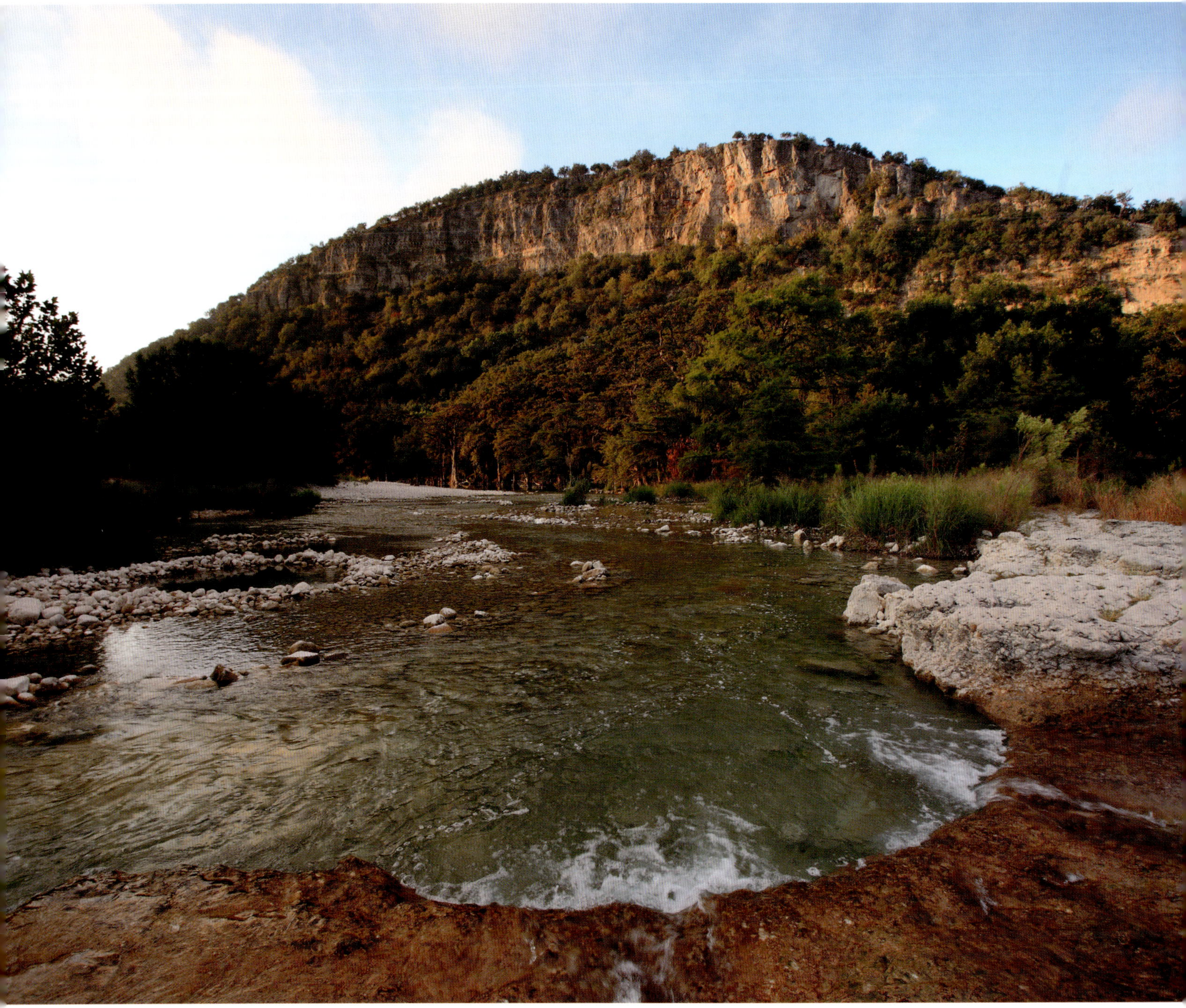

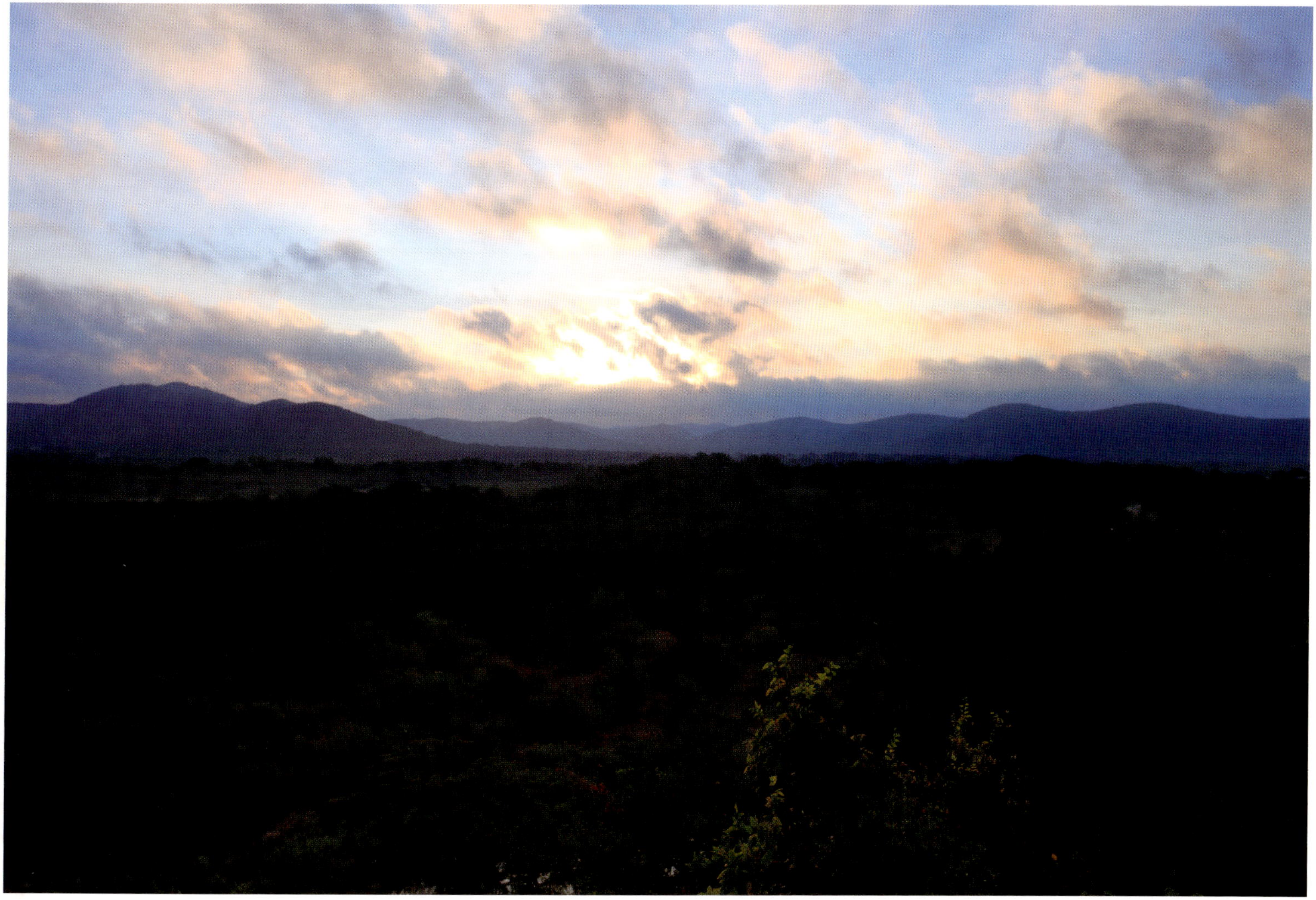

◀ The craggy, weathered face of "Old Baldy"—a landmark limestone bluff—rises above the clear Frio River, catching the morning light in Garner State Park.

▲ Looking east from an overlook in Garner State Park, the rising sun showcases silhouetted layers of distant undulating peaks just beyond the verdant Frio River Valley.

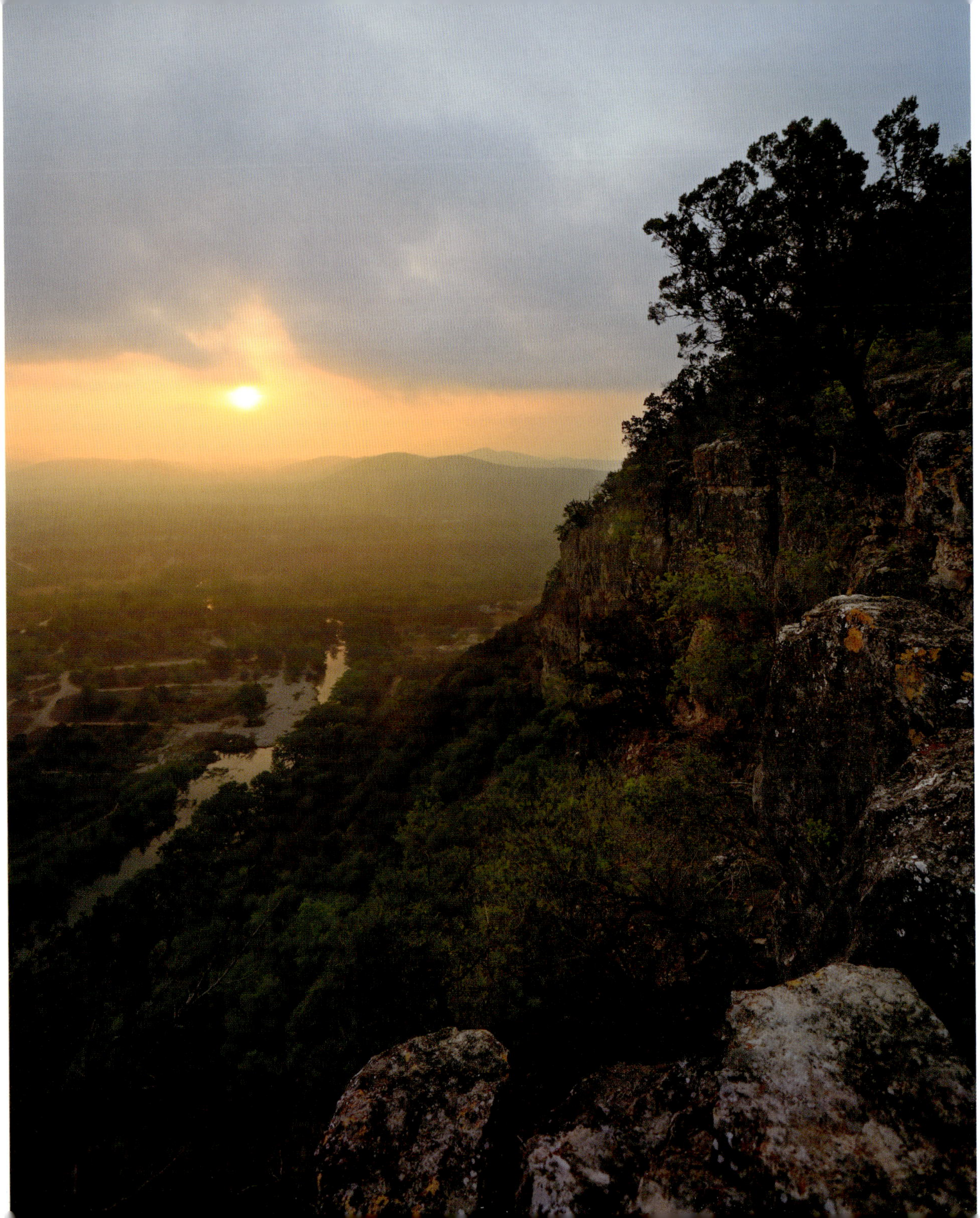

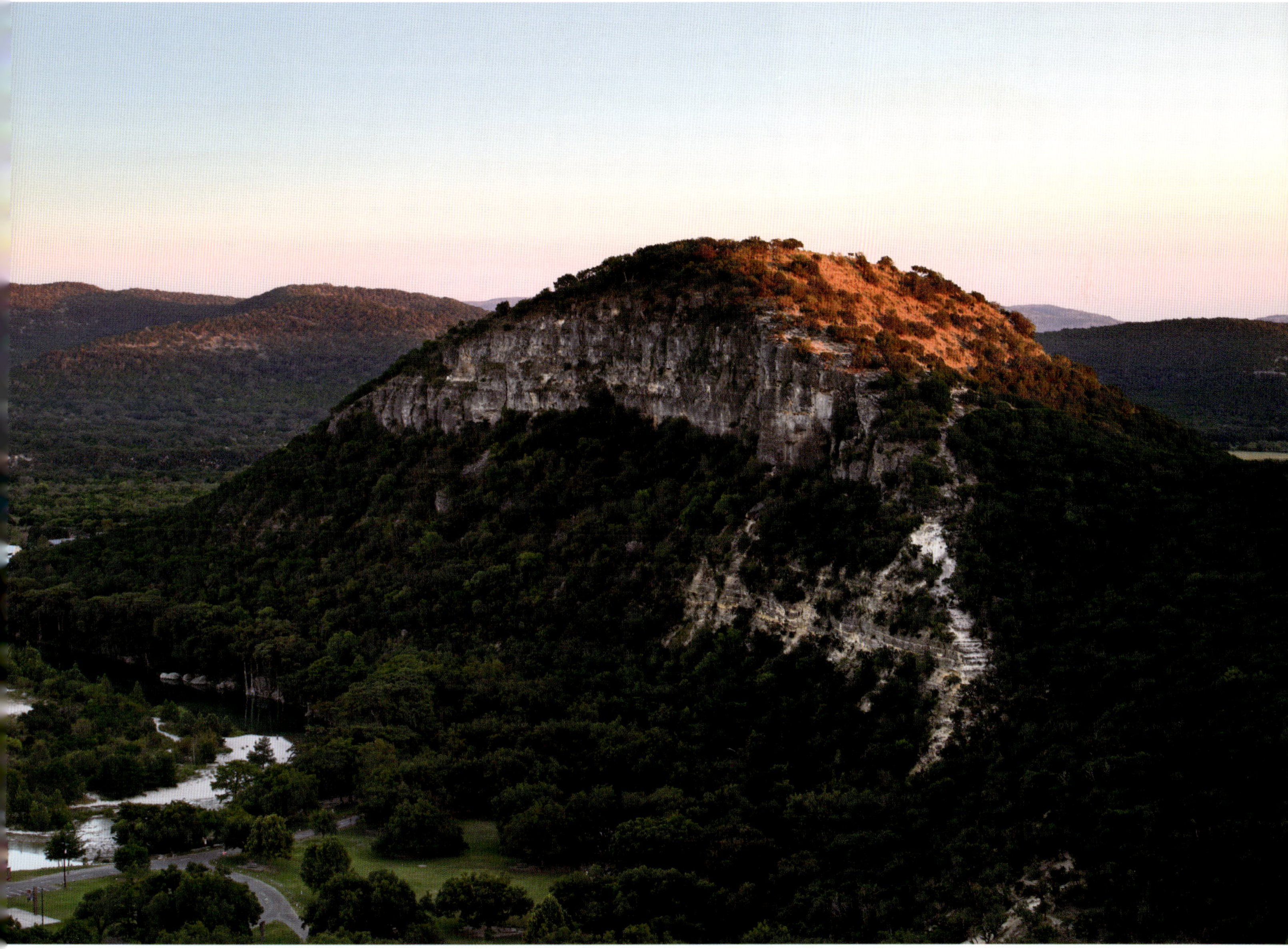

◀ The rising sun momentarily pierces dense morning fog, bathing the scenic Frio River Valley in a warm light. This view from the summit of Old Baldy makes for a breathtaking panorama in Garner State Park.

▲ Seen from a distant peak, the fleeting alpenglow after sunset grazes Old Baldy, accentuating its half-dome profile.

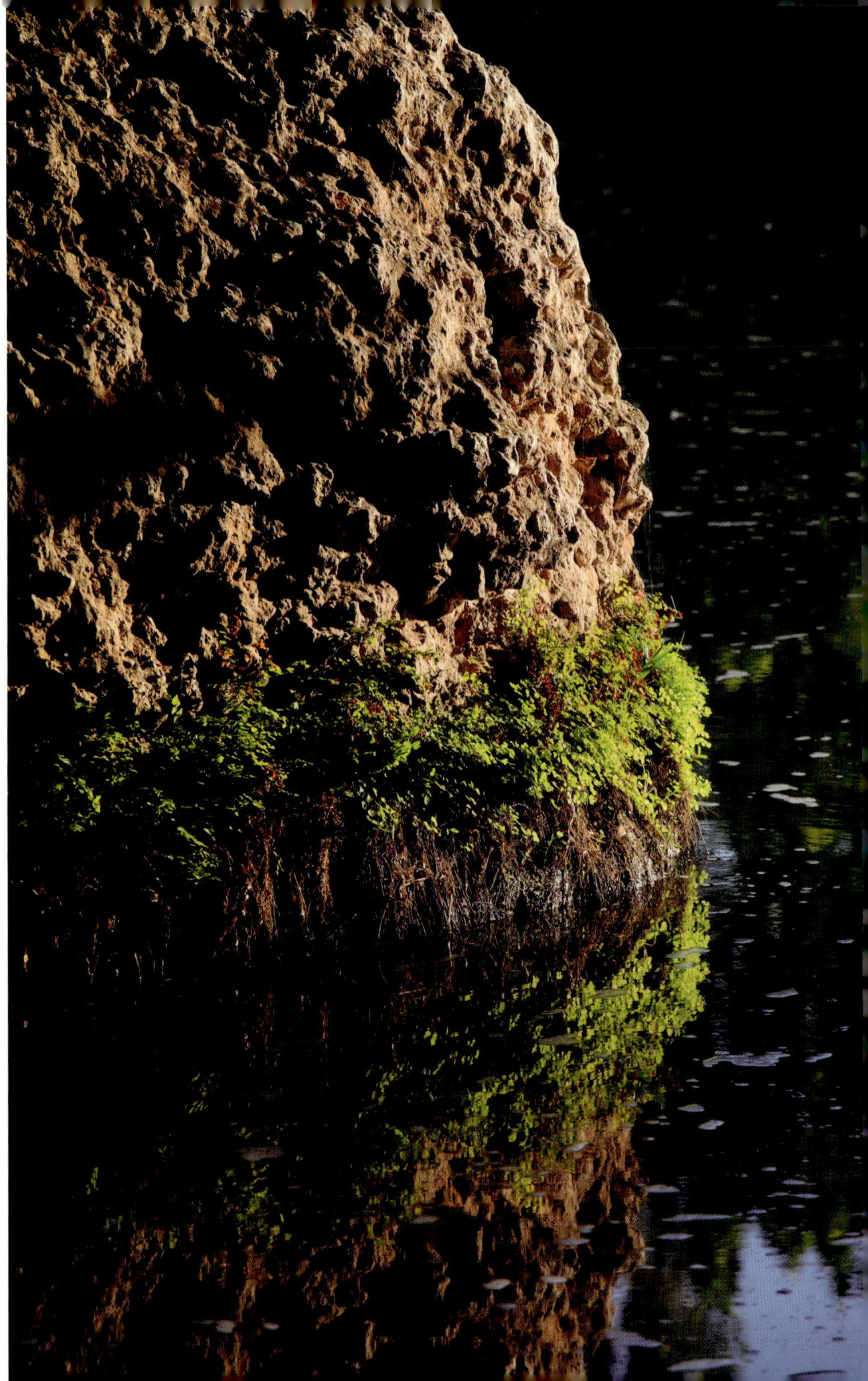

▶ On a calm section of the Frio River the water's still surface reflects maidenhair fern growing around the base of a limestone island.